Rape in Chicago

WOMEN IN
AMERICAN HISTORY

Series Editors
Anne Firor Scott
Susan Armitage
Susan K. Cahn
Deborah Gray White

*A list of books in the series appears
at the end of this book.*

Rape in Chicago

Race, Myth, and the Courts

DAWN RAE FLOOD

University of Illinois Press
URBANA, CHICAGO, AND SPRINGFIELD

"Strange Fruit," written by Abal Meeropol (Lewis Allen, pseudo).
Used by permission of Edward B. Marks Music Company.

Library of Congress Cataloging-in-Publication Data
Flood, Dawn Rae.
Rape in Chicago : race, myth, and the courts / Dawn Rae Flood.
p.   cm. — (Women in American history)
Includes bibliographical references and index.
ISBN 978-0-252-03689-7 (cloth)
1. Rape—Illinois—Chicago—History.
2. Rape—Public opinion—History.
3. Rape victims—Illinois—Chicago.
4. African Americans—Sexual behavior—Illinois—Chicago.
5. Discrimination in criminal justice administration—
Illinois—Chicago.
I. Title.
HV6568.C4F56   2012
364.15'320977311—dc23   2011044551

To Jack

Contents

Acknowledgments

After more than a decade of research and writing on the topic of rape myths and rape trials in a modern city, I assumed that I would feel great satisfaction in finally sitting down to acknowledge those who have helped me along the way. Instead, I find myself overwhelmed by thinking about the widespread encouragement that I have received over the years and am nearly paralyzed in trying here to recount it all. I shall do my best.

No scholarly research would ever be completed without financial support, and I am fortunate to be able to thank several sources. The American Historical Association Littleton-Griswold Award for Legal History and the King V. Hostick Award for Illinois History at the Illinois State Historical Society supported early stages of the research presented here. Both the Department of History and the Gender and Women's Studies Program at the University of Illinois at Urbana-Champaign provided funding to help offset the costs of research and conference travel, and I am grateful that they were able to help get me started. The Social Science Research Council's Sexuality Research Fellowship Program, funded by the Ford Foundation, provided significant financial support, allowing me to take a year off from other duties and concentrate on thinking and writing. The SRFP also put me in contact with a broad array of scholars whose research on sexuality has inspired me in countless ways, and I cherish the friendships I made as a result. Support from the President's Research Fund at Campion College at the University of Regina allowed me to return to Chicago and get back into the archives after several years away. Subvention funds from the Humanities Research Institute at the University of Regina aided in the final production of this manuscript.

I have also had the good fortune to receive extensive support from friends and colleagues at a number of different institutions over the years. The gender and history reading group at the University of Illinois at Urbana-Champaign provided an intellectually stimulating space to discuss new ideas. Friends in the Women's Studies Program and the Department of History at the University of Wyoming at Laramie and in the History Department at the University of South Florida at Tampa also offered unending enthusiasm for my work. The comments and questions I received during annual meetings of the American Historical Association, the Social Science History Association, the National Women's Studies Association, and the American Association for the History of Medicine helped me identify more clearly what I had to say about the difficult topic of sexual violence. I would also like to thank Maria Bevaqua, E. Frances White, and the editors at the *Journal of Women's History* for helping me sharpen the focus of this research. I thank the *Journal* for allowing me to reprint portions of my article "'They Didn't Treat Me Good': African American Rape Victims and Chicago Courtroom Strategies during the 1950s," (vol. 17, no. 1, Spring 2005), which appear here in Chapter 3. Thank you to Laurie Matheson at the University of Illinois Press, whose confidence in this project and whose patience with my many questions has helped the book come to fruition. Thank you as well to Lisa Lindquist Dorr and the anonymous reviewers for the press, who took the time to offer thoughtful comments and critiques about this work. While certainly rewarding for everyone involved, the voluntary peer-review process can be a thankless task, and I very much appreciate the extensive efforts put forth by those who agreed to review this manuscript. For their support in the copyediting and production stages of publication, thank you to Julie Gay and Jennifer Clark. In these shrinking budgetary times, it is a pleasure to work with a scholarly press that takes such good care of its authors. Thank you to Katherine Jensen for her work on preparing the index.

Not all sources of encouragement and critique have been anonymous or distant. My Canadian colleagues have offered keen support for this "foreign" topic, and I would especially like to thank those who listened to and remarked on portions of it presented at the University of Regina History Department Colloquia and Campion College's Idle Talk Series. Special thanks to Jeet Heer for reading most of this manuscript at an early stage and offering his valuable impressions about it. Several other individuals have also read all or portions of this research, and my work is better for it. Thank you to Leslie Reagan and Liz Pleck for showing me how to do it: without them, I know I would not have been able to start, much less finish, this book. Thank you as well to the many professors at the University of Illinois at Urbana-Champaign whose intellectual curiosity never ended at their own areas of research, especially Mark Leff, David Roediger, Paula Treichler, Adrian Burgos, Dana Rabin, Antoinette Burton, Kristin Hogansen, and Diane Koenker.

Friendships with young scholars that began so many years ago have continued to sustain me, even as our lives have spread us far apart today. I would especially like to thank David Krugler and Elisa Miller, who read this entire manuscript and offered extensive comments that have certainly improved it. Dave has been a constant source of experience and wisdom in all matters academic (and quite a few nonacademic ones), and I am grateful that he is willing to share it with me. Elisa has graciously responded to the many questions that plagued me throughout the long revision process, and she continues to remind me today that these ongoing struggles are worth it. Thank you as well to my sexuality research friends David Johnson and Brian Donovan, who know all too well the trials and tribulations of publishing in this area. Thank you to Lara Stepleman for providing me a southern refuge and a reason to go on holiday and get away from it all at various times over the past decade.

In Chicago, I would like to thank Phil Costello and Jeanne Child at the Clerk of the Circuit Court of Cook County Archives at the Richard J. Daley Center; the staff at the Chicago Historical Society; librarians in the Municipal Reference Collection at the Harold Washington Library Center; and archivists at Northwestern University. I would also like to thank Amy Lewis, whose knowledge of wine and Chicago restaurants made my research visits there much more enjoyable, and whose support for my scholarship means more to me than she likely realizes. For long distance research assistance after I took up residence outside the United States, I owe tremendous thanks to Mike Sherfy and Karen Phoenix. To the many others too numerous to name here, thank you; any failings in this book are entirely my own, although I have tried to do justice to your insights and questions.

The support of family and friends outside of academia has been a remarkable source of inspiration to me over the years. I would especially like to thank my parents, Bud and Jan Flood, who may not have always understood the long process of scholarly publishing, but who have always applauded my attempts at it. Finally, to Jack Mooney, who first introduced me to the city that I now know and love so well, despite the unsettling research topic that drew me there. Thank you for sharing with me your apartment building, your bar, your sailboat, and your friendship. I am fortunate (but not surprised) to have you, and now your lovely wife Marilyn, in my life. I am confident that our connection will continue no matter where we end up, and it is to you that this book is dedicated.

Rape in Chicago

Introduction

"An Accusation Easily to Be Made"

Rape. The word itself grips the public imagination with a sense of horror, fear, and perhaps even morbid fascination. Familiar responses include sympathy and support for the victims, outrage at the perpetrators, and an understandable concern for personal safety. But sometimes other thoughts sneak in as well: what was she doing walking by herself at night? Why did she get so drunk at that party? If she had avoided those things, then thoughts likely shift onto a different terrain: he's so creepy he must have done it, just look at the way he ogles and insults women every day. And if the sexual violence is interracial, although statistics prove this is less common than crime among individuals of the same race, the more uncomfortable response is perhaps to expect, but not to excuse, it. These are some of the hidden thoughts about rape that no one likes to admit that they might think, but which include questions historically shaped by a public adherence to rape myths in American culture: myths that routinely define the boundaries of believable victims and likely suspects.

To begin any discussion of sexual violence, rape trials, or criminal jurisprudence in an Anglo context is to acknowledge the oft-cited statement of seventeenth-century British jurist Matthew Hale, who categorized rape as "an accusation easily to be made and hard to be proved and harder to be defended against by the party accused, tho [*sic*] never so innocent."[1] Hale was concerned with what he believed were too many false prosecutions of robbery and rape under past monarchs, and he cautioned authorities against allowing public concerns about sexual violence to mistakenly shape the application of (then) present-day common law. Hale may have been the first to articulate this belief, but his words are regularly brought up in rape trials in the United States even today, and they capture myriad assumptions about sex and gender relations in modern society. Hale's characterization, however, misses an important exception rooted in the distinct history of American race relations: a belief that African American men have an inherently criminal sexual nature and that, if accused of rape by any white woman, they must be guilty. These assumptions are the straw men of the modern American judicial system when it comes to prosecuting sexual violence—but straw men that have proved difficult to knock over. This book reevaluates the ways in which individuals negotiated the extraordinary challenges of being victimized by or accused of sexual violence in modern Chicago, with an eye toward unpacking rape myths and criminal prosecutions. Central to this analysis are the ways in which racial status intertwined with gender and class privilege, or the lack thereof, and how ideas about appropriate or unacceptable sexual behaviors shaped the narratives told in the modern courtroom.

Underlying Hale's cautionary definition of sexual violence is the idea that women lie about it. An ideology of rape throughout history is that such an accusation "easily made" was also likely made up. It was from this early legal interpretation that dominant rape myths scrutinizing women, and privileging the words of men, emerged. State authorities—including the police, hospital workers, attorneys, and courtroom officials—have been previously cast as especially reluctant to trust women who accused men of sexual violence. Instead, they believed that women who *really* wanted to resist rape could effectively do so. Other rape myths include the belief that the crime only occurs in the "ghetto"; that all rapists are unusually depraved or sex-starved; that rape is a crime of sexual passion; and that women make false accusations out of spite or revenge.[2] The exception to beliefs about lying women constitutes a different kind of American rape myth, emerging out of a hegemonic society desperate to keep control of a multiracial, free population. Since the nineteenth century, most whites believed that the only possible true victim of rape was a sexually chaste, white woman attacked by a black stranger in a public space she could not avoid during normal, daytime activities. Convictions of black men so accused were virtually guaranteed, especially in Southern courts, even while criminal prosecutions were also shaped by social factors such as class status, family connections, or a victim's personal reputation.[3] These latter factors routinely affected rape prosecutions in Anglo courts since the time of Hale, resulting in a wide variety of punishments, acquittals, and legal compromises that reflect the profound impact of historic rape myths on criminal realities over time.[4] Popular rape myths continued to persist in the mid-twentieth century and, as this study demonstrates, regularly shaped urban rape trials and their outcomes.

The myths did not go unchallenged, however. In their challenges, individuals involved in successful rape prosecutions in Chicago, whether they were legal authorities or everyday men and women, revealed ways in which they understood and claimed their rights as American citizens. In seeking redress when personal protections failed, as they so often did in the cases of women sexually attacked or men mistakenly accused, individuals pursued a different type of protection throughout the mid-twentieth century. Many looked toward the only official avenue left available to them—the criminal justice system—in order to seek protection of their rights and responsibilities as American citizens, when protection against violence perpetrated on the street (or in an alley, or home, or parked car) failed. Female victims sought the protection of the State during trials, even after their personal safety and bodily integrity had been violated. They opened their lives to judicial scrutiny, confident in the righteousness of their claims. Accused men looked for protections as well, in the form of defense strategies that targeted the State's prejudicial investigations and interrogations as well as making use of judicial safeguards against the wrath of mistaken (or lying) women.

For different individuals to claim such rights, regardless of their social status or the circumstances surrounding the violence they encountered, demonstrates how gendered assumptions of chivalry did not automatically dictate who was awarded or denied State sanctioned legal protections. As scholars have effectively demonstrated throughout different historical periods, the criminal treatment of rape has been shaped by a number of assumptions about the appropriate sexual behaviors of men and women.[5] These assumptions have, historically, been based on the premise that white women's sexuality needed to be controlled. Their innately lustful, deceiving natures required harnessing, lest their wicked ways destroy pious colonial communities or call into question familial inheritances.[6] As women increasingly claimed moral piety in the aftermath of religious Great Awakenings in the American colonies, their sexual chastity still needed to be carefully guarded—by male relatives when necessary and sometimes by women's lies as well.[7] By its very nature, controlled white female sexuality shaped the sexual behavior of men. Respectable white men needed to restrain their sexual appetites, even if those appetites were whetted by women's moral failings. Potential rape victims were thus at the mercy of chivalric men and paternalistic institutions. Some victims were more easily shielded than others.

Slave men and women did not fit into this sexual paradigm. Their sexuality was simultaneously both controlled yet also believed by whites to be inherently uncontrollable. As human property, their right to unfettered sexual access was governed by masters, who sought to increase slave stock exclusively through familial breeding after the foreign importation of slaves to the United States ended in 1808.[8] In a society built upon assumptions of white superiority over other races, black sexuality was foreign, savage, and not easily proscribed by the demands of morality. Admitting that some slaves, or even some free blacks, might have (hetero)sexual desires that privileged monogamy and the family unit would have recognized social equality in a racially divided nation; such a belief was unthinkable for all but the most committed abolitionists in the young American nation.[9]

After the Civil War, racist thinking about African Americans continued to influence prosecutions of sexual violence even as individual black men and women resisted stereotyped misperceptions about their behavior. Black men's sexuality became innately predatory in white minds, at least when it was directed toward white women. White beliefs about black women's promiscuity mirrored those about black men: theirs was an especially seductive sexual personae, necessary to keep up with their men and to, regrettably in many white minds, entice otherwise controlled and controllable white men. The opposite mentality of passive and asexual African Americans—more prevalent for some black women than among the almost always potentially dangerous black men—further restricted beliefs about black sexuality.[10] These ideas accompanied familiar concerns about rape more generally and lent weight to racial myths that dictated viable victims and prosecutable offenders. When men's and women's real lives did not mirror dominant assumptions about sexual violence, as they so often did not, strategies for both the prosecution and defense worked to construct a mythic truth in the modern rape courtroom.

My expectations about sexual violence, and my initial interests in this project, were informed by modern feminist ideology in the late twentieth century. As such, I assumed that women were rarely believed if they came forward with rape allegations. Like other white feminists from the Midwest, my racial privilege also precluded a more nuanced understanding of the racial rape myths embedded in American society. I understood that black men were often unfairly prosecuted for attacking white women and that black women were even less likely than white women to be believed when alleging rape, but I assumed that this type of discrimination was regionally specific and more typical of an earlier period than in modern Chicago. I began the project wanting to know more about what happened to women when they came forward and participated in formal rape prosecutions. Authorities believed some women who charged rape and prosecuted some men for these crimes. Who were they? What effects did rape myths have on the pursuit of legal recourse for victimized women? What defense arguments emerged to challenge State strategies, and how did these arguments make use of familiar racial assumptions about black men and sexual violence?

I turned to the court system to seek plausible answers about what happened when ordinary people encountered the complexities of criminal justice in the United States as unwilling participants on both sides of the adversarial system. As this book demonstrates, male authorities—including police, physicians, judges, and attorneys—were neither particularly cruel nor especially dispassionate toward women who testified in rape trials. Instead, they responded to women's efforts to seek judicial protections by helping them in ways that have been overlooked by contemporary critics, who argue that the prosecution of sexual violence always resulted in women's "re-victimization" when they reported rapes.[11] This research also engages the racial rape myths affecting investigations of sexual violence in a region not generally associated with these assumptions, revealing how African American women and men asserted their own rights both as victims and the accused. Their efforts expose elements of an equality struggle complicated by factors of gender and sexuality that contemporary scholars are only beginning to more fully explore.

An analysis of a set of sex crime trials that were initiated in Chicago between 1936 and 1976 demonstrates that many women during this period reported sexual attacks and found support for their claims from those around them. Beginning the research prior to World War II and extending it into a decade when lobbying efforts resulted in significant rape law reform allows me to examine sexual violence within the context of the many social changes that affected trials in the United States during the mid-twentieth century. For those cases that did go forward to conviction, trial narratives had a familiar ring, suggesting that proverbial rape myths influenced successful prosecutions even when individual case circumstances deviated from a recognizable script. While some authorities remained skeptical of women who reported rapes, police and prosecutors pursued numerous investigations, even in cases that defied rape myths. Implementing chivalric assumptions of masculine protection, they guarded the female victim as the central figure in their cases in the years surrounding World War II, even if her life did not fit precisely the portrait of a so-called believable victim. Although not all victims could be adequately protected from sexual attacks, they could be (and were) protected from verbal attacks in the courtroom, at least until national concerns about the prevention and prosecution of crime changed the acceptable parameters of trial proceedings.

The criminal courtroom does not exist in a vacuum, and the legal and social context in which trial participants acted changed throughout the period under study here. The widespread social reform movements of the 1960s and 1970s had a significant influence on the treatment of the oppressed, including their treatment in the criminal courtroom. During the 1960s, as judges began to accord the accused a greater protection of their rights, prosecutors shifted trial emphases. They added more corroborative testimony to support victims' claims, thereby assuming less faith in their trial narratives and less effectively restraining defense attorneys and judges from interrogating women's sexual histories. While this shift did much to erode the power of female witnesses in the courtroom, so too did it erode assumptions about chivalry that dictated which women deserved State protection and which did not. Instead, prosecutions of rape took on the complexity of trials of other types of violent crimes, bringing the category of sexual violence into a new legal realm. In this realm, male authorities did not assume women needed to be shielded from the constraints of the adversarial judicial system, but rather embedded them within it. For the women who found themselves caught up in this system, their experiences were often contradictory; although their claims to legal recourse were taken seriously, their trial encounters remained difficult to negotiate. The 1970s intensified the corroborative elements of rape trials even while a vocal feminist movement further shaped judicial strategies and sought to improve the treatment of rape victims both inside and outside courtrooms.

Investigations and criminal trials were never easy for rape victims to endure, but women have always come forward to report rapes and have insisted that they were not complicit in sexual violence, despite public and judicial scrutiny. Almost exclusively, male authorities were not always sensitive to the difficulties women faced when talking publicly about private instances of sexual violence, but victims often found support in unlikely places. Neighbors and strangers helped them, by calling police and even seeking out or sometimes detaining suspects themselves. Physicians and nurses aided women in emergency rooms, displaying varying degrees of sympathy in their efforts. Investigators and prosecutors responded to rape victims and helped them pursue legal recourse against their attackers, in spite of the challenges such efforts entailed.

This did not occur in every case, of course. Many women never told anyone about being sexually attacked, and those who did faced numerous obstacles in gaining State support. Sometimes police found women's allegations "unfounded," or they mistreated victims during their investigations by assuming women's complicity in sexual attacks.[12] The "unfounded" category problematizes rape investigations, as its definition relies on myths that conflict about standards of consent and generally fails to recognize attackers known to victims. This study, however, is not a comprehensive history of sexual violence. Rather, it is an analysis of how changing investigations, medical support, and the trial procedures surrounding rape demonstrate the ways in which American citizens claimed the right to, and not just the rewards of, judicial protections. Analyzing cases that ended with convictions challenges the belief that rapists were never punished because authorities thought all women lied about sexual violence. It engages rape myths on their own terms, seeking to understand how individuals resisted them or made use of their power in venues just as restrictive as the myths themselves. It demonstrates how Americans of different social positions attempted to avail themselves of the rights defined in the U.S. Constitution and implemented through the criminal justice system, even if some had greater access to those rights than others. This research also reveals that the State pursued many rape cases even when the circumstances of the attack did not mirror public expectations about sexual violence. As feminists focused on anti-rape activism by the early 1970s, they admitted that some convictions happened but believed those rare occurrences to follow a strict pattern that this study begins to complicate.[13] Prior to this period, witnesses negotiated the justice system labyrinth in order to assert their individual rights, and in doing so they defied ideologies that constructed some rape victims as more believable than others and some defendants as more criminally prone than others.

The site of this project is the diverse, urban population of Chicago, a city that housed an active and multifocused reform movement since its early-nineteenth-century incorporation. Migration patterns of African Americans from the South coming to industrialized cities during the twentieth century have moved the focus of race relations beyond their original Southern borders; accordingly, many scholars have looked at Chicago in order to analyze modern race relations.[14] Leaders in Chicago's black community pursued civil rights throughout the twentieth century, challenging discrimination in policing and employment while fighting de facto segregation in housing and public spaces.[15] Chicago Legal Aid, one of the first public aid societies to be established in the country in 1930, evolved from Progressive Era women's efforts to protect abused women and children.[16] The city's dynamic reform history continued into more recent decades when, in 1967, Chicago women formed some of the nation's first feminist consciousness-raising groups, whose purpose was to define and combat patriarchal oppression.[17] Of particular interest to these women, and to the modern feminist movement, was the legal and social treatment of rape victims. During the 1970s, Illinois implemented laws to guard against the kinds of character attacks that Hale's entrenched definition of sexual violence encouraged.[18] Further Illinois reforms provided a model for new sexual assault laws adopted throughout the nation during the 1980s.[19] Chicago thus provides an effective setting to explore the complex history of sexual violence and criminality in the United States, as well as race and gender power dynamics.

Rape statutes in Illinois and throughout the nation evolved from Anglo common law precedents regarding male property, revised to incorporate republican notions of citizenship and rights. Initially conceived of as a crime against male property rights, nineteenth-century medical jurisprudence ultimately reshaped legal considerations of sexual violence as a violation of individual female bodies.[20] The Illinois Revised Statutes, originally codified in 1874, defined rape as "sexual intercourse with a female . . . by force and against her will."[21] Throughout the nineteenth and early twentieth centuries the law was revised several times to incorporate different details, including raising the legal age-of-consent in 1887 and again in 1905, thus creating a new criminal category known as statutory rape, which negated questions of consent about youthful victims.[22] The following decades saw further revisions in the language and categorization of sex crimes, but at its core, rape remained a crime of "sexual intercourse with a female . . . by force and against her will."[23]

Case law also shaped the evaluation of rape trial evidence. As the courts took up more criminal cases in the growing population of Chicago in the late nineteenth and early twentieth centuries, authorities placed a stronger emphasis on clarifying jury instructions.[24] Their efforts attempted to safeguard the rights of the accused but also, in keeping with Hale's familiar pronouncement, tried to protect the integrity of the law. By nature of their existence in the public sphere, jury members were familiar with rape myths; their official duties, however, were governed by laws and not by popular beliefs. This did not mean that juries found it easy to adjudicate crime and, during the early decades of the twentieth century, the task of evaluating witnesses and evidence fell to them. Although Illinois courts allowed nineteenth-century defendants to waive their constitutional right to be heard by a jury, the majority of defendants did not avail themselves of bench trials until well into the twentieth century.[25] It was not until the 1930s that the majority of local jurisdictions even allowed bench trials for felony defendants.[26]

Important to judges or juries evaluating forcible (or nonstatutory) rape cases was the veracity of the victim's narrative. Several early-twentieth-century court opinions allowed testimony about a woman's general character to shape the assessment of trial evidence. Some also recognized, in light of mythic assumptions about lying women, that a victim's previous "unchaste character" did not automatically preclude the possibility of rape.[27] Throughout the mid-twentieth century, case law precedents generally required corroboration of rape victims' testimonies, although many also recognized that women's sincerity could be positively appraised without corroboration, depending on individual case circumstances. This meant that a victim's testimony regarding her lack of consent, "if clear and convincing," could be enough to ensure a rape conviction.[28] However, judicial opinion also allowed that consent, "no matter how reluctantly given," negated a necessary element of the crime and thus could not sustain a conviction.[29]

Closely connected to a lack of consent that was necessary to prosecute rape cases successfully was the required proof of forced penetration. Here as well, legal precedents varied on what constituted actual force. Prior to the 1960s, most convictions were upheld on the basis of some evidence of a woman's resistance and a man's physical force to overcome her will.[30] Case law also acknowledged that resistance could be allayed or even futile, given the circumstances of an attack, the presence of a weapon, or the paralyzing fear of the victim.[31] It was not until the early 1960s, however, after significant public attention to the expanding problem of criminal sexual violence, that courts regularly accepted that a lack of resistance was not the same as legal consent and that the level of force necessary to complete the criminal act of rape varied significantly.[32] The main elements of proving that a sexual attack had happened, "by force and against her will," were importantly connected to rape myths, insofar as the latter expected women to be less than honest when speaking publicly about private sexual matters, even if those matters involved forced sexual trauma.

The language of the statutes and of case law precedents failed to reflect the difficulties that rape victims, of any race, encountered as they faced potential skepticism about the accusations they made. Moreover, the neutrality of this language erased the reality that African American men were those most often prosecuted for sexual violence. Historian Peggy Pascoe argues that the alleged colorblind nature of the American judicial system actually reinforces racial discrimination because it does not recognize the ways in which white authorities prejudicially investigate crimes.[33] Civil rights activists took up this issue of discriminatory criminal prosecutions, for rape and other crimes, in a post–World War II push for equality legislation in Chicago and throughout the nation.[34] Systematic organizing on behalf of sexually victimized women came to Chicago somewhat later. Unlike other crimes that did not automatically question the actions of victims, the standard of proof in rape cases strictly scrutinized women because the crime turned on the issue of their consent. Rape law did not uniformly attempt to shield victims from public scrutiny until feminists in the 1970s lobbied for reforms.[35] This did not mean that women did not come forward with accusations of sexual violence that they successfully helped the State prosecute, regardless of their socioeconomic, racial, or marital status. Nor does it mean that black rape defendants were not vocal in their demands for civic protection against racial rape myths that cast them as sexually criminal. As this book demonstrates, rape myths operated at many levels, yet individual actions and trial strategies had the potential to undermine them effectively.

The central myth that governed both statutory and case law questioned just whom to believe when allegations of sexual violence became public. Suspicion toward women who accused men of rape persisted due to confusion about the crime and about the ability of women to resist it. As sexual intercourse was not, itself, against the law, and because medical experts disagreed about the level of resistance that would prevent it, rape occupied a unique position within the criminal code.[36] Considered particularly atrocious when it actually (though infrequently) occurred, most people also thought women falsely reported rape more often than not, as its legal definition relied on Hale's seventeenth century interpretation of sexual violence as "an accusation easily to be made and hard to be proved."[37] An analysis of women as inherently deceitful in sexual matters is beyond the scope of this study, although it should be noted here as a vital factor that shaped rape myths and made successful criminal prosecutions hard to achieve.[38] Although other major categories of violent crime might have been difficult to connect to a specific defendant or required extensive evidentiary support in order to prosecute them successfully, rarely were they questioned in the same way that authorities scrutinized women's rape accusations. Simply put, murder had the proof of a dead body; robberies and kidnappings were charged when something or someone went missing; assault occurred predominantly against male victims with visible or extreme injuries, since the police did not effectively punish domestic violence throughout much of the twentieth century.[39] Beliefs about rape as a rare crime compounded the issues that victims encountered when they came forward to report sexual attacks, even as prosecutions of them increased throughout the decades following World War II.

The seventeenth-century common-law understanding of rape has informed its historical presentation ever since. Modern assessments of the legal history of rape began in 1951, when Morris Ploscowe first published *Sex and the Law*, tracing Anglo common law precedents and reform in American rape law.[40] Feminist scholars took up the topic in the late 1960s and 1970s, seeking to understand how jurists felt it might have been "easy" for women to make the accusation and why authorities believed it to be a difficult crime to prove. To feminists, the answers were simple: empowered men did not trust inferior women who cried rape. They analyzed the origins of this mistrust, offering an early basis for gendered legal scholarship. In *Sexual Politics* (1969), Kate Millett presented a literary criticism of how sexism pervaded social relations and informed contemporary politics, thus effectively limiting prosecutions of sexual violence.[41] Susan Brownmiller was one of the first feminist researchers to examine the long history of sexual violence, when she published *Against Our Will: Men, Women and Rape* (1975). Brownmiller considered how sexual violence operated globally as the primary tool by which "*all men* keep *all women* in a state of fear."[42] She argued that keeping women in a constant state of fear of sexual violence forced them to passively depend on the protective mercy of men who would not rape them.[43] Many feminists lauded her groundbreaking analysis, yet others were critical of its lack of racial perspective as she downplayed how white Americans had used rape accusations to justify racial violence against African American men. Radical activist and scholar Angela Davis encouraged white feminists to consider the position of racial minority women in the anti-rape movement and to broaden their critique of gender oppression to include the racist and imperialist nature of the patriarchal American power structure, especially when it came to sexual violence.[44] These activist-scholars established an important framework for understanding the relationships among gender, race, rape, the status of women, and the law.

The expansion of women's and gender history as fields of scholarly inquiry considers the many ways in which acts of sexual coercion and their prosecutions, or lack thereof, have affected individual lives and social relations. Some women defied social expectations and demanded protection against rape, even if their socioeconomic, sexual, or racial status defied notions about the right to such protection. Many women were unsuccessful in those demands.[45] Some men fought allegations of sexual violence by invoking those very stereotypes about female promiscuity that modern feminists, rightly, began to challenge in the 1960s and 1970s. Some were successful in doing so.[46] Some men attempted to invert expectations about their sexual criminality by challenging the broader parameters of a judicial system that treated them unfairly. Some failed at those challenges.[47] Rape myths are based not just on Hale's seventeenth-century assertion, but they are also shaped by how social relations differentiate power and authority over time. This book continues such an exploration, analyzing the ways in which women defied the limitations of chivalry that denied legal protections to rape victims perceived as illegitimate, as well as how men attempted to subvert a racially prejudicial justice system during the mid-twentieth century in Chicago.

An important element of social power negotiations includes the connections between racial and sexual violence prevalent in the United States throughout its history. In reminding white feminists in the 1970s and 1980s to recognize these connections, scholars of African American life look to a longer history of black female activism that consistently challenged racial rape myths.[48] By attempting to expose the ways in which white Americans used interracial rape accusations as a justification for racial violence against black men, African American women have long voiced their concerns about civil rights and personal safety.[49] Their critique of a racist ideology that cast African American men as "beast rapists" included challenges to white (mis) perceptions about black women's sexual promiscuity.[50] The "jezebel" stereotype, stemming from a long history of masters' unchallenged sexual access to female slaves, convinced many white authorities that African American women were "un-rapable."[51] These racial rape myths, although predominantly associated with social relations in the American South, affected criminal prosecutions and defense strategies throughout the nation. They were both played out, and challenged, in modern Chicago.

The ongoing historical discussion about sexual violence illustrates how individuals intervened in and were shaped by the legal process. The creation of the category of statutory rape, prosecutions of incest and sexual abuse within the family, and the growing body of literature about male victims of sexual violence suggest that the history of rape law is fraught with change inspired from below, rather than exclusively imposed from above.[52] A public discourse condemning sex crimes was historically connected to the State's duty to protect its citizens, even if all citizens were not considered entirely equal.[53] Such inequities were pronounced in the courtroom strategies that prosecuted or defended against rape, due to the uniquely gendered nature of the crime. Prior to statute revisions in the 1980s, the legal definition of rape in Illinois (and other states) specifically required penetration of the female genitals by a penis.[54] As well, the crime's historic connection to the many myths that shaped predominant understandings of sexual violence compounded the potential for bias in the courtroom. Chicagoans who found themselves unwillingly enmeshed in the justice system had to negotiate confusing legal concerns as well as the ways in which popular myths shaped sex crime trials throughout the mid-twentieth century.

Equality under the law is an important theory shaping the U.S. Constitution; inequality, however, has long been the legal practice in most American jurisdictions. Disproportionate numbers of racial minorities and indigent men were convicted of sex crimes in Chicago and throughout the nation, yet these men publicly challenged the stereotypes and myths that directed investigators to them. Examining the treatment of African American rape defendants and the strategies they used in court reveals how racial prejudice intervened in modern Chicago rape investigations. Rape defendants were often victimized by a discriminatory justice system that, to this day, unfairly targets racial minorities and the poor.[55] Chicago rape cases that were appealed show the ways in which there were, potentially, many victims in court: women who faced an arduous physical and emotional recovery from sexual attacks; defendants who faced prejudicial investigations and abusive treatment at the hands of criminal authorities; expert witnesses who routinely had their authority challenged during trials; and everyday people forced to adhere uncomfortably to the constraints of the adversarial system. This is not to suggest that degrees of victimization were equally traumatic, but it does begin to complicate assumptions about how rape trials unfolded.

As a study of rape trials that ended in guilty verdicts and how the myths embedded within them operated, this book is not limited to women's experiences in court. Rather, I consider here the actions and words of other courtroom witnesses—including medical experts, investigators, defendants, and defense witnesses—as well as community responses to urban crime and sexual violence. Trial testimonies, presented in support of either side of a case, produced particular truths that were shaped by wider social forces. The adversarial justice system, predicated on the idea of illuminating a single truth about any alleged crime, in fact exposed myriad truthful constructions from a variety of courtroom witnesses. That their words were given different weight, as evidenced by the outcomes of these cases, attests to the ways in which language and the seemingly neutral rules of the court engendered profound power relations.[56] This study does not judge the truthfulness of testimonies or the accuracy of trial results, but rather analyzes how and why individuals acted the way they did in mid-twentieth-century Chicago courts. A broad analysis of courtroom testimonies, placed in the context of a modern urban society, demonstrates how rape was connected to changing gender and race relations in Chicago that came to emphasize the claiming of rights over a paternalistic awarding of protection.

Crime data make it difficult to know how many rapes are not brought to the public's attention. The Federal Bureau of Investigation in the United States annually compiles reports of crime and estimates that rape is the most severely underreported among violent crimes.[57] In an attempt to address the discrepancy between reported and unreported crimes, the U.S. Bureau of Justice Statistics first organized the National Crime Victimization Survey in 1972, which continues to poll one hundred thousand Americans annually in order to ascertain additional information about violent crimes. The survey reveals that 64 percent of rapes go unreported and that even fewer women report attempted sexual assaults.[58] Inconsistent criminal data recorded in Chicago prior to 1960 also make it difficult to fully understand how many actual rape investigations resulted in criminal convictions.[59] In spite of statistical limitations, existing data reveal a significant racial imbalance in reporting. Researchers estimate that as few as one in fifteen African American women who have been raped report it.[60] Angela Davis suggests that society's persistent racism contributes to this discrepancy insofar as white men occupy a space of racial and gender privilege that black women know they cannot effectively challenge, and so they do not report interracial rapes.[61] Moreover, because of the broad association between sexual violence and the mainstream feminist movement, some researchers suggest that African American women are also reluctant to report intraracial rapes for fear of being cast as traitors, or tools of white society, conspiring to oppress black men.[62]

However, not all African American women viewed silence about intraracial rape in that way. Despite historical studies that analyze sexual violence exclusively in terms of African American men's predatory sexual nature against white women, the majority of rapes occur between individuals of the same race.[63] As historian Danielle L. McGuire suggests, "There are moments in history when the pain of violation or the opportunity for justice forced [black] women to come forward to speak out against their [black] abusers."[64] African American women who accused African American men of rape in Chicago during the mid-twentieth century thus found themselves in an uncomfortable alliance with predominantly white law enforcement and judicial authorities, as the civil rights movement and broader black political community often remained silent about these sexual crimes. In spite of the difficulties they faced, many women of all races came forward to report rapes and forced authorities to listen, demanding protection and justice as capable citizens with rights judiciously and legislatively defined.

Civil rights activists in Chicago took their arguments about legal racism into the courtroom during rape trials, using the cases as a platform from which to challenge discrimination and demand reform. The claims that African American men were arrested and charged with rape for little more than being found in historically segregated neighborhoods suggest that we look beyond the Jim Crow South when discussing the racialized nature of sexual violence. Moreover, an analysis of the arguments about racial discrimination that surfaced during the trials considered here moves a discussion of civil rights beyond the more familiar terrain of Southern voting rights and desegregation, or unfair housing practices. More than 80 percent of the cases analyzed in this project involved defendants who were not white.[65] The racial construction of the trials goes far in explaining why, in the years during and immediately following World War II, defense attorneys focused primarily on instances of prejudicial abuse at the hands of white Chicago police officers rather than interrogating the potentially unchaste character of victims. Racial rape myths had long undermined the respectability of black manhood, and black rape defendants in Chicago consistently found their masculinity threatened by abusive police and a racially discriminatory justice system.[66] Nonetheless, they fought for their innocence using the rhetoric of manly protection, rights, and public citizenship.

Rape trials expose the messy ways in which gender, race, class, and sexuality cannot be regarded without overlap. No single demographic or social category ever consistently trumped any other in determining trial outcomes, no matter what rape myths instructed the public to believe. This research avoids the limitations of a strict linguistic reading of trial testimonies, in order to consider more broadly how individuals represented themselves when talking publicly about private issues of sexual trauma, and how legal counsel chose to represent them in court.[67] The conclusions presented here recognize the persistence of rape myths governing trial proceedings in modern Chicago, while delineating the ways in which ordinary individuals undermined and altered those myths. While the circumstances of individual cases might encourage defense attorneys to pursue derogatory questions about a woman's sexuality, it was not until the mid-1950s—more than a decade after the war that opened the public sphere to American women in new and lasting ways— that they began to more extensively cross-examine victims about their past sexual actions. In the 1960s, judicial decisions that protected the rights of the accused further changed defense strategies by expanding challenges to biased investigations and intensifying the scrutiny of victimized women.[68] In the trials that took place during the 1970s, courtroom strategies shifted once again to incorporate arguments that reflected ongoing social activism in the city, particularly informed by modern feminism and a radicalized civil rights movement.

Sex crime trials, where for many years the only female participants were likely to be the victims, present an expansive opportunity to explore how the gendered nature of the courtroom inhibited some social challenges even while encouraging others. Women, and the authorities charged with protecting them, regularly defied social and legal conventions when issues of sexuality were publicly interrogated. In the only other type of criminal indictment mandating the involvement of women in all cases—abortion prosecutions— courtroom strategies constructed aborting women as victims, rather than accomplices, of this crime. This allowed prosecutions to go forward without being undermined by defense arguments about unchaste women.[69] Civil law involving abortion cases was a different matter. Certain conditions allowed

some women and their families to sue over botched abortions that resulted
in severe injury or death. Others forbade such torts in order to punish what
they defined as women's immoral sexual transgressions, suggesting that the
judicial presentation of women, no matter the rule of law, "was unstable, contradictory, and contested."[70] The treatment of women during mid-twentieth-
century Chicago sex crime trials follows a similar trajectory. Although rape
myths shaped public suspicions, prosecutors and complainants worked to
challenge such skepticism, especially when women's everyday lives did not
easily fit widespread beliefs about sexual victimhood. And while prosecutors
sometimes mounted arguments that were rooted in rape myths, their trial
strategies also reflected timely social concerns, thereby defying some of the
expectations they purported to uphold.

   This research is based primarily on testimony taken from sex crime transcripts produced from appeals that came out of Cook County Circuit Courts
during the mid-twentieth century. Courtroom testimony is recorded during all trials, but formal transcripts are only produced when a conviction
is appealed. In order to appeal a case, attorneys (or in rare cases, convicted
defendants themselves) had to present a costly series of legal briefs citing case
law about why certain elements of trials were conducted improperly. These
formal documents, along with a copy of the original transcript, were then
submitted to higher courts for consideration.[71] Social agencies might help
cover the costs, but the burden fell primarily on the individuals involved.
After World War II, the National Association for the Advancement of Colored People (NAACP) began paying closer attention to criminal convictions
when it could be inferred that they were based on racial prejudice rather than
factual evidence. Subsequently, the NAACP might cover the cost of certain
appeals.[72] Because its budget was limited, however, so too were the number
of appellate cases the organization could fund. The years under study here
begin in 1936 with the first preserved transcript for an appealed rape conviction.[73] At the same time, the Chicago Police Department began discussing
plans to organize a separate Sex-Homicide Division to investigate violent
crimes. Supporters of the plan connected these criminal categories because
investigators found that rape often had the potential to lead to murder.[74] I
read and analyzed every transcript of rape, attempted rape, and crime against
nature in Chicago appealed before 1959: a total of thirty-four cases.[75]

   The appellate process changed when the Illinois Supreme Court held that
a lack of financial means denied individuals the right of "due process." The
high court required the State to provide money to produce a copy of a trial
transcript, or a less formal equivalent, to support appeals regardless of the
economic status of the petitioner.[76] After the State assumed the responsibil-

ity of funding the production of transcripts for indigent defendants, the number of sex crime convictions that were appealed in Cook County tripled during the 1960s. The volume of cases required that a sample of transcripts be analyzed: one-third of the recorded cases, for a total of thirty-three trial transcripts of decisions appealed between 1960 and 1969.[77] During the 1970s, appellate cases nearly tripled again, so one-eighth of the preserved trial transcripts from the years 1970–76, a total of twenty-six cases, constitutes the sample for these years.[78] This study ends with cases that began in 1976, although they were often tried in court a year or two later because of the slow pace of the American justice system. It was at this time that the Illinois State Legislature passed legislation that shielded rape victims from the types of courtroom interrogations that many authorities and women had been attempting to curtail for years prior to their official inclusion in the law. Supplemental analyses come from the print media, as it reported on sex crime convictions, legal trends, and representations of rape victims and defendants in the Chicago press during the years under study.[79] While several newspapers are referenced, the *Chicago Tribune* was the city's oldest and most widely circulated daily during the mid-twentieth century and thus provides the basis of the systematic print media analyses presented here.[80]

Cases can be appealed only if a defendant pleaded not guilty and was convicted, so the ninety-three transcripts that constitute the main sources used in this research do not reveal everything about the history of rape in modern Chicago. These transcripts do, however, provide important insights into the history of sexual violence, the persistence and defiance of rape myths, timely trial strategies and legal processes, and the changing status of women and men in the courtroom. Although limited by certain structural constraints, criminal records also reveal particular moments in individual lives that are rarely recorded in other places. The victims and defendants who appeared in these sources did not leave personal memoirs or deposit their correspondence in an archive for later researchers to discover; instead, they testified before courtrooms filled with strangers where their words were recorded verbatim. Interpreting the silences, objections, interruptions, and utterances that were "stricken from the record" (but which stenographers still wrote down) helps illuminate a broader history of personal experiences and a social, not just a legal, understanding of the trial system and the successful prosecution of violent sex crimes.

Throughout the project, the names of witnesses who testified in court and the individuals who appeared in government and media reports connected to rape cases remain as they appear in the sources. The data analyzed here are all matters of public record and do not legally require the use of pseudonyms when referring to the people appearing within them.[81] While the decision to use real names is perhaps controversial or even voyeuristic due to the nature of the study, I believe that transparency is important. Since this research seeks to understand the experiences of individuals who entered the system because of circumstances of sexual violence—and claimed, with varying degrees of success, protective rights of citizenship along the way—I felt it vital not to hide their identities. Too often "everyday people" are lost in the historical record because of a lack of preserved documentation about their lives: this book recaptures and respects ordinary people's voices, even if they only appear here because of personal trauma and violence.[82]

Linguistic choices made throughout the project reflect a historical understanding of sexual violence and race relations in mid-twentieth-century America. I have referred to the people victimized by sex crimes as women, victims, complainants, or complaining witnesses. I avoided the term "prosecutrix," as rape victims were sometimes called (unless citing the evidence directly), because it reflected the accusatory beliefs justice officials often directed toward women who reported rapes during the decades under study. Since the trials analyzed here all ended with convictions, whatever suspicions authorities may have held about victimized women were overcome, undermining the implications of that term. I have also avoided using the word "survivor" when referring to rape victims during most of the years of this study. When anti-rape feminists introduced victim advocacy efforts during the early 1970s, "rape survivor" first entered the public lexicon, although it rarely appeared in Chicago courtrooms even then. The legal terms used reflect the indictments filed: rape, crime against nature or deviate sexual assault, and attempted rape. I used the phrase "sexual attack" rather than "sexual assault" when referring to sexual violence more generally as the latter is a legal category that did not appear in Illinois law until 1984.[83] The word "assault" also downplays brutality: as the testimonies analyzed here often reveal high levels of violence, "sexual attack" seemed a more appropriate choice. As well, attack was the term consistently used in the print media to imply sexual violence before changing community standards allowed for the publication of more detailed descriptions of so-called taboo crimes.[84] This project considers, almost exclusively, race relations within and between white/ethnic Chicago communities and the city's African American population. There were other racial minorities populating Chicago throughout this period, yet the overwhelming majority of individuals appearing in the transcripts, and those discussed in the public discourse of rape, were either white or black. African American and black were used interchangeably in both the narrative and analyses, while

"Negro" and "colored" appear in quotes when taken directly from sources, reflecting standards of the times.

Reconstructing rape narratives from trial transcripts demonstrates how everyday people negotiated criminal policy when they formally engaged with unfamiliar proceedings. Most rape victims were ordinary women, uncertain as to how to act in court, and most defendants were similarly caught within this system. Expert witnesses and authorities, including physicians, police officers, and crime lab technicians, may have been more familiar with the adversarial system, but their testimonies also reveal the effects of persistent rape myths even as those myths came up against very real social change. Chapter 1 provides an overview of the experiences of women as they entered the justice system after reporting sexual attacks prior to the 1960s, when judicial decisions significantly altered trial proceedings. Victims' social differences were muted from a prosecutorial standpoint because of standardized investigative procedures—procedures much more rigorous, if not entirely sensitive, than previously understood by contemporary studies of sexual violence. Racial privilege shaped the majority of these successful prosecutions, in that African American women almost never appeared in court testifying against white men, and white women testified against black men far more often than they did against white rape defendants. Women's marital or class status did not preclude their central importance to the States's cases, demonstrating how many women challenged the limitations of chivalry, which awarded protections to only a select few, by standing up for themselves and being taken seriously when they reported sexual violence.

Chapters 2 and 3 consider racial rape myths and how they affected modern Chicago trials. A focus on defendants and defense strategies in chapter 2 reveals how African American men and their attorneys challenged assumptions about black criminality and forced urban authorities to confront these assumptions during the postwar years, when the civil rights movement expanded nationally. These men specifically asserted that the trial system they faced in Chicago mirrored a Southern system of (in)justice that had not yet fully abandoned lynch-mob violence. Although they were not successful in gaining acquittals, their efforts expand our understandings of racial discrimination and re-imagine the geographic boundaries of the criminalized black male body. Chapter 3 refocuses attention on the treatment of rape victims during the 1950s exclusively, when African American women began regularly appearing in court, challenging the idea that they did not trust the system, or that the State did not consider theirs to be winnable cases. Despite the State's efforts to portray black rape victims as deserving of protection and justice, defense attorneys maintained racist and sexist stereotypes in court, causing an evolution of the rape trial into the hostile territory that contemporary rape victims face and feminists continue to reform.

The book's final chapters analyze the strategies employed by attorneys both to prosecute and to defend against rape, as well as trial participants' resistance to rape myths in light of ongoing social reform movements. Chapter 4 considers U.S. Supreme Court decisions that guaranteed defendants' rights and their role in shaping the structure of rape trials at the local level during the 1960s. New judicial protections worked in favor of defendants yet simultaneously made trials even more difficult for victims, as legal requirements necessitated more precise corroborative testimony that overshadowed the narratives women produced. Chapter 5 considers how changes in gender and race relations played out in society and in Chicago rape trials during the late 1960s and 1970s. Outside the courtroom, feminists helped create victim advocacy services and provided much-needed support for women who came forward to report sexual attacks. Despite a long history of African American women's activism against racial and sexual violence, the radical feminist movement was plagued with a myopic focus on gender oppression that limited interracial cooperation in the anti-rape movement.[85] Such limitations did not mean that black rape victims did not make use of advocacy services, reflecting the potential for interracial feminist cooperation during this period. Such cooperation did not extend to relaxed urban race relations, however, as defense strategies continued to challenge the familiar prejudices of the Chicago police well into the 1970s.

This book places sexually violent conflict in Chicago at the center of uncovering how individuals negotiated prescribed sexual and social identities during a time of shifting gender roles and racial strife. Women of all races claimed the right to be protected against sexual attacks and helped the State legitimate their claims with legal recourse, even when their socioeconomic, marital, or racial status defied expectations about who constituted a believable victim. They found support within a judicial system that, historically, did not readily welcome female participation. African American men, challenging legal accusations of dangerous sexuality in modern Chicago courtrooms, participated in a long tradition of defying racist assumptions about their inherent criminality. While defense arguments rooted in the broader rhetoric of civil rights did not work in their favor in the cases analyzed here, the strategies employed to defend against accusations of rape nonetheless reflected black men's attempts to claim, as American citizens, protection against discriminatory practices. The unwilling participants in sex-crime trials challenged rape myths and asserted their rights within a judicial system notoriously uncomfortable with the collision of public and private that prosecutions of sexual violence entailed.

1. Rape Victims and the Modern Justice System

On the evening of November 21, 1936, thirty-eight year old Anna Brasy, a white woman who sang soprano in her church choir, finished practice and went home. She lived with her mother and brother in a Lincoln Square apartment on Chicago's north side. She went to bed, but later woke up when she heard her bedroom door open. She turned and saw a man standing over her. He was holding a knife and told her not to scream or he would kill her. After forcing her to remove her pajamas, he raped her. He brutally beat her, tied her hands with the cord from her bathrobe, and demanded money. She told him that she had some in her closet. Although the man agreed to leave when he heard this, after taking the money he continued to attack her. He started to choke her as well, but left abruptly as Brasy struggled to free herself. She woke her mother and brother. When her brother saw her condition, he called the police while Mrs. Brasy tended to her daughter. When the police arrived, one officer immediately took Anna Brasy to the hospital and another investigated her bedroom and the alley outside the apartment, searching for the perpetrator. After several months in the hospital, Brasy had still not identified any of the suspects that the police brought there for her to view. When her mother received an anonymous tip about the attack, Brasy informed the police. Shortly after, they arrested twenty-four-year-old Robert Conroy, a white man Brasy ultimately identified as her assailant.[1]

Anna Brasy's experiences were extreme, and public attention to the case reflects a great deal of concern about urban crime and violence, especially sexual violence, during the mid-twentieth century in Chicago. Although it involved a level of brutality that did not mirror all Chicago rape cases that ended up in court, the similarities between Brasy's experiences and those

of other rape victims—even those who did not spend months recovering in
the hospital—suggest that authorities pursued rape investigations more aggressively than previously understood. Although current assumptions about
the past have doubted the diligence with which male authorities investigated
rape allegations, court and media records prove this to be untrue. The State's
Attorney's Office in Chicago organized a Sex Bureau in January 1937 in order
to deal with sex crime cases in the city, forcefully responding to the publicity surrounding a series of attacks against women in downtown hotels since
the previous summer.[2] This initiative coincided with the establishment of
a distinct Sex-Homicide Division within the Chicago Police Department,
organized to "capture the night prowlers who have been raping and killing
women."[3] Five detectives were permanently assigned to the Sex Bureau, with
additional officers transferred in temporarily when difficult cases like Anna
Brasy's continued until a suspect was identified.[4]

With regard to identification of suspects, it is during this period that the
Bertillonage system of suspect identification via body measurements (named
after its nineteenth-century creator, Alphonse Bertillon) was being replaced
with fingerprint identification, although investigators continued to rely on
multiple forensic identifiers in their search for missing criminal suspects.[5]
In keeping with these techniques, the police kept on file "the fingerprints,
measurements, and photographs of every person accused of a sex crime in
the city" in the hopes of catching what a local newspaper called "moron attackers."[6] Such a derisive label and the published concerns about ongoing
attacks suggests that, in spite of Matthew Hale's historical warning about
unproven accusations, many people were alarmed about the realities of sex-
crime violence. Chicago authorities kept busy in an attempt to curtail sexual
violence in the city, and they responded to women's complaints, even when
victims were not so brutally beaten as Anna Brasy.

Extensive details of Chicago's many rape investigations are lost to the historical record, however. Investigations ended or grew cold when police could not
locate viable suspects, or charges might be dropped when a victim withdrew
her complaint, due to reasons often left vague.[7] Moreover, as part of the professionalization of the modern justice system, by the 1930s nearly 80 percent
of all Chicago defendants pleaded guilty, usually to a lesser offense than the
original charge.[8] Nonetheless, prosecutors brought forward and tried several
cases successfully, even if these were a fraction of the rape complaints investigated or even reported to the police throughout the mid-twentieth century
in Chicago. While commonly held beliefs about rape myths in many ways
shaped how indictments were presented in court, trials ending in convictions
did not universally adhere to public expectations about "real rape" victims

and violent sexual attacks.[9] Likewise, while it was once thought that women were reluctant to pursue legal recourse after being raped, in fact many victims willingly entered the bewildering space of the courtroom in order to claim their right to be protected against unprosecuted sexual violence.

Women's efforts to represent themselves as victims of crime rather than as instigators of sexually deviant contact indicate their rejection of rape myths. Moreover, the support they received from State authorities suggests that these myths were publicly contested in the decades surrounding World War II. Court officials allowed women to narrate their experiences of sexual violence without extensive corroboration during these decades, privileging their testimonies above that of other State witnesses. Many judges also prevented defense attorneys from straying too far from the specific details of attacks and criminal investigations by limiting questions about victims' personal backgrounds and sustaining State objections on these matters. The legal maneuverings of both prosecuting and defense attorneys affected the treatment of women during trials in different ways, of course, but rape victims maintained some authority in the courtroom. After all, it was their testimony that would ultimately make or break cases. During this period, women's courtroom efforts reveal how essential they were to the judicial process and how authorities took seriously their right to claim the protections of the criminal justice system.

Prosecutors emphasized victims' chaste and forthright character while building their cases, even when their marital, racial, or class backgrounds defied the expectations demanded of sexually victimized women. Downplaying victims' social differences during these years emphasized that the State did not automatically succumb to suspicions that certain victims (middle-class, chaste white women) were more believable than others (black, working-class, or divorced women). As the cases analyzed here demonstrate, prosecutors supported many different women in their pursuit of State protection. Defense attorneys were unable to destabilize these muted differences, at least until African American rape victims began appearing in court more regularly during the mid-1950s. Black women's social status was easier to interrogate within the confines of a system rooted in both racial and gender privilege. For a time, however, Chicago court officials respected rape victims' testimonies, avoiding particularly harsh scrutiny of their social circumstances in the courtroom. The overlapping experiences of women who reported rapes and helped the State successfully prosecute defendants highlight the ways in which they coped with their unwelcome involvement in the judicial process and asserted their own, albeit limited, power in this venue. Although prosecutors may have relied on historic notions of chivalry and of awarding protection to a select few, victims' efforts to claim security within the public sphere of the judicial system expanded a culture of rights for all women.

Throughout the mid-twentieth century, Chicago police investigated thousands of reports of rape and other violent crimes. In the years leading up to a departmental reorganization in 1960, Chicago police arrested rape suspects in an average of almost 67 percent of all investigations, which compares to the 72.5 percent average arrest rate for felonious homicide investigations between 1936 and 1959.[10] These data correspond to changes in the modern city. During the crisis of depression and the early years of World War II, investigations of violent crimes were downplayed in favor of other national concerns, even as authorities expanded the apparatus that dealt with reports of sexual violence. Still, Americans' attentions lay elsewhere during these years, which was especially true for crimes that involved victims whose veracity was already potentially suspect, like women who reported charges of domestic or sexual violence.[11] Rape arrests in Chicago during the early 1940s were also limited by investigative difficulties, as a transient military population shipped in and out of the city, making it difficult to find alleged perpetrators. Enlisted suspects also could have been turned over to military police, which held jurisdiction over civil crimes at this time. The 1920 Revised Articles of War gave the U.S. military jurisdiction over all crimes allegedly committed by servicemen and women, whether on or off base. Its World War II–era court docket was crowded because of the existence of the largest American military force ever assembled at home or overseas. Civil prosecutions of enlistees and officers became possible only after 1950, when the revised Uniform Code for Military Justice replaced the earlier Articles of War.[12] Not coincidentally, the number of arrests for violent crimes in Chicago expanded significantly after World War II as well.

In spite of investigative difficulties, hundreds of Chicago women regularly came forward with reports of sexual violence, influenced by their changing status in the public sphere. During the 1930s and especially after the United States entered World War II, women joined the paid labor force in greater numbers than ever before, challenging gender role expectations in American society.[13] As more women entered new public arenas, they relied less on the traditional, and sometimes false, security of domestic boundaries. Instead, women displayed an expectation of the protections accorded American citizens, reflected in their willingness to defy questions about their sexual culpability and report rapes to authorities. They continued to do so in the years following the war, when rape complaints and investigations never again fell to prewar levels.

Table 1. Differential Arrest Rates for Rape, Felonious Homicide* in Chicago, 1936–1958

Year	Rapes Investigated	Rapes Cleared by Arrest (% Arrest Rate)	Homicides Investigated	Homicides Cleared by Arrest (% Arrest Rate)
1936	143	89 (62%)	344	187 (54%)
1937	158	95 (60%)	354	195 (55%)
1938	146	85 (58%)	278	153 (55%)
1939	174	88 (51%)	342	222 (65%)
1940	134	71 (53%)	306	200 (65%)
		5-year average: 56.8%		5-year average: 58.8%
1941	154	62 (40%)	297	195 (66%)
1942	177	81 (46%)	289	169 (58%)
1943	237	124 (52%)	228	139 (61%)
1944	363	190 (52%)	249	170 (68%)
1945	409	249 (61%)	280	186 (66%)
		5-year average: 50.2%		5-year average: 63.8%
1946	448	308 (69%)	295	164 (56%)
1947	473	329 (70%)	258	132 (51%)
1948	623	450 (72%)	418	244 (58%)
1949	737	575 (78%)	352	290 (82%)
1950	635	464 (73%)	331	290 (88%)
		5-year average: 72.4%		5-year average: 67.0%
1951	697	509 (73%)	332	290 (87%)
1952	627	428 (68%)	449	375 (84%)
1953	535	376 (70%)	432	379 (88%)
1954	471	327 (69%)	419	350 (84%)
1955	536	361 (67%)	436	352 (81%)
1956	583	378 (65%)	434	368 (85%)
1957	596	404 (68%)	413	350 (85%)
1958 **	532	352 (66%)	412	359 (87%)
		8-year average: 68.3%		8-year average: 85.1%
Totals:	9588	6395 (66.7%)	7948	5759 (72.5%)

Source: Chicago Police Department, "Annual Reports," 1935–1958. Data published as raw numbers; percentages tabulated by author.

* refers to murder, negligent manslaughter, non-negligent manslaughter

** data unavailable

Helping to explain the increase in rape reports and arrests in Chicago by the end of World War II was public attention to women's activities, including concerns about female sexuality. Such anxieties were embodied in the wartime image of the "Victory Girl," who sought sexual adventures out of a sense of patriotism and to explore newfound freedoms, but whose exploits had the potential to undermine the sexual health of fighting men and, indeed, the moral health of the American nation.[14] Wartime newspapers lamented an increase in female criminals, chastising the amateur "pick up girl," who was crowding out her professional prostitute counterpart in Chicago's jail cells.[15] Moreover, critics noted the alarming rates of sexual attacks being reported during the later war years and connected these violent crimes to the violence of war.[16] Women's sexual activities and contested status may have led some men to believe that they could push flirtations beyond the consensual stage, resulting in more instances of attempted and forcible rape, or at least more reports of sexual violence by this period. Chicago's growing population affected criminal statistics as well; there were simply more people in the city by the end of the 1950s than there were at the beginning of the 1930s.[17] Consequently, there were more crimes to investigate and more criminals to pursue. The investigation and arrest rate for forcible rapes in Chicago grew much faster than did the city's population, however, suggesting that local authorities were prioritizing a problem once downplayed.

Telling Someone

Few women called the police directly after being raped, opting instead to report the attack to a neighbor, a family member, or sometimes to strangers. Both men and women helped rape victims in traditionally gendered ways, without automatically dismissing their claims or succumbing to the suspicions that popular myths directed them to feel. Women offered immediate aid and emotional support, while men played the protective role of intermediaries who called police, or initiated an amateur search for the perpetrator. In Brasy's case, her brother called the police immediately after he saw his sister's brutalized condition. After Mary Elson, a middle-class white woman, was dragged into an alley and raped in Chicago's downtown "Loop" neighborhood in 1946, she asked the man who found her to take her to her nearby church, where she expected help from her priest. The man was "good enough to take her to the police station" instead and the police called Elson's priest, who accompanied them to the hospital where she was later examined.[18] Forty-three-year-old Marguerite Thorpe, a divorced, working-class white woman, was attacked in 1948 while waiting for a bus on the southwest side. She told the first woman she saw on the street after it was over. This woman took her into a friend's nearby apartment, where the women attended to Thorpe and the husband called the police.[19] Maurice Brown, an African American resident of the Wells housing project near Chicago's south side Bronzeville neighborhood, ran to her mother's home when she was raped in 1951. A male neighbor overheard Brown's panicked claim and, while her mother called the police, he went to the alley where she said she had been attacked to see if the assailant was still there.[20] Both men and women volunteered assistance to victims and helped alleviate some of the isolation that women felt after being raped. None of the courtroom testimonies from these witnesses suggest that rape myths about lying women diminished the support these victims received after they were attacked. Indeed, newspaper articles from the period are filled with details about Chicago clubwomen demanding action to "curb moron crimes" and praising the efforts of those who kept vigilant watch for suspects after rape victims filed reports.[21] Even if a woman's rape allegation did not make it to trial, it is clear that many Chicagoans demanded support and protection for female residents against sexual violence.

Police followed a standard procedure when they responded to a report of rape. Their duties were to observe and to take statements from everyone who was possibly involved in a case, including victims, suspects, and any other relevant witnesses. The officers in Chicago's Sex Bureau had to, as one detective explained, "make proper preparation of the case for the State's Attorney's office."[22] This was often difficult for police because victims were understandably traumatized by sexual attacks and could not always talk about them right away. When investigating Mary Elson's complaint, police later testified in court that "she was very nervous and unable to talk," but that the officer quickly "tried to get as much information as [he] could."[23] Although legal precedents did not demand it, reports made without delay were usually viewed with less skepticism than those from women who waited to report sexual attacks.[24] Police interviewed victims several times during the course of an investigation, but immediate statements helped prosecutors build stronger cases because these women did not have time to think up excuses about why they were on the street or at a tavern before they were attacked.

An investigator's job meant not only interviewing witnesses but also determining the extent of a rape victim's physical injuries and assessing her demeanor. Their observations were important for later courtroom testimony concerning the truthfulness of women's complaints. Police expected rape victims to be upset; as female sexual chastity was highly valued even in modern American society, its violent ruin was understandably devastating for sexually victimized women. An officer's testimony about a woman's traumatized responses to what were, to him, standard investigative questions helped validate her accusation. Police were not necessarily unsympathetic when they encountered distressed victims, but they had to find out what happened, and part of that process required interviewing victims who were neither calm nor immediately forthcoming about their experiences. A police officer corroborating the 1949 testimony of rape victim Margerite O'Neill, a waitress who worked in the same north side working-class neighborhood where she was attacked, told the court "she was in a hysterical condition" when they first talked to her.[25] When the police responded to a call from teenaged Joan Skuzinski in 1952, an officer testified "she was crying and seemed to be hysterical . . . [and] she told us two men had raped her."[26] If the police could testify that an alleged victim was "hysterical" or "dazed," this suggested to the court that she had been sufficiently traumatized and was probably telling the truth about being raped.

Medical testimony also provided important corroboration for women who reported rapes, although its inclusion at trials during the mid-twentieth century was inconsistent. Police knew more about this than victims, who generally went to the hospital after being raped only because officers took them there. Police did not, however, take an alleged rape victim to the hospital as a matter of standard practice, but only if her physical injuries seemed to warrant it. When police arrived at a crime scene in the middle of Chicago's black business district in 1952, they found Ernestine Collins, an African American woman who had two black eyes and was bleeding from a head wound. An officer took her to the hospital and later told the court why: "for her condition and to see if her complaint was justified."[27] In Collins's case, the injuries to her head, not her rape complaint, demanded primary attention. Ann Burtner, a white woman, testified in 1943 that she called police after a "colored" man broke into her apartment in Chicago's south side Packingtown neighborhood and raped her. Neither the State nor defense counsel asked Burtner about a medical exam, nor did she or the investigating officer testify about any hospital visit.[28] When police questioned Alice Goolsby, an African American housewife and mother, about the rape she reported to them in 1955, she chose not to go to the hospital. As an officer testified, "She didn't see fit to go."[29] When the defense attorney asked Goolsby's husband if he took his wife to a doctor after the attack, he simply said "no."[30] As in the case of Anna Brasy, however, police took severely injured victims to the hospital for treatment. While there, they were also examined for their rape complaints.

Female family members or friends often accompanied women and the police to the hospital. When African American teenager Dorothy Mae Hayes was raped in 1946 in a neighborhood just west of downtown, her cousin drove Hayes and her mother to Cook County Hospital right after she reported it.[31] One of the women who helped care for Marguerite Thorpe after finding her on the street on the southwest side accompanied her and the police to the nearby Jackson Park Hospital.[32] Emily Warbende's female supervisor at a south side orphanage went with her to the Englewood Hospital in 1950 after Warbende, a white woman who lived and worked at the orphanage, was raped in her bedroom there.[33] Later, they might testify for the State, as in the case of Flora

Frazee, who went with Thorpe to the hospital and later appeared as a witness against rape defendant Lorce Jones.[34] These women stood up for victims and told the court what they believed had happened to victims of sexual attacks, thereby challenging myths that assumed most women lied about rape.

Going to the hospital with a victim provided some emotional support after a rape, but women faced medical examinations alone. Rules of privacy and professional privilege excluded friends or family members during rape exams.[35] A police officer waited, perhaps behind a curtain or outside the room, ready to collect forensic evidence gathered during the procedure. Of course, the physicians (mostly men) and nurses (almost exclusively female) who performed the exam were there, but women were isolated from concerned friends and family during this time. Some women had no one, other than the police, to accompany them to the hospital after an attack. In 1952 Ann Robinson had recently moved to Chicago and lived alone at the Wabash Avenue YMCA, a temporary residence for many of the African American migrants who settled in the city during and after World War II.[36] When she reported a rape, the police alone took her to Cook County Hospital, since she had no close friends or family members to accompany her.[37] Similarly, Ernestine Collins, who was raped outside a south side tavern after spending time there with friends, waited inside while the bartender called the police. The bartender later testified how he had warned the man who eventually raped Collins to leave her alone "because she was not bothering anyone," yet neither he nor any of the other black male patrons volunteered to go with her to the hospital after she was attacked.[38] While some women may have been hesitant to go to the hospital with only the police, others were undoubtedly grateful for their help and sought treatment that would later help support the State's cases.

Medical examinations of victims provided important circumstantial evidence corroborating women's allegations of sexual attacks. The elements required to legally prove rape included a woman's resistance and the penetration of her genitals by "the male sex organ."[39] No universal standard defined adequate resistance to prove rape, but physicians could offer their opinions about force, resistance, consent, and penetration if called to testify. The inclusion of medical evidence during this period strengthened the State's cases by corroborating women's words with experts' opinions, but it was not yet a mandatory part of successful rape prosecutions.[40] Prosecutors could use physicians' testimonies that proved intercourse at least had happened, thereby challenging defendants who claimed that they never had sex with the women testifying against them. Hospital visits following a rape became more commonplace by the 1960s, at which time prosecutors regularly began presenting more corroborative evidence, including medical reports and expert testimony, to support women's rape allegations.

At mid-twentieth century, medical examinations in rape cases consisted of observing the patient, performing a pelvic exam, and taking blood and vaginal samples for laboratory tests. Physicians often noted the psychological condition of a patient, observed any external bruising or cuts, and looked for the presence of spermatozoa. Physicians testified about all of these matters, as well as about the appearance of stains on a woman's clothing, and fluid in or around her vagina. By the 1930s, medical experts could easily observe motile spermatozoa under a microscope, and a chemical test could isolate seminal fluid on fabric as early as 1878.[41] British common law required evidence of "emission" to prove rape in order to overcome concerns about "accusation easily made and hard to be proved." But American physicians throughout the nineteenth century lobbied hard for courts to recognize that penetration itself, as "an uncivilized act of aggression," could be enough to sustain a rape conviction.[42] Early in Illinois history, State officials agreed, although it was not until nearly a century later that the legal concept of penetration without emission as sufficient to prove rape was entrenched in case law.[43] Even without such a requirement, testimony about the presence of sperm on a woman's body or clothes could help support her rape allegation, even if identification techniques connecting that sperm to a particular suspect were still decades away.[44]

While physicians could corroborate a victim's claim of intercourse, they could only offer opinions about her lack of consent. The consent standard was the key to every rape conviction. If a woman said yes or if the defense effectively argued that she failed to resist, thereby tacitly consenting in the eyes of the law, prosecutors had no case. Recalling the admonishment that rape was hard to prove, many physicians believed that a rape would be nearly impossible to complete if a woman resisted to the utmost of her ability.[45] The inclusion of medical evidence in sex crime trials was thus a tricky proposition for the State. When physicians testified in rape trials prior to the 1960s, they regularly speculated about victims' resistance, or lack thereof, during alleged attacks. Their testimonies could help corroborate women's words or could be spun by defense attorneys as evidence that alleged victims failed to resist and thus perhaps actually consented to sexual activities after all.

It was difficult for a physician to determine how hard a victim fought off an attacker, but the presence of vaginal bruising or injury to the hymen suggested at least some resistance on her part, which supported a claim of sexual violence. The physician corroborating Mary Elson's accusation told the court about "bright blood" and "profuse bleeding from a laceration of the hymen of recent origin."[46] A physician testifying in the 1951 rape trial of John Ingraham and James Ethridge indicated that he found evidence of recent healing around the edges of the hymen when he examined the victim, a student at the south side's largest and virtually all-black Wendell Phillips High School.[47] When Mary Ann Texter, a twenty-four-year-old African American bookkeeper, reported that she was sexually attacked near the south shore of Lake Michigan in 1957, the physician who examined her testified that her hymen was partially covered with a blood clot. This finding, he explained, was "nature's way of attempting to repair" a recent injury.[48] In addition to its evidentiary value, this type of medical testimony reminded the court that sexual attacks involved severe physical violence as well as emotional trauma. It is doubtful that anyone hearing this kind of testimony would be unable to at least begin to question myths that assumed women's complicity in such violence.

Prosecutors did not abandon rape myths entirely in using medical evidence to build their cases, however. Expert testimony about injury to the hymen went beyond corroborating a victim's resistance and invoked social beliefs about the importance of a woman's purity, specifically her virginity, in determining her lack of culpability in a sexual attack. Anna Brasy's physician testified about the extent of her many injuries, including injury to her hymen. He told the court that when he first examined Brasy, her hymen was bleeding in a number of places, "as though it had been torn in the last few hours."[49] He admitted that while the hymen did not stay intact throughout a woman's life, he was of the opinion that Brasy had never had intercourse before, effectively supporting her rape accusation.[50] Medical testimony about a recently injured hymen suggested that a woman was chaste and thus unlikely to consent to sex with anyone, in keeping with mythic perceptions about the most believable of rape victims. Brasy's testimony that the violation happened when a stranger broke into the family home after church choir practice intensified the physician's opinion about her chastity.

Details about religion helped the State present a more complete picture of the victim of a sexual attack, beyond what physicians or investigating officers talked about in court. A woman's religious status might also help allay suspicions about her public activities and could counter myths about female sexual promiscuity that defense attorneys tried to exploit. Rita Gray Goldberg testified against Charles Hughes in 1948. She told the court that it was just past midnight and she was on her way home from her family's nightclub business when she was attacked outside the elevated train (El) stop in her neighborhood, just west of downtown. Although the prosecutor never questioned her directly about her religion, he did ask her to spell her last name, which was unnecessary as the court stenographer had the correct spelling on other documents. This question helped stress her religious affiliation, though, which was a familiar one in a city that housed both a significant Jewish population and many liberal Catholics who actively opposed anti-Semitism.[51] Joan Skuzinski accepted a ride home from a tavern after she and a friend went to a dance in 1952. She later accused the drivers of rape. When she testified, the prosecutor made sure to establish that she was a recent graduate from, specifically, Lourdes Catholic High School before asking her any other questions about the sexual attack.[52] Courtrooms were strange and sometimes hostile environments for women who spoke out publicly about intimate and traumatic details of their disrupted lives, aware that their status as victims of sexual violence was intensely scrutinized. Bringing up their religiosity was a way for prosecutors to elicit sympathy, rather than skepticism, toward rape victims who testified in court.

As the different rape cases that went forward to appeal demonstrate, however, the specter of certain rape myths was sometimes more creatively invoked at trial because women's lives did not always adhere to popular directives about their credibility. Some, like white church choir soprano Anna Brasy, fit easily into the paradigm of an authentic victim of sexual violence. Others, like black tavern-goer Maurice Brown, contradicted several elements of this paradigm, even though she also helped the State convict the man who raped her. Chicagoans actively protested the growing menace of "moronic" sex crimes in their city. Yet numerous editorials and letters in the newspaper also differentiated between the crisis of sexual violence and the sexual misunderstandings that happened when women went out looking for a pick up or accepting favors such as drinks, dances, or rides home from men they had just met.[53] These "tavern rapes," as some critics dismissed them, relied on traditional adherence to standards of appropriate female behavior that were beginning to break down in the years surrounding World War II. Prosecutors whose cases relied on the testimony of women whose actions did not always reflect idealized femininity had to look for ways to summon the community's outrage about rape, and not their consternation about loose or lying women. So they made use of medical evidence such as bleeding hymens to prove that women resisted and were physically injured by sexual violence but also to imply that, no matter what their prior actions might have been, they were still chaste and unlikely to have consented to sexual activities. Judges and juries could (and did) believe these women, regardless of any other details about their lives or the circumstances of cases that might have contradicted the expectations of valid complaints coming from "real rape" victims. In spite of its corroborative value, however, medical evidence was not always available to the State.

Significant obstacles discouraged many women during this period from pursuing medical treatment following a rape. In over 40 percent of the Cook Country Circuit Court transcripts analyzed for the years 1936 through 1958, complaining witnesses did not mention a hospital visit and prosecutors presented no medical evidence at all.[54] Victims sometimes avoided medical treatment for economic reasons. Throughout the first half of the twentieth century, few Americans could afford to go to the hospital. At the onset of the Depression the average cost of a clinic visit, for physical examinations and a variety of tests and treatments, was about five dollars—at a time when new minimum wage laws guaranteed only forty cents per hour.[55] Visits to hospital emergency rooms, after which women might be admitted for further care, were even more expensive than clinics, and the added costs of laboratory tests prevented many rape victims from seeking medical attention.[56] While some victims' physical injuries required treatment, and medical institutions absorbed these costs prior to the advent of voluntary health insurance plans, if a woman was not severely injured after a sexual attack, she might hesitate to go to the hospital, fearing its prohibitive cost. By the early 1950s, nearly half of all Americans remained uninsured. For those with insurance, their coverage was limited to only about fifteen percent of an average hospital bill.[57]

In addition to monetary difficulties, some victims avoided post-rape medical examinations because they were hesitant to expose themselves, both literally and figuratively, to even more male authorities than they had already encountered. A review of medical publications from the late nineteenth and twentieth centuries suggests that doctors and medical writers were often less than sympathetic, and sometimes coldly dispassionate or even cruel, toward the rape victims under their care.[58] While physicians considered pelvic examinations standard medical procedures, their patients' experiences were anything but common. Police and physicians testified about questioning women in emergency rooms while they were "lying on examination tables . . . talking, hysterical, disheveled, dirty, in shock," recreating a scene that emphasized the trauma and isolation rape victims suffered following an attack.[59] Women also had to deal with the social taboos that examining procedures disrupted, in addition to the emotional and physical aftermath of sexual violence. Even under potentially joyful circumstances, such as during childbirth, many women felt uncomfortable having male physicians examine their private organs.[60] When researchers developed the "pap smear" test for detecting cervical cancer in the 1940s, campaigns encouraging women to get screened and to get over their discomfort at the procedure demonstrate how difficult it was for women to abandon their modesty, even in the name of good health.[61] In cases of rape, the discomfort of female patient-victims

could be compounded by physicians' internalized suspicions toward potentially lying women.[62] Female doctors, who may have alleviated women's
distress over having pelvic examinations, rarely staffed emergency rooms.
Physicians who specialized in the treatment of rape victims and wrote articles
about forensic rape exams were usually men who had no idea what women
faced after a sexual attack. Their gender, and the myth—especially popular
among medical experts—that a woman could avoid a sexual attack if she
truly resisted, contributed to the insensitive and wary attitudes that many
physicians expressed toward rape victims.[63]

Yet raped women did go to hospitals, and the attitudes and actions of
physicians varied. Some were sympathetic toward patient-victims and treated
them with sensitivity and care. In a rare courtroom appearance by a female
attending physician, Dr. Yolanda Sanchez testified on behalf of the State for
forty-seven-year-old white, widowed rape victim Ann Mack in 1955. Before
she presented any forensic details, she first informed the court that she "found
the patient to be nervous."[64] Sanchez's choice to begin by testifying about
Mack's emotional condition rather than with her medical findings suggests
a gendered empathy with the victim. Some male physicians also expressed
sympathies about their patient-victims in court, rather than displaying the
neutral dispassion or the suspicions and implied hostility that was prevalent
in the medical literature. Before examining Ann Robinson the night she
was raped, one of the interns at Cook County Hospital's emergency room
made sure his patient was modestly covered, since the police were present
during the exam.[65] Dr. Albert Weiss specifically told the court in 1959 that
he examined Joyce Ray, a nineteen-year-old white student nurse at the University of Chicago, only after he "gave her the necessary medical care for her
marked nervousness."[66] The reactions of physicians and other medical staff to
patient-victims were highly individualized. In spite of the critical tone of so
much medico-legal literature about women's allegations of sexual violence,
universal condemnation (or praise) for medical professionals who dealt with
forensic rape examinations is difficult to sustain historically.

If police successfully pursued a suspect, victims might quickly identify
their attackers, sometimes even before they left the hospital. Bringing a possible suspect to the hospital so the victim could identify him did not always
result in an arrest, though. Anna Brasy's was one such case. While police had
found a knife at the scene, and a pair of men's shorts with blood on them in
a nearby alley, they had difficulty connecting them to a viable suspect.[67] An
officer testified that police brought over fifty suspects to the hospital for Brasy
to identify during the months she recovered there.[68] Almost one year after she
reported the attack, and several months after physicians released her from the

hospital, the case remained open. Only after Brasy told the police about an anonymous call to her mother did they find and arrest Robert Conroy. They placed him in a lineup with nine other white men at the Belmont Avenue police station, and it was here that Brasy identified Conroy as the man who had attacked her the previous year.[69]

In all criminal investigations, the State expected police to find and arrest alleged perpetrators. Throughout mid-century, Chicago police made arrests in nearly 67 percent of all reported rapes, many of these within a few weeks of the complaint.[70] The police were not so lucky in Anna Brasy's case, as it took much longer than that. The delay and the numerous failed identifications suggest several things about rape investigations in Chicago. Initially, the police actively investigated the case. They interviewed several lakefront fisherman in order to identify the boning knife recovered at the scene, and questioned many different suspects. The police wanted to find Brasy's attacker quickly, both because of the extremely violent nature of the crime and also because the idea of a white man prowling the alleys of Chicago's north side and attacking innocent white women was disturbing to the city's middle-class, white population. Crime was not supposed to occur in their neighborhoods, but only in other areas—presumably the neighborhoods that housed the city's African American and transient populations, although crime reports were beginning to spill over these traditional community boundaries as well.[71] During the time that Brasy recovered, police were also busy looking for another rape suspect, a "colored" man who climbed into the windows of white women staying in downtown hotels and south side apartments.[72] These cases had caused enough panic that the police department finalized their coordination of the Sex-Homicide Division, a distinct unit that went operational in September 1937 and worked with the newly organized Sex Bureau to deal with reports of sexual violence in the city. The division employed detectives to investigate criminal reports but also employed seven social workers to help women victimized by sexual violence, a trend familiar in a city with a long history of this kind of reform activism.[73]

Women had to identify the men who raped them: at the scene, in the hospital, through photographs, or in a police lineup. Police struggled with apprehending the correct suspect in rape cases. Since the victims were usually the only witnesses to the rapes they suffered, their descriptions alone dictated those whom officers pursued. Police arrested men for rape according to how they looked or because of their immediate presence in the area of an attack. If that presence was unexpected, as in the case of an African American man on the streets in a historically white neighborhood, the exact descriptions victims provided might matter less to arresting officers, who were familiar with racial rape myths that assumed black men's guilt for interracial sexual attacks. The police did not always find perpetrators right away, though. Both Ann Robinson and Joan Skuzinski recognized their assailants from pictures after failing to recognize anyone in the suspect lineups arranged for them.[74] Lilie Corfield, an African American woman, attended several lineups at the south side Englewood Police Station during the weeks after she was attacked in November 1957. Corfield eventually identified Gerald Chatman at one of the many lineups she attended. A second victim and several witnesses who had seen Chatham near where the rapes had occurred confirmed this identification.[75]

Delayed identifications demonstrate that victims refused to abandon their important role in a rape investigation, despite the psychological difficulty of repeatedly having to revisit their attacks. An African American victim, Charlestine Mills, attended many lineups after reporting that she was raped in 1955. When she ultimately recognized her attacker at one of them, she testified that she viewed the men for some time before identifying the defendant in order to be sure about it.[76] While other felony investigations also suffered from delayed or difficult identifications, the nature of prosecuting sex crimes placed women at the center of their own conflicting emotions. They wanted to help police find the right suspect while simultaneously trying to put the events of a rape behind them so that they might get on with their lives. Not all rape investigations ended in trials, however, because not all victims were willing to continue with investigations that went on for months or even years. Such frustrations were highlighted by press coverage of rape charges dropped due to women's failure to return to court to testify against their attackers.[77] Their desire to get beyond the sexual traumas that brought them to the justice system in the first place was made all the more problematic because many Americans believed popular rape myths about lying women. Yet many Chicago women continued to demand their right to legal protections, even if they had been unable to protect themselves against sexual attacks. They were resolute in their determination, and the police did not automatically dismiss most complaints or fail to follow through with difficult investigations even when victims' social backgrounds or experiences of violence contradicted rape myth expectations.

A victim's reluctance to identify the wrong man could, however, stymie police investigations. In many cases, detectives pursued suspects for weeks, sometimes months, only to be denied an arrest by the word of a woman. The local news was filled with articles detailing how rape charges were dismissed because victims failed to adequately identify suspects.[78] The State could not initiate criminal charges without a defendant. Rape convictions depended on the testimony of victims, who, because of the wording of the statutes, were always women.[79] Without their cooperation with male authorities and their participation in a judicial process that was not generally welcoming to victims of sexual violence, rapists went free. Police took women's identifications seriously and investigated rapes as best as they could, but they had to depend on the statements of women offered in the midst of personal trauma. The entire male-dominated and rape-myth-informed criminal justice system thus hinged, uncomfortably, on the words of women and the identifications made by them. Their efforts represented deliberate participation within an institution that did not easily accept their input. Women's persistence here is important and also reflected a personal defiance of rape myths that they might have once believed themselves and a willingness to claim the right to avail themselves of legal recourse through the justice system rather than wait to be protected by chivalrous men.

Going to Trial

Prosecutors presented rape cases in a courtroom very differently than the investigations of them unfolded. Officers investigating a rape could gather information in a much less formal manner than attorneys in court, who had to abide by the rules of an adversarial system that required a structured presentation of evidence at trial. At midcentury, police were bound by few of the constitutional protections the accused in the United States today deserve and enjoy. They questioned suspects and recorded statements as individuals made them, usually without attorneys governing their conduct or without the accused knowing that they had the right not to talk to the police at all.[80] Police brought in suspects and hoped that victims would identify them, which sometimes required holding several lineups. Conversely, attorneys questioned trial witnesses who, while in court, had to respond to exactly what was being asked. They were not supposed to offer information beyond what was asked or to clarify their answers without prompts from attorneys. They might have done so in earlier venues, like when they first spoke with police, for example, but during trials their testimonial narratives were more restricted. Prosecutors had to build a case out of information from witnesses, predominant among them the victims themselves, and they presented a constructed scenario at trial to prove the defendant was guilty "beyond a reasonable doubt" of the crime with which he was charged.[81] How victims fit into that construction demonstrates the many ways that women challenged rape myths, even while prosecutors and defense attorneys both sought to exploit these myths in different ways.

During a rape trial the victim, called the "prosecuting" or "complaining" witness, usually testified first, followed by the arresting officer in the case. State witnesses who appeared in court less often included physicians and family members or friends to whom victims initially talked about attacks, but prosecutors did not always include their testimonies at trial. The law did not require corroboration of a woman's rape allegation if it was "clear and convincing."[82] It was, however, sometimes advantageous for both the State and the female victim when there was a man who had called in a report of rape, because that allowed men to testify in a setting in which their gendered authority was more explicitly valued. Rape myths directed suspicion toward most female victims, and supportive male witnesses helped alleviate doubts in court. The brother, male neighbor, or priest who called the police and later testified at trial did not suffer the same wariness that the American public or defense attorneys usually held toward women who reported rapes. The court valued these men's testimonies in ways that were not undermined by popular assumptions about sexual violence and lying women.

The people who testified in rape cases knew what they were supposed to talk about, but unless they had appeared in court before, they could not have been fully aware of the limitations they encountered during trials. Courtroom narratives were not the first time victims described their attacks to male authorities. Indeed, they had done so many times before—to police, physicians, family members, and friends—but the trial venue was different. It was particularly upsetting for victims, who were the center of State's cases and thus at the center of the court's attention. They, of course, knew firsthand the traumatic details of rapes that they had to talk publicly about in a courtroom full of strangers, itself a taxing prospect. Moreover, they had to do so in such a way as to overcome the myriad doubts against them, while simultaneously adhering to unfamiliar trial rules. Transcripts illustrate that some women were better prepared to testify about their attacks than others, which was only partially explained by witness preparation. In 1908, the American Bar Association (ABA) established a "Canon of Professional Ethics" that defined appropriate lawyerly conduct.[83] It took some time for it to be adopted nationally, but by the mid-twentieth century, Chicago attorneys were bar certified and operating according to the rules. Rape victims knew what questions they would face from prosecutors in court and how they were supposed to answer them, but often they did not anticipate how defense attorneys could manipulate or directly challenge their testimonies.

The modern U.S. criminal trial is based on an adversarial system where opposing sides present arguments designed to illuminate the "truth." Although British common-law precedents formed the basis of American case law, the

U.S. legal system incorporated additional elements structured according to citizenship rights articulated in the Constitution.[84] Protections under the Sixth Amendment, for example, guaranteed that someone accused of a crime has a right to face his or her accuser publicly—a difficult proposition for the victim of any violent crime.[85] Some of the system's contemporary detractors suggest that it is particularly trying for rape victims to fairly participate in public trials. Gendered styles of communication allow male witnesses to fit more easily into the adversarial, almost combative, structure of the courtroom, while women are often more familiar with using language to "build relationships . . . and mediate disputes."[86] Contemporary trials certainly constitute one way to mediate criminal disputes, but their rules simply do not accommodate building relationships. While individual men's and women's communication styles do not always fit neatly into such binary categories, this division is especially useful in analyzing a rape trial setting where victims and court officials were divided by gender in almost all cases. When all of the elements of a rape trial were combined—defense attorneys versus victims; men versus women; private recollections versus public display; and the consequences of emotional trauma versus the requirements of criminal testimony—they worked together to present uniquely gendered challenges for victims of sexual violence.

Rape victims whose cases ended with convictions had to deflect or escape entirely the social blame they may have encountered when they first reported an attack. Other women were not as successful in subverting rape myths, and newspaper articles detail many sex crime cases acquitted at trial or refused an indictment by the grand jury.[87] It was not always clear why some sex crime indictments ended the way they did, but newspaper coverage often clarified how juries refused to believe women who alleged rape if the women had been drinking with defendants, if they claimed the attack took place in the man's home or hotel room, or if they had otherwise allegedly enticed defendants into sexual activity.[88] Adherence to popular rape myths shaped the outcome of these types of cases, as community members assumed some women's behavior did not reflect that of a believable victim. In other words, Hale's seventeenth-century characterization of rape as an accusation easily made and hard to be proved still haunted twentieth-century courtrooms. At the same time, the local print media regularly published criminal statistics that highlighted the efforts Chicago authorities made to curb sexual violence in the city. The high arrest rates for sex crime suspects did not translate into similarly high conviction rates, but neither were conviction rates appallingly low during this period. Indeed, throughout the years surrounding World War II, the *Chicago Tribune* reported on hundreds of rape convictions and sentencing practices, as well as highlighting sex crime conviction rates that hovered around 50 percent.[89] Depending on their editorial tone, reporters used this information to demand higher accountability among authorities and stricter legal action against sexual violence, or to quell community concerns about the stresses of urban living at a time of significant population growth and sweeping social change. Either way, these reports suggest that not everyone in Chicago assumed that all women lied about rape.

Women who faced the foreign environment of the rape courtroom in the trials analyzed here had to find ways to assert their rights, knowing full well that historical assumptions were not on their side. Challenging the adversarial rules and producing their own narratives of rape allowed women to regain some control over their lives and to assert their rights within the justice system. Victims like Anna Brasy might not have been able to effectively resist being sexually attacked, but they could attempt to resist testimonial boundaries by offering explanations for questions that went unasked during trials. Even though attorneys never brought it up directly, victims regularly explained how they "allowed" themselves to get raped. Even if the circumstances of their cases did not precisely reflect rape myth expectations, in court women expressed the need for, and their right to, State protection. This was not the kind of protection offered out of chivalry to only certain victims, as reflected historically in limited rape prosecutions. Their diverse social backgrounds and the varying details of their attacks reveal how women throughout Chicago claimed justice as a constitutional right, in spite of the obstacles they faced in doing so. Moreover, by simultaneously resisting the linguistic constraints of the courtroom while attempting to conform to agreed-upon standards of believability, women presented themselves at trial in an acceptable way even though the system forced prosecuting witnesses to talk publicly about the social taboo of sexual violence.

Anna Brasy's courtroom appearance represented the final part of her involvement in the criminal justice system. Brasy's testimony first established her activities during the night of the attack; she came home from choir practice and went to bed shortly thereafter. Next she described the layout of her bedroom and the street light shining in her window, emphasizing to the jury how she was able to see her attacker, despite the fact that she was raped in the middle of the night.[90] Considering the amount of time and number of suspects it took for police to find the man Brasy ultimately identified, this context was extremely important. Proper identification was also important because the public defender in the case never questioned the premise that Brasy was raped; he only denied that it was his client who had raped her. After

Brasy identified the defendant as the man who attacked her, the prosecutor asked her what happened.

By braving the system to make known their attacks, many rape victims helped the State gain convictions and proved themselves to be capable citizens, articulating not only their own visions of the law but also of appropriate standards of sexuality and gender roles. They asserted in court that they had not been doing anything wrong, nor did they behave in any way that could be construed as consenting to sexual activities. Victims usually testified about the details of attacks in response to a single question. By eliminating numerous distinct inquiries about the charge, which divided a rape narrative into a series of impersonal encounters, prosecutors allowed women to recount their attacks without diminishing personal trauma. These accounts give insight into the experiences of women in the courtroom, in addition to exposing the actual events of sexual attacks that were successfully prosecuted during this period.

The details that rape victims presented in court were explicit, and sometimes difficult to imagine. Brasy testified that she woke up when she heard her bedroom door open and felt a shadow over her bed. A man threatened her with a knife against her throat, which effectively stalled any resistance on her part. As she told the court, "I know I screamed but it was not very loud." The jury later heard from her mother and brother that they did not wake up then, suggesting that her screams were quiet or muffled.[91] Next, she described the attack, beginning with the defendant's intent: "The first thing he said, 'I am going to fuck you,' of course I was just paralyzed with fear then."[92] Although the judge upheld an objection to Brasy's fear-induced paralysis, the jury heard her say how afraid she was. Victims on the witness stand commonly offered unsolicited testimony, such as describing their emotional response to a rape, in spite of trial rules prohibiting such comments.

Testifying about forced participation represented a way for rape victims to challenge assumptions about their culpability in an attack. By describing herself as "paralyzed with fear," Anna Brasy denied the implication that she did not resist sexual activity strongly enough, or at all. Victims consistently spoke about their fears of rape, and many also testified that perpetrators threatened to kill them or that the presence of a weapon curtailed their resistance. Marguerite Thorpe testified that she felt what she believed to be a knife in the defendant's pocket and that he "put his hand over my mouth and told me if I made any outcry of any kind that he would kill me."[93] Similarly, Maurice Brown told the court that the defendant threatened to kill her if she screamed while he held a knife against her throat.[94] Ernestine Collins explained how she "played like I wasn't going to do . . . anything about it" so she could escape further injury after she was raped.[95] Aware that resistance was a required legal element to prove rape, women also insisted that the circumstances of an attack shaped the nature of their resistance. Suggesting murder as a consequence of fighting back helped women counter perceptions about their passivity, which was often exploited by defense attorneys as tacit consent. Murder was something men understood better than rape, which helped women clarify their experiences of sexual violence in the masculine courtroom setting. Moreover, Chicago investigators also agreed that rape and murder had the potential to be connected when they established the Sex-Homicide Bureau while Anna Brasy recovered from her sexual attack.

Victims' testimonies also reflected their efforts to shape bodily discourse into a formal narrative that reflected gendered standards of respectability. After first quoting her attacker's words, "I am going to fuck you," Brasy switched to a more technical description. She could begin her narrative with a crude word because it was not her own, and this emphasized the social distance between Brasy and the defendant. The prosecutor quickly moved her away from such graphic language. He asked, "he had sexual intercourse with you?" Brasy confirmed it and continued, more formally. She described how he "put his mouth to my vagina and then he turned me over and attacked me again in the rectum."[96] When the prosecutor asked her to clarify what she understood by "intercourse," Ann Robinson testified that she meant, "they attempted to put their penis [sic] into my vagina."[97] Sometimes the language of a victim's testimony was a bit less technical, but no less descriptive. When asked what she meant by having "an intercourse" with the defendant, Marguerite Thorpe told the court that he had "stuck his privates into my privates."[98]

Testimony about sexual matters was particularly trying for trial witnesses, especially for the women at the center of the State's rape cases. Not only did such testimony recall for women traumatic past events, but it also brought attention to a difficult topic at a time when frank discourse on sexuality and the body was only just beginning to expand in the public sphere. The demands of respectability denied women the right to discuss explicit sexuality in public, even if such discussion was necessary for rape prosecutions. Most victims appearing in the trials analyzed here negotiated such difficulties by using formal language to describe sexual attacks, either initiating the words on their own or following the lead of prosecutors. This helped them preserve their status as respectable women, even if justice officials or juries may have been suspicious of the circumstances that brought them to the court's attention in the first place.

Brasy's testimony functioned in numerous ways. It proved the necessary legal elements of a rape and a "crime against nature."[99] It allowed her to talk about sensitive issues in a clinical way and thus establish an authoritative voice that mirrored forensic experts who sometimes also testified about sexual violence. It provided her with a sense of emotional distance while she recalled the details of the attack and helped her explain her inability to stop it. Finally, Brasy declared her own class position and her violation by a lower-class man. He told her, "I am going to fuck you," she told the court "he put his mouth to my vagina . . . and attacked me again in the rectum."[100] The victim here presented herself as a respectable woman in contrast to the defendant, who spoke in a "course [sic], uneducated manner" and who demanded from her "unnatural" sexual acts, implying that his socioeconomic status was beneath hers.[101] Brasy's testimony was powerful and complete, and she was an effective prosecuting witness.

Other victims faced more antagonistic court officials during a rape trial. Defense attorneys, who were supposed to challenge the State's cases, might try to do so by questioning women's sexual respectability or by arguing that they had likely consented to intercourse and, therefore, were not really raped at all. Such strategies reflected the kinds of rape myths that governed much thinking about sexual violence and represented some of the most hostile insinuations that women endured in court during this period. When Margerite O'Neill testified against Coleman Sepe, the public defender repeatedly asked her if she "came into these taverns [near the site of the attack] quite frequently, but most of the time in the escort of some man?" When O'Neill testified that sometimes she also went out alone, he asked if "it would be after midnight, is that right?" He also repeatedly asked her how, if his client ripped off her undergarments as she had claimed, why "in no place in these panties was there any evidence of a rip?" as he showed them to her and to the court.[102] The defense attorney's clear implication was that O'Neill must have initiated the sexual encounter, or at least consented to it, as the defendant insisted she had. After all, he established that she was familiar with seedy taverns, was known to date different men, and wore skimpy underwear that she allegedly removed herself as part of a consensual sexual act—arguments all meant to undermine the victim's respectability, and thus her veracity, in sexual matters. Rose Bojko, a Ukrainian immigrant who barely spoke English, faced a defense attorney who repeatedly objected to her stilted testimony. Instead, he suggested she act out the rape she claimed had happened in the back seat of his client's car in 1953.[103] This request would have forced Bojko to relive the rape in a way that police statements or trial narratives did not. Moreover, the

defense counsel's proposal for such a performance would have demanded that
the victim present herself in a sexually provocative manner, undermining
the central element of every rape prosecution: the lack of a woman's consent.
Luckily for Bojko, the judge agreed with the State's objection to this outlandish
proposal, declaring such a demonstration to be "distasteful" and protecting
the victim from compromising herself like that in court.[104]

Stenographers produced shorthand notations of every question and inter-
ruption that occurred during trials. Although transcripts present only the
words of trial participants, one can hypothesize about rape victims' emotional
experiences in the courtroom. The prosecutor usually began by informing
victims that they needed to speak loudly so that the court could hear all of
their testimony. Some women had to be reminded to speak up, indicating
discomfort at both speaking in public and reliving the trauma of a sexual
attack in the trial venue. Almost immediately after Margerite O'Neill began
to tell the court what happened to her the night she was raped, the public
defender interrupted to ask that she "please talk up loud enough for me to
hear too."[105] Defense attorneys for Frank Teti and Dominic DiBiaso repeatedly disrupted rape victim Ann Robinson's narrative with complaints that
"she is talking so fast" they did not understand her testimony.[106] During her
description of the night she was gang raped in 1957, the African American
complainant, Hazel Morrison, had to tell the court several times that the
defendants called her "a fat mama" and said that they wanted her.[107] Recalling the details of a rape was harrowing for any victim under most (if not
all) circumstances, but doing so in an unfamiliar setting that did not readily welcome female participation, or in a public venue where respectable
women did not speak of such things compounded their difficulties at trial.
The obstacles women overcame in helping the State pursue legal recourse
against rapists were embodied in their hesitant voices and repeated, difficult
testimonies. Authorities' cooperation with women, even with those whose
lives did not mirror preconceived notions about believable victims, demonstrates that rape myths about deceitful or sexually provocative women were
not universally held. The cases analyzed here featured a variety of women
from many different backgrounds, suggesting that not all rape victims were
reticent to participate in a system that modern feminists would later target
as a source of abuse.

Women's confidence in their own abilities to cope with the aftermath of
rapes and to claim judicial protections against them helped shape attorneys'
responses as well. When Mary Elson testified, no one asked her to repeat
herself or speak louder. Elson's courtroom confidence did not diminish during her cross-examination either. At one point, in response to the public de-

fender's question about identification, she referred to him by name indicating that she "wasn't fit to positively say anything that day, Mr. Collins."[108] Despite her audible and confident testimony, however, the prosecutor asked Elson if she would like a drink of water.[109] This undoubtedly helped her calm down, but it also interrupted an intense cross-examination built upon mythic beliefs about lying women. As Joan Skuzinski described how she attempted to resist a particularly violent attack, the judge gave her a chance to compose herself when he declared that "well, we will give her a little recess, a five minute recess here."[110] In the same way that some physicians displayed sympathy and sensitivity toward the rape victims they examined, State officials also reacted to women in a highly individualized manner, tempering the atmosphere of male privilege that the courtroom fostered.

Many women found rape trials, and their role within them, confusing. For example, defense attorneys insisted that victims avoid the term "rape" because that was a legal determination up to a judge or jury. They routinely objected to women asserting that they had been raped, thus distracting and frustrating them. When Emily Warbende testified several times that she was raped, either the defense attorney objected or the prosecutor interrupted, "No, no, not rape, what did he do?"[111] Ann Robinson also asserted that when she talked to a police officer, she told him, "I was raped." Over defense objections, Robinson insisted, "That is what I told him."[112] Similarly, Joan Skuzinski explained that when the police arrived at her home, her mother wanted to know why. Skuzinski testified that she told her mother, "I was raped," and repeated it even after defense counsel objected.[113] How victims understood their experiences of sexual violence did not easily fit into the constraints of the American judicial system, but their courtroom efforts nonetheless demonstrate women's willingness to come forward and endure repeated examinations in pursuit of State protections. In doing so, they found support in a number of unexpected places.

* * *

Although no two sets of circumstances that surrounded a rape were alike, public expectations about sexual violence followed a pattern that appeared in many of the cases successfully prosecuted during this period. The attack of Ann Burtner presented a more familiar rape scenario than that of Anna Brasy. Burtner's injuries were not as severe as Brasy's, and her description of the suspect was not unexpected. Burtner was a white, married woman who was pregnant with her second child in 1943. Her husband was also white, and worked as a truck driver. She was at home with her sick baby when an African American man invaded her bedroom. The defendant, Samuel Wright, testified that he worked as a janitor for his brother-in-law, and that he was a recent migrant to Chicago from Mississippi, where he had finished the seventh grade.[114] His racial status and lack of education were consistent with white expectations about the men who usually committed rapes. Despite Burtner's advantageous racial and social status, she had a difficult time, and the judge had to interrupt her testimony with encouragement to "compose yourself now."[115] Repeated courtroom questions about the details of rapes were necessary for convictions but nonetheless illuminated the obstacles that women faced when they reported sexual violence, even for those women whose attacks presumably conformed to racial rape myths.

Despite the efforts of defense attorneys to prevent victims from using the word rape in court, the women who appeared in these transcripts continued to insist that they had been sexually attacked. They came from different Chicago neighborhoods, occupied various socioeconomic positions, held diverse religious faiths, were both black and white, and were married, divorced, single, childless, or mothers. What they had in common was sexual victimization and a persistence to claim their right to State protection when it happened. They sought support and expected police to investigate their attacks, sometimes sought medical care, and repeated their stories to prosecuting attorneys who brought charges against male suspects. They demanded that police, prosecutors, judges, and juries listen to their words and their experiences, and punish defendants accordingly. Not all victims chose to report rapes, but many did. Some of them also had their voices heard in court, in spite of rape myths that regularly questioned women's complicity in sexual violence. The responsiveness of prosecutors during this period contradicts the assumptions of feminist activists and writers, who argued that little was done to aid victims prior to the anti-rape movement of the 1970s.[116] It was the sometimes-uneasy cooperation and trust between male authorities and female victims that resulted in rape convictions throughout the mid-twentieth century. This trust would eventually be undermined by changing judicial standards, but for a time women asserted their rights in the courtroom even if they had lacked sufficient protections outside of it.

The confrontation between private sexual trauma and its public presentation in the structured courtroom setting reveals how distinctly gendered sex crimes were awkwardly situated in the masculine sphere of the criminal trial, and how difficult, but not impossible, it was for female rape victims to navigate this terrain successfully. Many women entered and dealt effectively with the constraints of the justice system after brutal circumstances forced them into that position. As central witnesses for the State, women received help from police, prosecutors, and judges, but women did not sit back and

wait for justice to be awarded to a select few. They claimed their rights, cooperated with criminal investigations, and successfully intervened in criminal
proceedings that had long dismissed the majority of women's allegations of
sexual violence. The various social positions of the women discussed here
suggest that expectations about believable victims did not prevent the State
from taking up the cases of women who did not easily fit into the rape myth
paradigm. The commonalties among different women's actions and reactions
to sexual violence and the limited power they claimed during these traumatic
episodes deserve recognition for what they represented: many rape victims
persevered in court and helped the State gain convictions in spite of the
difficulties they encountered in doing so. Just as women persevered against
durable rape myths, so too did black defendants and their attorneys struggle
to overcome one of the most unrelenting of related racial myths—that of the
black beast rapist.

2. The Power of Racial Rape Myths after World War II

Southern trees bear a strange fruit,
Blood on the leaves and blood at the root,
Black body swinging in the Southern breeze,
Strange fruit hanging from the poplar trees.

Pastoral scene of the gallant South,
The bulging eyes and the twisted mouth,
Scent of magnolia sweet and fresh,
And the sudden smell of burning flesh!

Here is a fruit for the crows to pluck,
For the rain to gather, for the wind to suck,
For the sun to rot, for a tree to drop,
Here is a strange and bitter crop.[1]

In 1939, jazz singer Billie Holiday first performed *Strange Fruit,* an emotionally intense song about African Americans lynched in the South. Holiday released the song that year on an independent label because her regular one, Columbia, was not interested in it. By the end of World War II, the recording had sold over fifty thousand copies and was well publicized in the left-wing press. Holiday's numerous performances across the country made it a sensation, and it became her signature song.[2] Passersby on Forty-Seventh Street, in the heart of what was known as the "Harlem of Chicago," often heard it as music drifted out of the jazz clubs and entertainment spots that featured stars such as Nat King Cole, Sarah Vaughn, and Holiday herself, who often performed on Chicago's south side.[3] Jazz artists recognized the song as "the first unmuted cry against racism" in America.[4] Although lynching had been a theme in black fiction, theater, and art, it had not figured prominently in music prior to Holiday's recording. Certainly, such overt lyrics had never before been directed at white audiences. White Americans who enjoyed Holiday's performances of *Strange Fruit* generally resisted the song's message about discrimination and racial violence. Others missed it entirely, as was evident in a famous recollection of one request, made to Holiday in a Los Angeles nightclub in 1950, to "sing that sexy song . . . the one about the naked bodies swinging in the trees."[5] She refused.

While no black men were formally lynched in Chicago in the twentieth century, the lyrics in *Strange Fruit* evoked the kind of discriminatory treatment that African Americans throughout the nation recognized. Although black male sexuality had been condemned as savage and potentially dangerous throughout American history, it was after Emancipation that African American men were represented as a particular threat to the social order, especially in Southern states. In the late nineteenth century, white Southerners regularly discriminated against and attempted to control a newly free black population. Of special concern was the threat of racial miscegenation: the fear that African American men, free to pursue economic and social equality no matter how thwarted their attempts may have been, would also want sexual access to white women.[6] A related belief was that no white woman, no matter how lowly or depraved, would ever willingly consent to interracial relations, in spite of significant evidence to the contrary.[7] White Southerners used these fears to rationalize extreme violence against African American men and used the excuse of rape to justify the lynchings and vigilantism that supported the racial status quo. By World War II, instances of lynch mob violence had decreased significantly, but the specter of interracial sexual violence continued to govern trial proceedings, even outside the Jim Crow South.[8] Many Americans continued to believe that black men were sexual predators and likely perpetrators of rape if accused, especially but not exclusively, by white women.

Among the many injustices African Americans suffered throughout the twentieth century was a systematically racist criminal justice system. An almost entirely white police force often arrested the first dubious looking black suspect found near the scenes of reported crimes.[9] In postwar rape trials, black men in Chicago tried explicitly to defend themselves against the system's racism. In the cases analyzed here, they were unsuccessful and convicted. White judges and juries who heard allegations against African American rape defendants did so with full knowledge of historical rape myths that constructed black men as sexual predators. Consequently, they handed down swift and severe punishments against African American men so accused. Black Chicagoans related to Holiday's song on a different level than whites because they understood that the system did not have to endorse vigilante violence in order to be racially discriminatory. Black defendants and their attorneys accused white justice officials accordingly, sometimes using the metaphor of lynching that Holiday sang about so poignantly. They regularly documented the abusive character of Chicago's police force and used postwar rhetoric that valorized domestic life in order to present themselves as respectable family men, seeking justice against false accusations and mistaken arrests. They pointed out similarities between court convictions, lynchings, and mob violence and, in doing so, accused Chicago court officials of unfairly imposing a Southern system of discriminatory (in)justice upon them.

As postwar Chicago rape trials that were appealed make clear, interracial sexual violence involving white victims and black defendants was not limited to Southern jurisdictions. Indeed, white women testified against black men more than twice as often as they did against white men in the sex crime convictions appealed during the decade following World War II. In only one case an African American victim testified against white defendants, and white men were involved in less than a quarter of the total appellate cases filed between 1946 and 1955. In other words, nearly 80 percent of the convictions in the immediate postwar years were appealed on behalf of African American men.[10] By the mid-1950s, rape cases involving white women and black men dropped out of the available transcripts almost completely, reflecting the realities of sexual violence: that it was (and is) a crime most often committed among individuals of the same race, in contrast to expectations about the prevalence of interracial sexual violence. The treatment and presentation of African American women as victims of rape will be analyzed in depth in the next chapter, but it is relevant to note here that the charges of racial discrimination heard in postwar rape trials suggest that victims did not have to be white for Chicago authorities to exploit beliefs about sexually dangerous black men.

Targeting biased policing became an important part of civil rights activism in the years following World War II, as the movement became increasingly vocal in its demands for equality. Chicago's civil rights leaders accused police of ignoring crime in minority communities while aggressively pursuing black suspects charged with crimes in and around historically white neighborhoods.[11] They were not entirely correct, insofar as police data reveal that the highest arrest rates in the city actually took place in black districts.[12] However, while the Chicago police arrested similar numbers of black and white rape suspects every year, African American men constituted only around 11 percent of the total male population in the city during this period.[13] These data expose a significant racial imbalance in policing sexual violence.

The efforts of civil rights leaders, and of the black men facing rape charges, very much reflected the troublesome position sexual violence held in the American imagination. The issues were compounded by publicity surrounding a postwar "sex crime panic."[14] Timely newspaper headlines called for a "war upon sex crimes," and numerous pieces demanded stricter laws to punish sex criminals and harshly criticized lax sentences for convicted rapists.[15] Reports in Chicago reflected widespread criminal trends during this period: more and more women of all races brought forth allegations of sexual violence after the war, and police investigated the majority of their complaints. The "unfounded" rate for forcible rape averaged 17 percent during this period, higher than the unfounded rate of other violent crimes, but lower than previously assumed. Following World War II, the founded rate for forcible rape in Chicago averaged 578 cases investigated per year, as compared to 209 cases per year in the previous decade (see table 1).[16] While crime data do not record the race of victims reporting, available transcripts reveal that African American women successfully helped the State prosecute rape in approximately 40 percent of the convictions appealed during this period, a fact not widely recognized in existing historical scholarship on sexual violence.[17]

While postwar Americans expressed a great deal of relief to return to everyday life without the stresses of overseas military conflict or the earlier economic crisis of the 1930s, things on the home front had changed. Part of the growing movement in support of racial equality meant challenging widespread judicial discrimination. Trial strategies reveal how black defendants rejected assumptions about their predatory sexuality and claimed rights rooted in the promises of American citizenship, much as women claimed justice by successfully pursuing legal recourse against sexual violence, in spite of the skepticism they sometimes faced. As men, as fathers, and as those asserting arguments about unfair investigations and erroneous prosecutions, black rape defendants in postwar Chicago represent one important element of modern civil rights activism. Although their goals of acquittal ultimately failed, black defendants, their attorneys, and the broader civil rights movement tried to bring the racism of the criminal justice system to judicial and public attention following World War II.

Victim Status and Troublesome Identifications

On April 5, 1946, Mary Elson left her church in downtown Chicago at about 10:30 PM and headed home. A light drizzle fell as she walked up Washington Boulevard to catch a streetcar. Before she reached her stop, someone grabbed her from behind and dragged her into an alley. As she tried to scream, the attacker covered her mouth with "terribly strong" hands. She begged him not to hurt her. As he knelt over her, Elson fainted. When she regained consciousness, she was being raped. The next thing she remembered was being told to "go that way." She got up and staggered onto the street where the driver of a passing car stopped at the sight of a distraught, bleeding woman with torn clothing and took her to a police station.[18]

Elson's recollections about that night effectively prevented the types of questions about sexual purity that rape victims often faced in court. She testified that she was leaving St. Malachi's Catholic Church when someone grabbed her and dragged her into an alley. She described to the court, in some detail, a set of broken rosary beads that she had lost the night of the attack. She also indicated that she had asked the man who initially found her to take her back to the church so that her priest might take her to the police station. This priest came to the station after she arrived and accompanied her and the police to the hospital that night.[19] The prosecutor carefully took the time to outline Elson's religious activities perhaps because she was attacked while she was alone, at night, on a downtown city street—all markers that directed suspicion toward adult women claiming rape. Most people, however, would have expected a white, churchgoing woman like Elson to resist anonymous sex, much less sex in an alley with a "colored" stranger.[20] Elson testified that she was single and had never been married, implying that she was a virgin. The State corroborated this testimony with medical evidence that indicated Elson had experienced significant vaginal trauma from the attack implying, in agreement with her marital status, that she had never had intercourse before being raped.[21] As shown in numerous trials analyzed here, medical testimony about sexual trauma and physical injuries helped support a victim's claim of rape. However, the State did not rely on this evidence alone to gain convictions.

Mary Elson's situation left little doubt that she was not complicit in the rape she suffered. She was a compelling victim, and her courtroom testimony was clear and convincing. She testified that after she was grabbed, "[I] screamed as loud as I could" and tried to "pull his fingers away with all the strength I had."[22] With the details of the law clarified to her, Elson knew that both distinct resistance and a lack of consent were necessary parts of a rape conviction.[23] She therefore testified accordingly. Although she was alone on the street after dark, the fact that she was on her way home from church—not a tavern or dance hall—when she was attacked made extensive cross-examination on this topic useless for the defense. Unlike other victims who were often forced to explain what they meant by "attack," authorities in this case interpreted her testimony as indicating a sexual attack, and left it at that.[24]

The public defender disputed the State's allegations against his client by challenging the victim's memory. Legally known as impeachment, defense attorneys tested witnesses' recollections by posing specific questions about any information they gave police and prosecutors in pretrial interviews. If the particulars of an earlier statement differed from a victim's testimony in court, the defense could more viably argue that the she could not have been raped. They maintained that most victims would remember, in explicit detail, such a violation if it had actually happened, again invoking rape myths about lying women.[25] Impeachment was a basic legal strategy, and attorneys routinely tried to confuse complaining witnesses with extensive questions about the location of attacks, the positioning of lights, names of streets, or other incidental details about rapes. It was a potent defense strategy for rape trials, given how popular myths cast doubt on most sexually victimized women anyway. Despite Elson's repeated references toward religious piety, the defense attorney initially tried to imply that she perhaps instigated the encounter by asking her about being out on the street, alone, at night. She repeated that she was on her way home from St. Malachi's and "wasn't a bit nervous or afraid" of the neighborhood. Quickly switching tactics, he asked her if there were lights in the alley, and did she actually see her attacker? Elson responded, "Washington Boulevard is always quite light you know."[26] Elson's testimony reflected her understanding that she had not undermined her respectability by defying gender norms in her personal life. This church-going virgin made it difficult for the defense to exploit rape myths about deceitful, promiscuous women. Moreover, she made clear to the court that, while out alone at night, she had not crossed any geographic boundaries into a de facto segregated neighborhood where she might have purposely encountered potential sexual criminals.

The urban geography surrounding rape allegations particularly interested Chicago attorneys defending African American clients. Elson was raped in an alley, like many other sexual attacks involving white victims and black defendants tried in Cook County courts during the mid-twentieth century. Marguerite Thorpe testified that a "Negro" attacked her while she waited for a bus and dragged her into an empty lot in the nearby Greater Grand Crossing neighborhood where she was raped in 1948.[27] In 1949, police pursued a black suspect whose modus operandi was to attack young women as they pushed their baby carriages on side streets with little traffic and easy access to alleyways in the Woodlawn area.[28] Ann Mack told the court in 1955 that as she approached her car after finishing an evening shift as a telephone operator, "four boys," one who was "light-skinned and the rest dark-skinned," came up behind her. They threatened her with a gun, pushed her into the vehicle and drove her to a secluded spot in the Englewood neighborhood where, she testified, they gang-raped her.[29] All three of these south side neighborhoods experienced significant changes throughout the 1940s and 1950s, as Chicago's black population expanded and many whites moved away to escape residential overcrowding, falling property values, and rising crime rates.[30]

Defense attorneys dealt with these geographic details in a number of ways, including trying to manipulate victims' testimonies in order to cast suspicion on their activities prior to an alleged rape. By questioning women about their presence on the street or near alleys at night in different neighborhoods throughout the city, they implied that women were potentially complicit in the attacks they reported, because they should not have been traipsing throughout Chicago by themselves. Defense efforts to shape trial arguments in this way, however, were usually blocked by prosecutors or judges, who attempted to shield white victims especially from the extensive character attacks that women, of any race, faced more regularly by the 1960s.

In rape cases, defense attorneys presented either consent or alibi arguments to defend their clients' innocence. A consent defense suggested that the victim wanted to engage in sexual relations with the man on trial or failed to sufficiently resist his advances, thereby tacitly consenting to them. Sex with consent, by definition, was not rape. Among the few white defendants who appealed their rape convictions during the immediate postwar decade, their attorneys in all but one case used consent defenses.[31] Attorneys for Frank Teti and Dominic DiBiaso argued consent in the case the State brought against them in the rape of African American victim Ann Robinson.[32] The defense strategy in this seldom-prosecuted type of interracial case exploited a particular racial rape myth that will be explored more fully in the next chapter—namely, that black women were sexually promiscuous and thus unlikely rape victims, and that authorities should be especially wary of their charges of sexual violence. White defendants, however, were not severely, if at all, punished for the rapes of black victims in Chicago or anywhere else in the United States throughout the mid-twentieth century.[33] Of the approximately one hundred sex crime convictions of white defendants that were not appealed, as reported in the *Chicago Tribune* in the decade following the war, none of them indicated that the victims were anything but of the same race as their attackers.[34]

Race and socioeconomic status shaped perceptions about criminality throughout the United States during the mid-twentieth century. When the crime involved was rape, ideas about both trustworthy victims and likely perpetrators compounded racially lopsided prosecutions. The same historical ideology informed criminal defense strategies. To suggest consent was risky in combating white women's allegations against African American men. While Chicagoans may have disagreed about the possibilities of white women consenting to sexual relations with black men, they did not easily accept such liaisons, thereby making this type of defense very unlikely to inspire an acquittal.[35] In her study of twentieth-century interracial rape cases in Virginia, historian Lisa Lindquist Dorr reveals how black men so accused were convicted most of the time. Defense attorneys rarely argued that their black clients' interracial relationships were consensual, and, moreover, African American men were reluctant to admit that they might have had white lovers because they were afraid of antagonizing the white jury members charged with deciding their criminal fate.[36] The "metalanguage" of race, as historian Evelyn Brooks Higginbotham asserts, has a "powerful, all-encompassing effect on the construction and representation of other social and power relations, namely, gender, class, and sexuality."[37] In the postwar rape trial courtroom, this metalanguage ensured that it was, at best, highly unlikely for a white woman of Elson's social class, marital status, and religious piety to have consented to sex with a poor, black man like the one who ultimately stood trial in this case. His only defense, valid or not, was one of mistaken identity.

Attorneys in most interracial rape cases thus relied on alibis in an effort to defend their black clients. They could argue this type of defense in two related ways: by providing evidence to prove the defendant was not where the victim said the rape had occurred, and by trying to prove that she was mistaken in her identification. They had difficulties presenting both types of arguments because of the inconsistent reliability of alibi witnesses, but also because of the prejudices of courtroom officials. Prosecutors, defense attorneys, and judges were all occasionally frustrated by witnesses from different socioeconomic or racial backgrounds who did not share their privileged status or values. In the 1951 case against John Jackson, the judge repeatedly wondered why the prosecutor could not call supporting witnesses, insisting that there was "no reason for these people not being here."[38] A number of the State witnesses in this case were residents of the Ida B. Wells housing project, a fact that the judge seemed to blame for their failure to appear in court. The first Ida B. Wells Homes, located exclusively within the south side "ghetto," opened in the early 1940s. By the war's end the project was quickly becoming overcrowded and associated with the growing crime rate in the city, in spite of community efforts to maintain its status as a complex of clean and modern homes for respectable black families.[39] Even more often, alibi witnesses who did appear in court on behalf of indigent black defendants, who constituted the majority of those who appeared before the Chicago bench, suffered racial and class prejudices during trials.[40] Moreover, indigent defendants relied on court-appointed attorneys and public defenders, who had high caseloads and often found it difficult to prepare elaborate alibi defenses.[41] The trial involving Mary Elson's attacker, Harrison Stewart, was one such challenging case.

Public defenders were cognizant of the racial prejudices their clients faced, but they also struggled with their own elite status in relation to the social position of the majority of rape defendants considered here. Defense counsel faced some setbacks in the Stewart case. More than once he had to ask the court for more time in order to substantiate the defendant's alibi. As he indicated during one motion, "It is pretty hard to get these people lined up," referring to potential witnesses from the taverns and cabstand that Stewart frequented around the time of the attack.[42] Defense attorneys recognized the logistical problems alibi witnesses faced, sometimes not having vehicles to get to court or having trouble arranging time off from work so that they might testify. But arguments like those presented by Stewart's lawyer were couched in the language of class bias.

This is not to suggest, however, that all criminal defense attorneys equally subscribed to socioeconomic prejudices or to racial rape myths that cast black men as dangerous sexual criminals. John Branion was the first black attorney to serve in the Chicago Public Defender's office and defended many of the African American men convicted of rape during the postwar years.[43] His courtroom efforts continued a long tradition of civil rights activism in Chicago that had grown, along with the city's African American population, throughout the twentieth century. Employment opportunities during and after the First World War, as well as a chance to escape the socially restrictive and racially violent South, encouraged black migrations northward. Chicago became a popular site where newcomers settled.[44] This process accelerated during and after World War II as industrial centers like Chicago needed workers and the mechanization of agriculture pushed more and more black sharecroppers out of the South.[45] Chicago's chapter of the National Urban League helped ease rural migrants' transitions to city life, while the local National Association for the Advancement of Colored People (NAACP) office attempted to address racial grievances. Among the issues taken up by the NAACP, especially in the years following World War II, were discriminatory criminal investigations and prosecutions.[46] John Branion was a part of this effort, as the organization specifically referred cases to him when they found black men arrested for prejudicial reasons, especially when they were mistakenly accused of raping white women.[47] Branion and other defense attorneys worked to overcome the entrenched racial rape myths that shaped Chicago trials. Without reliable alibi witnesses, they tried to do so by redirecting suspicions—away from their clients and toward flawed identifications and discriminatory police investigations—even while they were mostly blocked from challenging the veracity of white victims alleging interracial attacks.

As required in criminal investigations, rape victims provided descriptions that police used to locate suspects, but they did so during a particularly upsetting moment in their lives. Their descriptions were not always very detailed or specific. When questioned about what she had first told the police about the man who raped her, Mary Elson testified that he had a face that was "full and wide," and that he was "very dark."[48] When pressed, she said little more, and the public defender complained that in her initial statement to the police "she took notice of his face . . . but she doesn't identify any characteristics of the face as to this being the man."[49] When Elson pointed to the defendant at the trial, it was the first time anyone had ever directly asked her to identify Stewart.[50] When questioned about a lineup, Elson admitted that the police never arranged for her to view any suspects. Police held lineups when suspects were not identified at the scene of a crime or through photographs and in cases where the victim did not know her attacker.[51] Stewart's case fit that profile, although Chicago police never put him in a lineup for Elson to view. The defense attorney in this case highlighted in court the dubious circumstances of his client's arrest.

Attorneys relying on alibi defenses argued that rape victims mistakenly identified their African American clients, who were then unfairly arrested. Prior to federal defendants' rights decisions of the 1960s, the personal bias of segregated police departments more easily shaped local investigations. Courtroom arguments about discriminatory lineups and the mistaken pursuit of black men who happened to be found in historically white neighborhoods demonstrate how Chicago's de facto segregated boundaries were beginning to break down following World War II, thereby threatening the expected social order. The 1948 case of Lorce Jones, a black man who was convicted for the rape of a white woman, Marguerite Thorpe, offers an example of defense strategies that directed judicial suspicion toward the police rather than focusing it on the victim who reported a rape. Shortly after they were called, the police arrested Jones, whom they found walking down a street near the scene of the attack. When they brought him to the apartment where Marguerite Thorpe lay recovering, she identified him as the "Negro" who raped her. The people who first found the victim agreed with this identification, even though none of them actually saw the violence.[52] Jones may not have lived in the neighborhood where Thorpe was raped, although he nevertheless might have, as this area's black population expanded by 80 percent in the years following World War II.[53] Or he could have lived very close by, within a few blocks of the crime scene. Surrounding the area were historically black neighborhoods, including Washington Park, the center of Chicago's black business district and home to many important civil rights leaders in the city.[54]

The defense argued that the solidarity among the prosecution's witnesses from this white border region resulted in a case of racial prejudice that ended with charges being filed against the wrong man—the first black man police found in the area. Jones's attorney (the familiar John Branion) claimed that the victim was wrong about his client. According to Thorpe, it was dark in the vacant lot where she was raped. She did not provide the police with much of a description of the man who did it because, as she told the court, she was "too hysterical and shocked" to mention anything more detailed than his race. She insisted that she struggled with her attacker and scratched his face.[55] This detail supported the resistance element required to prove rape, but it also offered a particular mark of identification to look for on potential suspects. In press coverage of a highly publicized rape "crime wave" in the Chicago suburb of Evanston a few years earlier, several newspaper articles detailed how "fresh scratches" led to the arrest of numerous black suspects.[56] Police kept their eyes open for such things, when applicable. The arresting officer told the court, however, that he did not notice any scratches when he picked up Jones.[57] If Thorpe's attacker had been white, investigators would have looked more closely for those scratches. If the first person they saw when they looked around the neighborhood was an African American woman, her presence there would not have inspired the same type of wariness as that directed at Jones. The fears in the minds and hearts of white Chicagoans and white police were not against the city's entire African American population but instead were inscribed on the bodies of black men. These men, whom many white residents and police believed to possess predatory sexual qualities, had to be stopped from prowling forbidden streets and preying on forbidden women.

Thorpe's atypical identification demonstrates how police prejudice could intervene in their investigations. Although Branion sympathized with the victim, telling the court, "It is a terrible thing . . . when a woman cannot walk the streets unmolested," he also argued that the police apprehended a random black man because they found him walking down the street in a white neighborhood.[58] He challenged Chicago authorities to raise investigative standards so that African American men would not be subjected to the kinds of prejudices that had, historically, ruined or even ended their lives when they were falsely accused of interracial sexual violence. Indeed, the local press was filled with reports about Southern jurisdictions where black rape suspects were killed by vigilante mobs unhappy about court proceedings.

These articles underscored the differences between the apparently backwards South and the more enlightened processes of criminal justice in Chicago.[59] Defense arguments on behalf of black Chicago rape defendants, however, contradicted these distinctions and instead pointed out the potential bias in local sex crime investigations. Thorpe may have recognized the defendant as the man who raped her, but she did so while "hysterical and shocked," lying on a couch in a stranger's apartment rather than at a police station from a lineup of several possible suspects.[60] Especially if they found someone right away, police relied on distraught rape victims to quickly identify whomever they brought to her.[61] Any defense attorney knew that this had strong potential to bias identifications, especially when dominant white ideology presumed African American men's guilt when accused of rape by white women.

Bringing suspects to the victim for identification made it easier for police to discriminate against black rape defendants. Although the justice system in the United States eventually shifted some of the balance of power away from the State in an effort to protect the rights of the accused, during the decade immediately following World War II identification procedures were not quite so standardized.[62] Police could thus present black suspects to white rape victims in settings where defense attorneys argued that the identification was, at best, flawed and, at worst, entirely tainted. As we have seen, many victims carefully eyed suspects in lineups, photographs, or in other settings until they were sure that the police had the right man. However, the act of a police officer's bringing a single suspect to the victim for immediate identification implied his guilt, and victims sometimes went along with it, any uncertainties they may have had allayed by such circumstances.

The lack of standard identification procedures in Chicago rape investigations had the potential to expose suspects to a variety of discriminatory abuses. When Anna Brasy was brutally attacked in 1936, police brought more than fifty suspects to her hospital room, hoping she might identify the white man who had attacked her. She did not, but when they arrested someone ten months later, Brasy viewed a lineup of ten white men, from which she picked Robert Conroy, who was later tried, convicted, and sentenced for the crime.[63] Similarly, Rose Bojko ultimately picked the white man who raped her from a 1954 lineup with five other white men.[64] However, when Ann Mack identified one of the four African Americans she accused of gang rape in 1955, she picked him from a mixed race lineup, containing both "colored boys and white boys."[65] When Emily Warbende testified in the 1950 rape trial against black defendant Marvin Chukes, she described the lineup from which she picked him. Sixteen-year-old Chukes stood with six men, three white and two African Americans, all of whom, according to the victim, "were older men" than the defendant. While Warbende insisted that she was "no judge of ages," she also admitted that at least one of the men in the lineup looked to be around thirty years old.[66] The potential for investigative bias in this case, including a police lineup containing only one possible correct suspect—the black teenager Marvin Chukes—comes through clearly in testimony like this. While there is no way of knowing how many prejudicial lineups Chicago police held for the thousands of crimes they investigated every year, the evidence here suggests racial discrimination affected the identification of black rape suspects more often than when white men were so accused. Racial discrimination also carried over into the trial system, according to the testimonies of black rape defendants and the arguments of their attorneys, who increasingly made race a key point of debate in the postwar courtroom.

Legal Abuse and Civil Rights Demands in the Courtroom

Throughout the twentieth century, numerous civil rights activists, as well as the many black defendants engaged in the American criminal justice system, believed that system to be modeled on vigilantism. Interracial rape trials, especially, inspired critiques of criminal justice, even though courtrooms enjoyed the legitimacy of the law that lynch mobs, technically, did not. Early critics of lynching, like newspaper editor and activist Ida B. Wells, recognized how interracial sexual violence provided a false cover for white mob violence that targeted African American men. She charged that anyone who protected the hidden identities of violent mobs suffered from the same lack of civilization that white elites had traditionally used as an excuse to prevent racial minorities from achieving equality.[67] Wanting to disassociate from the uncivilized, authorities gradually began curtailing the activities of lynch mobs in the late nineteenth and early twentieth centuries.[68] Beginning in the 1920s, however, civil rights leaders accused Southern courts, especially, of providing the vengeance that thwarted mobs had missed as lynching began to fade from the landscape of a civilized society. By holding quick trials and by depending on all-white juries to impose mandatory death sentences for capital crimes, including rape, many supporters of racial equality pointed to the similarities between lynch law and State laws. Reformers of all races recognized the prejudicial and abusive nature of "legal lynchings."[69] Even today, the phrase "legal lynching" immediately brings to mind a very specific example of the relationship between sexual and racial violence and discriminatory legal proceedings.[70]

While Chicago was not geographically part of the Jim Crow South, racial prejudices affected the court system here too. Historical connections between racial and sexual violence shaped black rape defendants' claims about police bias and coercion in the city throughout the mid-twentieth century. They often accused the police of physical brutality, or of forcing them to confess to sex crimes that they denied committing. The lack of a lineup in Harrison Stewart's case meant that the State had other, more powerful evidence against him. In addition to Elson's almost flawless credibility, informed as it was by her racial and class privilege as well as by medical corroboration of a likely sexual attack, the prosecutor could use Stewart's own words against him. The defendant had signed a confession that the judge admitted as evidence in this trial.[71] No jury ever considered the validity of this document because only the judge heard Stewart's case and ultimately accepted his confession as the truth.[72]

Bench trials like Harrison Stewart's were common for postwar rape indictments and were especially prominent in the cases involving the African American defendants analyzed in this chapter. Chicago defendants followed a national trend, whereby nearly half of all those who stood trial for rape in the United States chose to waive their right to a jury by mid-twentieth century.[73] The move toward bench trials was part of a larger process of the professionalization of criminal justice; individuals increasingly relied on expert judgment during this period, rather than trusting the potentially uninformed opinions of their peers. According to the cases under study here, the difference between bench and jury trials split along racial lines. When Charles Hughes went on trial for the attempted rape of Rita Gray Goldberg, no jury decided whether or not he was guilty of the crime with which he was charged.[74] Neither did a jury hear the case against Maynard McAfee or consider evidence in the case against Ernest Davenport and Wesley Fields— all black men charged with raping white women.[75] Even in intraracial cases, most black rape defendants, including Willie Lewis, John Jackson, and Roger Williams, waived their right to a jury trial as well.[76] Indeed, nearly four times as often did African American defendants choose bench over jury trials than did white defendants facing sex crime charges prior to 1960.[77] This pattern broke down somewhat during the 1960s and 1970s, when black defendants began to look toward juries to decide their legal fate more often than they had prior to the expansion of appellate opportunities during that period. Before 1960, however, the majority of black rape defendants chose bench trials in the cases analyzed here. The brutal testimony of a rape trial, compounded by the usual racial status of both the victim and defendant, warranted defense attorneys' caution about juries. Not so the case for white rape defendants, as they could more effectively capitalize on both gender and racial privilege in the hopes of relying on juries to believe them over female victims, whom rape myths constructed as liars. Newspaper coverage of sex crime trials that were not appealed confirm this instinct: a number of articles critiqued judges who assigned lenient penalties to convicted black men, while others criticized juries for acquitting white defendants.[78]

Although no African American defendant or his attorney could guarantee how a judge would react to courtroom descriptions of sexual violence, most preferred their judgment to that of juries. They hoped that judges, as educated legal professionals, would rely on the rule of law and a balanced evaluation of evidence rather than succumbing to racial rape myths that assumed their guilt. When a defendant did not waive his right to a jury trial, defense attorneys recognized the racial problems that the system could present and tried to prevent potential jury bias. African Americans had the right to serve on juries and in Chicago many did, but prosecutors were not yet prohibited from constructing juries along racial lines during the immediate postwar decade.[79] When Golden McMath, an African American teenager charged with raping a white woman, went to trial in 1955, his public defender objected to the State's exclusion of all "colored" jurors.[80] The prosecutor argued that he had a right to use his peremptory (or "without cause") jury challenges, as did the defense. The judge sided with the State, and McMath faced an all-white jury that ultimately found him guilty.[81] Many African American rape defendants were part of the Southern migratory culture that constituted a sizeable portion of Chicago's postwar black community. Perhaps they compared white juries to the specter of white lynch mobs they had left behind when they left the South and preferred to trust their fate to professional white judges instead.

A signed confession, especially if the court deemed it admissible as evidence, provided strong evidence for the State that a defendant was guilty. If the police had not arrested the right man, why would he confess? Once there was a signed confession, why did this case even go to trial? Harrison Stewart and his attorney opted to go to court because the defendant denied the truthfulness of his statement, insisting that the police had threatened and abused him until he confessed. Recalling the lyrics of Holiday's famous song, the "scent of magnolia sweet and fresh, and the sudden smell of burning flesh" can thus be understood as an analogy to the discriminatory justice system that African American rape defendants in Chicago regularly confronted. On one side, they benefited from legal procedures rather than suffer immediate vigilante violence if accused by a white woman of rape. Conversely, what price did they pay for such justice in light of their accusations of racist discrimination and police abuse? Although most southern migrants to Chicago did not find the North to be the racial utopia they hoped it would be, they did harbor some expectations of equality because of the lack of Jim Crow laws in the Northern jurisdictions.[82] When they found that practice did not mirror ideology, black rape defendants spoke out about it.

The experiences of World War II inspired many African Americans to demand full citizenship rights, whether or not they were military veterans. Increased job opportunities and federal promises to limit employment discrimination, despite the prejudicial realities experienced by black workers on the shop floor, impressed upon African Americans their previously unrealized potential for civil equality.[83] Postwar changes in American life gave black men accused of rape a variety of arguments to combat those allegations. They defended their innocence using familiar anti-lynching imagery and rhetoric, informed by the context of the burgeoning civil rights movement. They also used traditional ideas about home and family, shaping what they understood to be appropriate social roles, in their own defense. Allegations about the validity of confessions like Harrison Stewart's raise questions about racial tensions in modern Chicago, and about how these tensions remained strongly linked to a national context of discrimination, increased reports of sexual violence, and traditional family and gender role expectations. Although arguments about judicial discrimination and police abuse did not work in favor of the black defendants considered here, that they were invoked at all reflects an important challenge to embedded ideas about sexual violence and race relations in postwar America.

Almost one month after Elson reported that she was raped, Chicago police officers went to the home of Harrison Stewart and took him in for questioning. They insisted that he knew what it was about and, over his protests of ignorance, demanded that Stewart tell them about his involvement in the sexual attack of Mary Elson. Stewart testified that during this interrogation he denied knowing anything about any rapes. After being questioned for a few hours and threatened many times, he indicated that the police also threatened his family. He claimed that they told him they would "lock up your wife and baby." At that point, Stewart testified, "That, I couldn't stand . . . why quite naturally me with small kids, I would have signed anything up to my death to save that kid and its mother."[84] Stewart's narrative conflicted with what the police had earlier testified to regarding the legitimacy of his arrest. In spite of laws against perjury, it is impossible to know who, if anyone, was completely honest about this in court. Whether wholly, partially, or not at all true, the defendant's pro-natalist appeal was very much in keeping with an emphasis on fatherly protection and familial support so prevalent in the

United States following World War II.[85] Harrison Stewart was not just an innocent black man abused by racist police, as his testimony suggested, but he was also a married father trying to protect his family from further harm by confessing to a crime he had not committed.

Other African American rape defendants described to postwar courts similar instances of police abuse and prejudice. Defense counsel in the case against Lorce Jones argued that his client woke up in the jail cell with a bruised lip and suggested that this was because the police had beaten him, after mistakenly arresting him in the first place.[86] Black men charged with raping black women also claimed that the police had physically abused them during investigations, revealing that discrimination was not limited to interracial cases. In 1954, police shot a black man whom they found near the Forty-Seventh Street El because of a report they received from a local resident who had heard his neighbor scream. The injured defendant claimed that he was unarmed, but the arresting officer testified that he saw a gun so he shot the suspect.[87] Although the shooting happened around 2 AM, the streets surrounding that El stop were populated with taverns, restaurants, and clubs; this area was busy at all hours, and it was unclear how the police, without having any suspect description, knew which man to pursue. Another African American defendant, Charles Johnson, told the court that the police questioned him several times about a 1955 rape case. Johnson claimed that almost twenty-four hours after he was arrested, an officer beat him repeatedly and promised him immunity if he confessed.[88] Although procedural standards permitted police officers to use force when necessary to arrest suspects, it is clear that these defendants testified about abuse beyond what the law allowed.

The use of force to arrest, detain, and interrogate suspects was always a part of police work in the United States, but that did not mean that officers could do anything they wanted. In the late nineteenth century, reformers lobbied to curb political corruption and promoted education as a prerequisite for professional employment, rather than allowing municipal appointments based solely on political patronage or informal apprenticeships.[89] One of the results of this trend was that the level of force the police could use during investigations lessened over time. In the 1920s, training manuals instructed officers to "draw their revolvers and be prepared to use them if necessary" when arresting suspects.[90] By the end of that decade, problems with excessive police brutality were more broadly exposed, if not adequately dealt with in Chicago, by the publication of a national report titled "Lawlessness in Law Enforcement."[91] In response, patrolmen during the 1930s were directed to "repel simple assaults with physical force and repel violent assaults by the use of deadly weapons if necessary."[92] This trend continued after the war. By the 1950s, arresting officers were taught to "not strike them [suspects] except in extreme cases in which your safety or that of the public is imminently endangered."[93] While changing national values helped eliminate some abuses, Chicago police depended on the standards set in their own precincts to conduct suspect interviews. Until the U.S. Supreme Court mandated it in 1964, police rarely allowed suspects to talk to a lawyer before or during interviews.[94] Without legal counsel present, detectives freely promised benefits to suspects if they talked and did not let them know they had the right not to answer questions at all. Forcing confessions out of unwilling suspects, however, had been illegal for over two decades by the end of World War II.[95] Although officers always denied beating or otherwise coercing African American defendants when they testified during rape trials, it is difficult to know what actually happened during interrogations that resulted in signed confessions.

At his trial, Harrison Stewart testified about numerous threats the police used to coerce his confession. The Chicago police knew Harrison Stewart: they arrested him in 1943 for murder, which likely influenced their decision to investigate him as a suspect in the Elson case.[96] Stewart told the court that the police threatened to "get a line and make me tell" about the rape.[97] He understood their meaning clearly when they threatened him by mentioning "a line," as in a line or length of rope used to lynch so-called black beast rapists. Stewart further testified that the police were rough with him and that "rather than have my wife locked up and me be beaten near to death," he signed a confession.[98] Other black rape defendants also complained about being forced to sign false statements. John Ingraham accused police of not letting him change details in a statement he insisted he never made. He testified that when he pointed out the mistake, the officer dismissed him saying, "I can't help that" and forced him to "sign it."[99] Ingraham and his friend, James Ethridge, were on trial for raping Jean McKee, who was also African American. Similarly, Charles Johnson, who was also on trial for raping a black woman, alleged that the police bullied him into signing a statement that, according to his testimony, he never read or had read to him, so he was unaware of what he had signed.[100] Although the black press regularly highlighted instances of police discrimination and abuse in jurisdictions outside Chicago, local officers also faced journalistic exposure.[101] The *Chicago Tribune* was more critical of the city's political administration than it was of its police force following World War II, but the newspaper nonetheless published a critical exposé on law enforcement in the wake of rising crime rates and investigative blunders, as well as informing the public about rape charges dropped due to investigative misconduct.[102]

Testimony about threats of lynching or brutality and abuse exposed racial discrimination, irrespective of regional geography. Encouraging news about the decline of lynchings in the postwar years could not erase memories of the highpoint of mob violence in American history, when over three thousand African Americans purportedly were lynched between 1880 and 1930, and the specter of interracial rape helped white Southerners justify the practice, even if the majority of lynching victims were never actually accused of sexual violence.[103] Black Chicagoans had lynchings seared in their collective consciousness, even if they had no direct experience of mob violence. The widely circulated "race paper," the *Chicago Defender,* systematically published accounts of lynchings, helping to create a national black consciousness about racial violence throughout the twentieth century.[104] Even the politically conservative *Chicago Tribune* published articles condemning attempted mob violence against African American rape suspects in Southern jurisdictions.[105] Accused black men and their attorneys sometimes used this imagery to support claims of innocence during trials. Golden McMath insisted that he had not raped white victim Ann Mack. His defense attorney carefully crafted his closing arguments for an acquittal. He appealed to the white jury's sense of fairness and duty by pointing out that in some places defendants are "sent off without any such trial. They string them up to the nearest tree [but] not so here."[106] The police also demonstrated their awareness of the connections between sexual violence, race, and vigilante (in)justice when they allegedly threatened Harrison Stewart with "getting a line" to make him confess to rape. When Stewart testified about this "line" in court, he invoked a strong black metaphor for white criminal justice: that it was extralegal, unfair, and inherently racist.

African American rape defendants attempted to assert not just their innocence in court, but their civil rights as well. When the prosecutor asked Stewart if he had signed the confession, he replied that he had done so only in an effort to protect his family. He claimed he wanted to "halt himself," but that he was afraid because he "wasn't able to whip the Chicago Police."[107] Stewart also tried to explain inconsistencies in his story when cross-examined about them. He asked the prosecutor, "Were you at the station when the police was beating me and knocking me about? You should take a look at the county jail and the hospitals."[108] When asked if he complained about his mistreatment, Stewart retorted, "What good would that do me?" and, at another point, "Frankly, I was afraid to say anything."[109] Over numerous defense objections, the judge admitted Stewart's signed confession into evidence against him. Despite federal protections against self-incrimination and judicial mandates against forced statements, it was up to local courts to determine the validity of confessions.[110] Chicago judges during this period routinely allowed them into evidence. Although defendants' testimony about police abuse provided a justification for legal appeals, the appellate court reversed only two of the nineteen original decisions appealed during the postwar decade and remanded them back to the circuit level to be retried. Both of these cases involved white defendants.[111] One case was eventually overturned because the higher court determined that the statements of the two white defendants tried together for a 1952 rape were made under duress.[112] The basis of this successful appeal was similar to the repeated claims of coercion made unsuccessfully by the African American defendants analyzed here.

In addition to allegations of police brutality and investigative misconduct, African Americans on trial for rape also used their status as fathers in an attempt to gain acquittals. When Harrison Stewart testified that he had only confessed in order to shield his family from the brutality of the Chicago police, he claimed a traditional gender role. Postwar rhetoric and ideology vigorously defined fathers as family breadwinners and protectors. The expectation that fathers provided for and protected their families frustrated many black men, who found such demands difficult to fulfill because of racial discrimination in the work force.[113] Yet claim such roles they did, in spite of the realities of postwar racism. Charles Johnson, a father of four, testified that he signed a rape confession in 1955 because police threatened and beat him but also because an officer promised him immunity if he confessed to the crime.[114] Legal immunity would have kept him out of jail, thus able to work and support his family. James Jeffery Jr., a married man with three children, asked his boss to testify on his behalf when he stood trial for rape in 1954. His supervisor of five years testified, in the language of the courtroom, that Jeffery "had borne a previous reputation of being a peaceful and law-abiding citizen," who dutifully supported his family all the time they were acquainted.[115] Just as African American defendants and their attorneys did, defense witnesses who appeared in court on behalf of black men accused of rape often made use of similar rhetoric involving both family support and judicial discrimination.

Some African American defense witnesses testified about experiencing police abuse themselves. Marie Stewart appeared in court for her husband, Harrison. She described at trial how the police just wanted to "talk" to Stewart the night he was arrested, but that they never brought him back to the family's home. They did, however, return later in order to search for evidence in their investigation. Mrs. Stewart told the court that the police threatened to arrest her if she did not cooperate, and she explained how she went along with them in order to protect the baby.[116] Marie Stewart's testimony presented a threatening image of abusive officers disrupting the sanctity of her home, not unlike the claims her husband offered about their similar actions at the precinct.

While the prosecutor questioned Marie Stewart and tried to portray her as a liar, she presented herself as a good citizen. She testified that she was a member of the Women's Army Corps during the war, emphasizing her patriotism and implying that she was honest and would not lie merely to protect her husband. Marie Stewart told the court that on the night Elson was raped, she met her husband at a tavern and they left together and spent the rest of that rainy night at home.[117] She explained how she had left their baby with a neighbor so she could meet him. The State's Attorney questioned that decision, remarking, "at 1:30 AM you took the baby out of its crib and took it over to the neighbor's home to leave it to go to a tavern?"[118] She indicated that the baby was already at the neighbor's because she and her husband had plans to go out that night. The prosecutor's accusatory question, however, placed Marie Stewart in a conflicted position: was she a good wife who defended her husband, or a bad mother who left her baby with a neighbor to meet her spouse at a bar? The judge ultimately dismissed Stewart's alibi, found him guilty, and sentenced him to life in prison. The appellate court upheld this decision.[119]

African American parents who testified on behalf of their defendant sons also shaped their trial narratives around family life and traditional authority, as well as police misconduct. Golden McMath's mother testified that when two patrol cars filled with several officers came to the family's apartment looking for a gun used in a rape for which her son had not yet been charged, she urged him to cooperate and respect their authority, even though the police did not tell her what was going on. She testified that she repeatedly asked the police "what happened" and "what have my boy did" but that they never answered her.[120] During the rape trial of Marvin Chukes, both of his parents took the stand to confirm their son's contention that he was at home, asleep, at the same time that the indictment against him charged that he was crawling into the victim's bedroom window. Chukes's father told the court that when his son came home between 10:00 and 10:20 PM, he "sat down beside me and watched the TV."[121] He further testified that after he went to bed, his son fell asleep on the couch. Mr. Chukes knew this because he woke up between 1:00 and 2:00 in the morning and "put a cover over his [Marvin's] feet."[122] The defendant's mother also testified for the defense. She reiterated her husband's claim that Marvin arrived home at 10:20 PM and watched television with the family. She explained as well that she knew her son could not have raped the victim in this case because she also got up during the night to go to the bathroom "and when I come out . . . both feets [sic] were under the covers."[123]

The verbal picture the Chukes painted in court echoed the rhetoric of the idealized American family of the postwar era. Despite fears of dominating technologies so prevalent during the Cold War, for better or worse, technology triumphed and television became a signifier of family togetherness.[124] Nonetheless, this ideal did not automatically convince authorities about the truthfulness of defense alibis. The judge ultimately rejected the testimonies of Mr. and Mrs. Chukes. Perhaps he found the alibi too constructed because of the couple's similarly detailed narratives. Perhaps he did not believe them because he understood that most parents, of any race, would say anything in order to protect their children, even if it meant lying in court. Or perhaps he found the claims of the Chukes, an African American family, implausible because they were *not* racially a part of mainstream America, no matter how hard they tried to present themselves as such by constantly mentioning television. For whatever reason, the judge did not believe Marvin Chukes and found him guilty of rape.[125]

It is not surprising that descriptions of idyllic family life failed to inspire acquittals for black rape defendants. Prosecutors inverted this type of testimony, suggesting that African American men had inherently criminal natures, in addition to predatory sexual qualities, that encouraged them to commit crimes in the name of family protection. They committed robberies and home invasions in order to get money for rent or food. They raped other women so they would not abuse their own wives. Attorneys who defended black men accused of rape constructed arguments about their innocence, as was their job. The particular strategies they employed demonstrate how African Americans could try to use mainstream public rhetoric, such as an emphasis on traditional family roles, in order to challenge discriminatory beliefs about black culture more broadly. The power of racial rape myths did not prevent black defendants or their family members and friends from defying negative characterizations in the courtroom, even if their defiance fell on deaf ears in cases that ended with convictions.

The final stage of any criminal trial involves assigning penalties to those convicted. The sentences handed down in the cases that went to appeal during the postwar decade reveal a bias against African Americans convicted of sex crimes, whether the violence was inter- or intraracial. In only two of eight cases under study here wherein white victims testified against black defendants were the sentences less than ten years: one involved the lesser indictment of attempted rape, the other a youthful offender.[126] In the remaining interracial cases, defendants were sentenced to an average of thirty years to life in prison.[127] In intraracial cases, African American defendants also received severe sentences, averaging twenty-six years, and in one case a black defendant convicted of raping a black woman received a life sentence.[128] In the cases involving white defendants under study here, their sentences averaged between sixteen and seventeen years.[129] Of course, not all sex crime convictions in Chicago during this period were appealed, and press coverage of sentencing rates reflects a similar racial bias in cases that ended at the circuit level. During the postwar decade, the *Chicago Tribune* reported on approximately 135 sex crime convictions, with charges ranging from indecent liberties with underage victims to attempted rape, to rape. While these articles did not cover all of the sexual violence committed in Chicago during these years or detail every conviction handed down, they do provide a more complete picture of local sentencing trends. According to press coverage, black men received, on average, twenty-eight-year sentences for the sex crimes for which they were convicted, while white men so convicted averaged fifteen- to seventeen-year sentences.[130] Sentencing trends, conviction rates, criminal investigations, and allegations of sexual violence all reflected degrees of racial bias, yet appealed cases in the decade following World War II demonstrate how African Americans in Chicago tried to resist judicial prejudices that had long been informed by racial rape myths.

* * *

When Billie Holiday sang *Strange Fruit* in jazz clubs around the United States after World War II, her performance awed audiences with its powerful and disturbing message. Imagining an American society without the bigotry that informed the brutality highlighted in the song was difficult, given that the pain of mob violence was ongoing when Holiday first recorded *Strange Fruit*. While lynchings had all but disappeared from the American landscape after World War II, the nation's collective consciousness retained these memories. Holiday's performances helped keep the hope of freedom alive, however, no matter how unsettling the song was to her or for those who heard it.[131]

Racial violence took new forms in the mid-twentieth century that did not exactly mimic lynching but that nonetheless evoked significant elements of ritual. Police, in their distinctive uniforms, might be equated with the hooded Klansmen who snatched black men from their homes or the streets on the basis of vague or fabricated suspicions about interracial sexual violence. The police did not have to hide their identities, however, as vigilantes preferred to do. As representatives of the State, police bias was arguably more sinister than what many Americans expected from Southern lynch mobs. Although not actually disguising those who wore them, police uniforms nonetheless masked individual agency. Their badges emboldened officers to protect the law and the honor of white women by targeting black men on the basis of existing racial and sexual ideologies. While the Chicago police did not resort to hanging rape suspects from "poplar trees," they sometimes threatened to do so and, in the process, erased the humanity of African American men by denying them their rights as fellow citizens. Chicago courts could not execute black rape defendants in the mid-twentieth century, but they could, and did, impose life sentences upon them while simultaneously assigning significantly less severe punishments to white men so convicted. While the justice system provided African Americans some hope of being judged fairly if they found themselves standing trial for rape, in the postwar decade the system represented, at best, a limited space for such hope.

Inspired by wartime promises of civil equality, African Americans in Chicago and across the nation agitated for rights that they had long been denied. White society resisted and criminal courts expressed a great deal of reluctance to attend to institutionalized racial discrimination. Authorities adhered to myths about predatory black male sexuality and sentenced African American rape defendants accordingly. Police arrested black men, sometimes only because they had been unfortunate enough to be found in exclusively white neighborhoods or border areas, and charged them with sex crimes against white women. Despite the fact that they had to testify before white judges or, less often, to predominantly white juries, the civil rights atmosphere of the time emboldened African American rape defendants to articulate their rights at trial, accusing police of bias and abuse. Although African American men evoked the imagery of lynching directly presented to white America through media such as Holiday's song, criminal trials muted the horrors of vigilante violence. The State presented evidence against black rape defendants, not mere accusations. Prosecutors expected defendants to lie, accused them of it, and offered police testimony to refute allegations of prejudice and coercion as presented by the defense.

Victims' accusations were downplayed in the face of defense narratives of racial discrimination, even though this strategy failed to convince the judges or juries considered here to acquit African American rape defendants. Although a few defendants suggested that women of questionable character consented to sexual liaisons with them, defense attorneys during the immediate postwar years rarely went too far in challenging the veracity of women who testified about being raped. Instead, they insisted that the police arrested the wrong man and that black defendants were, themselves, victims of racial discrimination. Social expectations, informed by traditional gender, class, and race relations, were important factors that affected both police methods as well as trial outcomes. Mary Elson publicly testified about her sexual trauma and was able to use effectively white racial privilege in order to do so, with minimal repercussions against her own character. While her trial experience was undoubtedly difficult, Elson's religious and appropriately feminine character undermined any plausible accusations that she might have instigated the rape or mistakenly identified the defendant as her attacker. Marguerite Thorpe and Emily Warbende also benefited from racial privilege in that the black defendants in these cases were convicted of rape, despite the questionable identifications made by the white women who accused them. Although victims were not immune from character attacks during the postwar years, in the cases analyzed here, protecting them as the State's central witnesses trumped expansive defense interrogations of them during trials. This type of courtroom protection would not last into the next decade, at least not to the same extent that it was employed prior to the late 1950s.

African American defense witnesses resisted white racial privilege in the courtroom as part of a broader agenda of civil rights activism. Utilizing familial norms to present themselves as respectable, and exploiting the questionable reputation of the Chicago police, they challenged racism in the criminal justice system and, by implication, within the broader urban community where they lived. Although Chicago had long offered civil opportunities for racial minorities, it also had a long history of de facto segregation and racial violence. African American defendants in the decade following World War II compared the city's courts with the Southern system of (in)justice that was expressed in Billie Holiday's *Strange Fruit*. The meaning of Holiday's song was recognizable to black Chicago residents, many of whom were Southern migrants themselves. The city's African American native sons were also familiar with a system that reinforced their inferior social position, especially when it came to racial rape myths that automatically defined them as sexually dangerous. They too were aware of and used the song's powerful message to articulate the need for social change.

While the nature of the adversarial system constrained trial narratives, it is clear that individuals who appeared in Chicago courts during this period were restricted in different ways. Their statements were scripted, both by attorneys using legal categories and by ideologies still present at the time. Because of the misperception that white women never consented to sex with black men, African American defendants had a limited range of options to defend against interracial rape allegations. They had to maneuver within these limitations, much as victims had to negotiate mythical expectations about their social status, sexual reputations, and sincerity in order to help the State prosecute accused rapists. Many black Chicago men who appealed their convictions in the postwar decade tried to establish alibis based on family ideals valorized at the time, and they regularly charged investigators with brutality and racial bias. African American defendants and their attorneys challenged the criminal justice system in the North and equated it with Southern-style illegal practices. At the same time they resisted being cast by white society as inherently criminal and sexually dangerous, whether or not they had actually committed the crimes with which they were charged. Less important to defense attorneys who shaped their strategies around charges of racial discrimination during this decade was the unbiased treatment of black rape victims, whom they considered obstacles to acquittals. The efforts of African American women to pursue their own claims of justice in court, however, also constituted a part of a postwar equality and rights struggle that has for too long been ignored.

3. Black Victims and Postwar Trial Strategies

In February 1959, Bernice Briggs appeared in court to testify against rape defendant Lawrence White, whom she accused of sexually attacking her the previous year. When she began recounting the circumstances that led up to the assault, Briggs quickly identified the defendant as the man who grabbed her while she was waiting for a taxi early one morning. He hit her head with an empty bottle, and, she testified, forced her to perform oral sex on him despite her pleas that she did not "know nothing about that kind of monkey business like that."[1] According to Briggs, her assailant pushed her down, hit her a few more times, and then began to rape her. She also testified that she was able to reach a switchblade she kept in her pocket, which she used to stab her attacker in the head, giving herself the chance to get away. When she reported the attack, the police called local hospitals to see if a man who fit the general description Briggs provided, and who might have been treated for a head injury, was at any of them. The Cook County Hospital staff indicated that they were caring for such a patient and promised to keep him there until the police arrived. Briggs went along, where she identified Lawrence White as the man who had attacked her that morning.[2] When the prosecutor asked her if she received any treatment for her own injuries at the time, she told him not just then but that she did "receive my treatment fourteen hours after that at the Provident and they didn't treat me good at that time."[3] The prosecutor dropped that line of questioning, and when White's attorney cross-examined her, Briggs's testimony never returned to the poor medical treatment she mentioned earlier during the trial. Lawrence White told the court a very different story. He claimed that he was mugged and stabbed, which is why he was at the hospital when the police arrested him.[4]

Briggs and White were both African Americans living in Chicago when violent circumstances brought them to the attention of the criminal justice system. The rape trial of Lawrence White clarifies some important shifts that had begun in Chicago, and within the justice system, during the 1950s: shifts that would ultimately come to affect the structure of the contemporary rape trial. According to his attorney, White was identified under questionable circumstances and furthermore was identified by a woman who had been "on some kind of relief . . . her word is good for nothing."[5] Although White's attorney questioned the actions of the Chicago police, which he claimed were blatantly prejudicial, he reserved his harshest scrutiny for the alleged victim. He used stereotypes of black women as sexually promiscuous, and of black single mothers and welfare recipients as dishonest, in an attempt to acquit his client. Because both the alleged victim and perpetrator were African American, the arguments that emerged during this trial abandoned strategies that revolved around racial discrimination exclusively but instead reinforced gender privilege in the courtroom. Even as the system was beginning to open up for defendants, who benefited from stricter rules of evidence that protected the rights of the accused, rape victims suffered more pointed character attacks during trials even after their bodies may have recovered from physical assaults.

Briggs turned to the police after she was sexually attacked and cooperated with their investigation, despite her misgivings about a system that mistreated her. As a sixteen-year veteran of domestic service and a welfare recipient, Briggs was certainly familiar with racial discrimination in a white-privileged society.[6] She received Aid for Dependent Children (ADC) for children who lived with her mother, so she also suffered the stigma of being an incompetent parent, suspect in her claims of State protection.[7] Briggs nonetheless trusted the justice system to do something about the violent attack she suffered. And the State responded, in spite of any reservations white society held about the status of African American women, whom many believed to be sexually promiscuous and thus unlikely rape victims.

That African American women successfully testified in intraracial rape cases challenges historical beliefs that their unchaste sexual nature made them undeserving of State protection or legal recourse following sexual attacks.[8] When they came forward to report rapes, black women encountered continuing silence from the activist minority community over their victimization. Moreover, in seeking aid from State authorities, they were unable to avoid the difficulties of cooperating with a system that did not, historically, treat its nonwhite members fairly. Such circumstances forced African American women who accused African American men of sexual violence into a difficult position. Should they stand up for themselves and pursue justice through a system that routinely denied racial minorities the full rights and privileges of citizenship? Or should they remain silent about the sexual violence they suffered because their attackers sometimes happened to be of the same race? The women here chose the former, but they were, for the most part, only able to do so successfully when accusing African American men, which compounded the personal difficulties they faced.

The proliferation of black victims appearing in Chicago courts during the 1950s suggests both that the State increasingly listened to them and that African American women were more willing to turn to the justice system to defend their rights. Although these women did not do so without difficulties, their voices are a part of an expanded culture of rights in which numerous groups and individuals challenged inequality in modern American society. As we have seen, convictions of black rape defendants in Chicago during this same period exposed charges of police abuse and prejudice. African American women also engaged this discriminatory system and did so in the face of broader black community silence. They asserted their rights as individuals deserving of justice and were supported by State authorities, just as many white women had been doing since before World War II.

Black rape victims, however, faced harsh treatment from defense attorneys who perfected derogatory strategies that questioned their words and actions. Unlike their white counterparts, they did not benefit as consistently from judicial shielding during trials, exposing how courtroom officials had not entirely abandoned racial myths about black women's motives or sexual promiscuity. Just as white Americans tended to fear the predatory sexuality of black men, so too did they tend to discount the possibility of sexual morality and integrity on the part of black women. Defense attorneys exploited this reasoning when cross-examining African American rape victims. The result was a rape trial that increasingly devalued all women's experiences of sexual violence, making their testimonies less crucial to the State's cases and ultimately positioning rape victims as targets of litigation abuse. This did not prevent women from claiming their right to State protection after reporting attacks, but it did help create a more hostile courtroom environment that anti-rape feminists in Chicago and across the nation eventually targeted for reform.

During the 1950s, African American residents made up roughly 15 percent of the city's total population but were the majority of witnesses who testified in rape cases appealed during this period.[9] The near singular attention to black perpetrators of interracial sexual violence, however, masked the sexual abuse of black women by white men. These victims were rarely able to seek legal recourse against their attackers. The persistence of racial rape myths regarding black female sexuality, which many whites believed made African American women overly promiscuous and thus unlikely to refuse consent to any sexual relations, prevented the State from effectively prosecuting most of these cases. But African American women also suffered sexual abuse at the hands of African American men. Scholarship has paid little attention to instances when black women turned to the same arena that had historically dismissed their victimhood, where they increasingly found authorities willing to take seriously their intraracial complaints.

The race of the individuals involved in Chicago rape convictions that were appealed during the 1950s shifted dramatically from those appealed in earlier years. Prior to 1950, there were only three appellate cases that involved victims and defendants of the same race in Chicago, while the remaining available transcripts were of interracial cases, with white women testifying against black men.[10] Between 1950 and 1959, there are twenty-six available transcripts of sex crime trials: of these, nineteen cases, or 73 percent, involved African American victims and, in all but one, African American men.[11] Of the remaining seven cases that involved white victims, the majority of them testified against white men.[12] While the data is necessarily limited to appellate cases because they alone produced full transcripts, some trends nonetheless emerge. At the appellate level, interracial rape cases decreased during the 1950s and black women appeared more regularly in court to testify, almost exclusively, against black defendants. Press coverage of sexual violence during the 1950s supports this trend. The *Tribune* sometimes reported that suspects were released, but in more than forty articles announcing the dismissal of charges or the acquittal of sex crime defendants during the 1950s, only three clarified that the accused were African American.[13] Thirty-seven presumably involved white defendants. Thus, white men rarely needed to appeal rape convictions, either because they did not go to trial or because they were more often acquitted. Even less often did white men find themselves in court facing accusations from black women, in keeping with racial rape myths about black female promiscuity and white male privilege. Appellate patterns during this period also confirm what contemporary researchers have long understood: in spite of myths about the prevalence of interracial sexual violence, the majority of rapes occur between individuals of the same race.[14]

Rape convictions were appealed for a number of reasons, all based on constitutional improprieties. An emerging defense strategy during the postwar years was to argue investigative bias, evidenced by issues like questionable identifications and police abuse toward alleged perpetrators, especially if they were African American. Informed by broader efforts within the civil rights movement that challenged discrimination in policing, Chicago defense attorneys like John Branion shaped their arguments in ways that would help convicted black men be heard by the appellate court. Claims of police abuse and discrimination against black defendants, however, were easier to make when victims were white. Interracial rape cases involving white victims and black defendants embodied traditional fears about miscegenation and the social status of African Americans. In cooperation with the NAACP, Branion especially used those fears to make distinct points about Chicago's strained postwar race relations in order to defend his African American clients. When rape victims were also African American, however, defense attorneys had to alter their strategies. Although they still accused police and prosecutors of brutality, misconduct, and discrimination, such arguments did not resonate with the same force as they had in interracial cases. The majority of defense attorneys, both privately employed and those within the Chicago Public Defender's office, were white men.[15] Their race and gender, as well as their professional status, made it easier for them to use stereotypes and myths about dishonest and wanton African American women in order to challenge the State's cases. In doing so, they undermined civil rights activism by verbally abusing black rape victims in court, even while they purported to uphold the virtues of equality by defending black men against discriminatory prosecutions.

The growth of the national civil rights movement after World War II depended on extensive participation by African American women, who had a long history of race activism. Their efforts during these years, however, focused less on distinct women's issues than they had before the war, and exclusively female groups began to lose much of their membership to organizations like the NAACP as the postwar movement gained momentum. Although black women in Chicago made the rising urban crime rate central to their community activism, their efforts addressed a broad spectrum of crimes (not just rape), especially as they related to postwar overcrowding in de facto segregated Chicago neighborhoods and discriminatory police investigations against black men.[16] Some early groups, like the National Council of Negro Women, survived into the 1970s only because its leaders capitulated to a broader civil rights agenda that focused on community service, rather than concentrating on the rights of African American women as they had done in the past.[17] The postwar civil rights movement thus centered on African American men and rights defined in the public sphere like enfranchisement and desegregation, despite the presence of a number of prominent female civil rights activists at the grassroots level.[18] Distinct black women's activism (re)emerged in Chicago along with the feminist movement of the 1960s and 1970s, although not without resistance among African Americans involved in the radical militancy of that period. But in the context of the civil rights movement of the 1940s and 1950s, issues like combating intraracial sexual violence against black women took a back seat to other concerns. Although African American women had actively worked for civil rights since the nineteenth century and always resisted having their voices silenced or their authority usurped, such resistance was muted as the mainstream civil rights movement found a more responsive national audience following World War II.

Given the well-documented history of white society's abuse of black women, it is ironic that some African American rape victims in Chicago found support from State officials rather than an increasingly vocal and active postwar civil rights movement. Or perhaps such faith, however tenuous it may have been, made sense during this period, when Chicago officials were linked to the "Daley machine." Although not elected mayor until 1955, Richard J. Daley had steadily moved up the ranks of the local political machine since the 1930s and became chair of the Cook County Democratic Party in 1953.[19] In doing so, he also assumed unofficial control of city hall during the final mayoral term of Martin Kennelly. Kennelly had become increasingly unpopular, especially among black voters, due to his lack of effort in challenging the segregationist tendencies of the Chicago Housing Authority, which faced a number of public-housing riots during the postwar years of urban population growth.[20] Yet it was also during the 1950s that Chicago claimed the title of "the city that works," at a time when other American cities experienced significant decay.[21] While Chicago had its own problems during this period, Daley's efforts to manage the city were often successfully efficient, albeit prejudicial and corrupt in many areas. For all of his segregationist tendencies, Mayor Richard J. Daley's efforts to address the needs of Chicago's black voters during the 1950s resulted in their unprecedented support for this big city "boss," at least for a time.[22] Moreover, the local news regularly reported on increased efforts to combat sex crimes during this period, specifically encouraging women to come forward to report rapes as a community service.[23] Potential embarrassment over reporting was, ideally, allayed by the *Tribune's* policy of declining to print the names of sex crime victims out of "the dictates of common decency."[24] Why anyone might feel embarrassed about being victimized by sexual violence had much to do with the widespread myth that a woman who wanted to avoid being raped could do so, if she really wanted to. While the experiences they described in court belied promises of personal safety made in the press or by the machine, the atmosphere of 1950s Chicago as a city that cared for its citizens inspired more black women than ever before to turn to local authorities for support and protection after being raped.

Although African American women who reported sexual attacks also found support from family members, friends, and neighbors, the broader activist community remained conspicuously silent about intraracial sexual violence. When the black press reported on sex crimes at all, it usually did so only to emphasize the innocence of African American men falsely accused of the rapes of white women. Occasionally, newspapers like the *Chicago Defender*—one of the nation's leading civil rights weeklies—might also point out the bias of the local police, who failed to rigorously investigate crimes against African American women.[25] This coverage, however, typically implied that their attackers were white, in line with traditional arguments about racial injustice in the United States.

Attention to intraracial sexual violence was rare in the local black press. If articles were published at all, they remained focused on broader accusations of racial discrimination related to particular cases.[26] One such instance was that of Gerald Chatham, who was convicted of raping two African American women in 1957. The *Defender* covered Chatham's sentencing hearing, where he "created havoc" in court by struggling with bailiffs, throwing a spittoon at a photographer, and breaking the arm off a chair. The reporter relegated the accusations against Chatham, made by black women, to the background of the piece while highlighting instead that his "berserk" behavior was "because he did not believe he would get a fair trial."[27] Chatham's 120-year sentence, far more severe than what most African American rape defendants received during the mid-twentieth century, underscored the article's emphasis on racial discrimination in the criminal justice sentence.[28] The broader movement and the attorneys who mounted civil rights arguments in support of African American rape defendants overlooked the violence suffered by African American women. However, black women's efforts to speak the taboo of intraracial rape demonstrate a challenge to some racial myths that automatically questioned the status of their claims, even while convictions against their attackers uncomfortably upheld other myths that cast all black men as sexually dangerous.

Another Side to Racial Rape Myths

White misconceptions about the predatory nature of black male sexuality were, in part, supported by an ideology that cast black women as either hypersexual or asexual. The stereotypes of the "jezebel" and the "mammy," rooted in slavery-era caricatures of African American women, denied them the right to claim a full range of human sexuality. This denial, in turn, left them without effective protections against sexual attacks. Asexual mammies were thought to lack enticing sexual characteristics and thus were not believably subjected to sexual violence. Who, after all, would attempt to rape a mother figure? Conversely, the jezebel image classified black women as sexually provocative. In her presentation of the myth of the "bad" black woman, historian Gerda Lerner posits that "by assuming a different level of sexuality for all Blacks than that of whites, and mythifying their greater sexual potency, the black woman could be made to personify sexual freedom and abandon."[29] If African American women seemed sexually unabashed, according to middle-class, white standards of monogamy, many believed it unlikely that they would have refused sexual advances from anyone, thereby refuting rape allegations that required resistance as a matter of law.[30] The "bad" black woman was thus eager for sexual exploits: she was neither chaste nor likely to mind if she were ravished.

African American women resisted this representation during the years following Reconstruction with numerous attempts to assert their modesty. They formed organizations like the National Association of Colored Women, founded in 1896, in an effort to combat inequality but also to combat stereotypes of black women as liars, thieves, or alleged prostitutes.[31] As women, black club leaders were less a threat to a patriarchal, white-supremacist society. They enjoyed more flexibility in demanding rights within the boundaries of the dominant system than did African American men, whose manhood made them particularly threatening to the social order.[32] Black clubwomen at the turn of the twentieth century thus found themselves at the forefront of civil rights activism as they promoted their own rights as well as the rights of the broader black community. These female leaders presented themselves as respectable, chaste women and tried to claim the same respect that white, middle-class clubwomen enjoyed. Many believed, or dared to hope, that asserting claims to respect would also encourage the achievement of full citizenship rights and social equality.

African American women resisted myths that limited their sexuality in other ways as well. During the 1920s and 1930s, black female blues and jazz singers became increasingly popular, providing white audiences with sexualized entertainment in segregated nightclubs. Women such as Ida Cox, Bessie Smith, and Billie Holiday sang of heartbreak and suffering, along the way claiming their right to be sexual individuals. They did not seek to promote a stereotype of wanton sexuality but instead demanded to be taken seriously as women and as people with a full range of emotions.[33] Whereas the predominant black female leadership of the day combated injustice through modest self-presentation, blues women instead asserted their power as fully realized sexual beings. As historian Deborah Gray White suggests, they were "arrogant and cynical" in the face of a prejudiced world, but they also "publicly affirmed black female sexuality with style and variety."[34] While this type of resistance offered African American women different options than the more conservative image provided by clubwomen of the time, it did little to challenge white beliefs about black women's promiscuity. By the postwar era, entrenched ideas about the myth of the "bad" black woman had encountered challenges from many sources, but the national civil rights movement did not focus on this issue.

Early in the morning on April 3, 1957, publisher Lacy Tyree heard glass breaking near his west side business and looked out the window to investigate. He saw barrels stacked beneath a window in a nearby building and a man running away from it.[35] One of the building's residents, Etta Jane Hardney, yelled for help as this man ran down the alley. She had been raped. The janitor from her apartment building went with Hardney to the police station, where he recognized the description she gave when reporting the attack. He believed it was Roosevelt Parker and told the police, who then issued a warrant for Parker's arrest. A few days later their suspect came in voluntarily, after he heard the police were looking for him.[36] When Tyree heard talk in the neighborhood of a woman raped by someone who broke into her first floor apartment, he went to the police station to report what he knew and described the man he saw running down the alley that night. Parker was already in custody and, after both Hardney and Tyree identified him from a lineup conducted at that time, the police charged him with rape.[37]

Just as white victims did, black women who reported sexual attacks relied on the support of family, neighbors, and friends. While the broader civil rights movement may have ignored the possibility that black men sometimes raped black women, Etta Jane Hardney's family and neighbors were not silent about this sex crime and got involved in its investigation. Her daughter, a door-to-door cosmetics saleswoman, also recognized Hardney's description. It sounded like a man she knew from the neighborhood who had previously helped carry her samples case a few times.[38] As well, their building's janitor promised the police that he could help them find Parker. Lacy Tyree later offered investigators information when he found out about the attack.[39] When Maurice Brown ran home after being raped in an alley near her south side apartment, a neighbor overheard her telling her mother what had happened. He went to that location where he found John Jackson, "laying up in the alley with one leg out of his pants, all his privates was out." He struggled with Jackson and managed to keep him there until the police arrived and arrested him.[40] When the other resident of a duplex that Juanita Lewis lived in heard her scream late one night and tell someone to "put the gun away, there's nobody here but me and you," he ran to the nearby El station to find help.[41] Although the reputation of the Chicago police for racial bias and brutality warranted caution from the city's black residents, when African American women were raped, their neighbors, family, and friends got involved and went to the police for help.

The burden of proof in criminal cases is on the State, and it helped prosecutors to have corroboration of women's accounts of sexual violence. Usually, the victims were the only direct witnesses to rapes, but not always. On a summer night in 1957, Hazel Morrison and two male friends were on their way to go fishing in Jackson Park. They searched the ground for worms with a flashlight but before they could find any, three men descended upon them and began to fight. One of Morrison's friends shone the flashlight up and hit one of the attackers with it before he fled, prompting the men to "catch that dirty son-of-a-bitch."[42] They knocked her other friend to the ground and then dragged her into the bushes where each raped her. Afterward they ran away, but not before all three victims (one of rape, two of assault) got a look at their attackers and were able to provide police with thorough descriptions of the three men. All three were arrested the following day on other charges, but since they matched known descriptions, the police called Morrison and her friends to the police station. From two separate lineups, they independently identified Robert Jackson, Johnnie Sinclair, and A. C. Harvey; all three were then arrested and charged with rape.[43] Much like family members who heard about attacks after the fact, black women could also rely on their companions to support them, in court if necessary. While the victim's testimony was central to the State's case, the court also appreciated external corroboration or additional eyewitness testimony if available.

To argue their cases successfully, prosecutors had to abandon myths about black women's sexual promiscuity and present African American victims as respectable women who were in court to seek justice and legal protection. Depending on the circumstances of a case, the prosecutor might emphasize black victims' respectability by questioning them about their family status, as in the cases against Gerald Chatham and Charles Johnson. The African American women who testified in these cases mentioned that they were married and had children.[44] This called the court's attention to their status as mothers, in line with the positive emphasis on family and motherhood during the postwar years. Rape victims were often married women who, the State argued, did not seek extramarital relations but instead suffered violent sexual attacks for which they were not responsible. Although the defense questioned Morrison's identification of her attackers, the prosecutor insisted, "The actions of these particular men would be indelibly burned into her mind." She was not seeking vengeance against the wrong men; instead, "she was honest and forthright from that stand, and everything that she told you [was] . . . exactly as it occurred."[45] Roosevelt Parker's attorney questioned the case the State presented against his client, arguing that the victim admitted to "no resisting, no screaming, no hollering."[46] The prosecutor disagreed, suggesting instead that she was a woman "who comes around and tells you, tells the whole world, look what this man has done to her. There is no one who would come and make that type of statement to hurt herself, disgrace herself" unless it were true.[47] This strategy worked for the State: the defendants in these cases were all convicted and sentenced to lengthy prison terms, reflecting the strength of the cases against them, despite the racial status of the victims.[48] Testifying publicly about private sexual traumas was difficult for any rape victim, regardless of her race, and prosecutors used that to underscore women's sincerity in the courtroom and gain convictions.

As in any felony trial, the circumstances of individual cases forced opposing attorneys to explain the same events in ways that either supported or challenged a woman's rape accusation. For example, a defendant could admit to having sex with his accuser but insist that she had consented, calling into question an allegation of rape even if both sides agreed that intercourse had occurred. This is what happened to Ann Robinson, an African American woman who had moved to Chicago in 1952, where she met two white men at a local beach. When she appeared in court to testify about being raped, she admitted that they had gotten along, and when they asked if she and a friend would like to go on a double date, she accepted. Robinson's friend could not go, so when Frank Teti and Dominic DiBiaso arrived to pick her up, she insisted that the three "go to a place where there were people [because] . . . you just don't go out with people you don't know."[49] The men apparently had something else in mind, because they drove for some time and parked the car where, as Robinson explained, "it was very deserted," and they gang-raped her.[50] Teti and DiBiaso had separate attorneys who both argued that Robinson had consented to the liaisons, one of them going so far to suggest, "she asked for what she got."[51] The prosecutor defended his case and asked the jury whether they were willing "to say that your daughters, your sons shall not have the right to go to the beach . . . without being bothered or molested?"[52] Similarly, the defense attorney for Dennis Kane suggested that victim Mary Anne Texter had actually consented to sexual activities. Texter testified that she had the defendant drop her off one block from her house after he allegedly attacked her; Kane's attorney suggested she did this because she did not want her mother to find out what she had been doing that night. He refuted the victim's allegation by asking her if it was only after she found out that his client was married, "that you decided to go to the police?"[53] The judge disregarded the implication and found the defendant guilty. Upon handing down his decision he suggested, "You have got a grown woman placed in a seemingly embarrassing situation. I think probably the reluctance to complain or make a situation known is perhaps natural, but within forty-eight hours she went to the police."[54] The judge in this case recognized, and forgave, the time that had passed between Texter's attack and her report of it to authorities, in spite of defense counsel's arguments about her sexual complicity.

Defense attorneys had to try to discredit prosecutors' cases and often attempted to do so through shaming tactics in the courtroom, asking questions that might raise judicial doubts, especially about black victims. When Ann Robinson testified against the men on trial for raping her, she was repeatedly frustrated in her attempts to explain herself because, as she tried to tell the court, the defense made her actions "sound the way it isn't at all."[55] After telling her "how these questions sound to your mind is not my fault," DiBiaso's attorney further objected to "this scene, these crocodile tears."[56] Although the judge threw out the insult, he sustained the defense objections because, according to the rules of the court, Robinson's answers were not responsive.[57] In 1958, Geraldine Horton testified that Charles Westbrooks had raped her. During her cross-examination, the prosecutor interrupted to find out "if counsel enjoys making the witness cry."[58] The defense attorney later apologized for being "a little rough" when questioning the victim. He told the court that he believed Horton had been raped but that he aggressively interrogated her only because he was concerned with "finding out who did it."[59] Recounting a rape was upsetting for any victim, especially because the courtroom was a male-dominated sphere that did not readily welcome female participation, even when women's testimonies were necessary to prove a case. The history of racial discrimination in the criminal justice system only compounded these difficulties for African American women.

Gender and racial issues, as well as individual styles, shaped how defense attorneys treated rape victims in the courtroom. Reflecting his commitment to civil rights, black public defender John Branion questioned black rape victims with a level of respect uncommon for many defense attorneys. Instead of interrupting Juanita Lewis when she testified against his client, or objecting to her statements as nonresponsive, he urged her several times to "just answer my questions please."[60] Judges never admonished Branion to step away from witnesses or to stop "hollering" at them, as the judge had to do when defense attorneys for Johnnie Sinclair, Robert Jackson, and A. C. Harvey cross-examined Hazel Morrison and her friends.[61] In a rare trial appearance in 1955, a female attorney defended Charles Johnson. She began her cross-examination of the victim, Alice Goolsby, by acknowledging that she knew Goolsby "had a very bad experience," and that she would try to be as brief as she could. When she questioned Goolsby about the rape itself, she gently tested the victim's recollection with the question, "And then you stated, Mrs. Goolsby, that he then proceeded with you in the act that I do not want to take you through again?"[62] This lawyer's gender tempered her attitude toward the victim, despite her efforts to convince the jury that the State was mistaken about her client's guilt.

Racial Stereotypes and Defense Arguments

Unlike the rare female or black counselor, most defense attorneys who cross-examined African American rape victims about their allegations attempted to use racial stereotypes to their advantage during trials. When they began regularly defending black men against black women's rape allegations, both private lawyers and public defenders could not exclusively rely on arguments that their clients were racially discriminated against, as had been a more common tactic in interracial cases involving white rape victims during the previous decade. Defense attorneys in black intraracial rape cases thus had to shift their strategies in court. They began to rely more heavily on stereotypes of black women's sexual promiscuity and their (often marginal) socioeconomic status in an effort to undermine the State's cases against black rape defendants. In doing so, they altered the atmosphere of the rape courtroom into a space where it became even more difficult for women to claim State protections without subjecting themselves to the kinds of personal interrogations that the victims analyzed here had been largely shielded from prior to this period.

Around midnight on September 4, 1956, Dale Barber was walking home from work when a man pulled up and offered her a ride. According to Barber's testimony, she refused, but the man forced her into his Pontiac and told her "not to try anything funny because if I did," she said, "he would shoot me." He asked her what she was doing out so late and, as she told the court, she asked him the same question. He indicated that he was looking to pick up a girl. Barber said, "[I] told him that he would not find any tramps in that part of town." She begged him to let her go and even tried to get out of the car when they stopped at a traffic light. He pulled her back in and drove to an alley where, she claimed, he raped her. She also testified, "He told me he was sorry he did the thing but he said he couldn't help himself," and then he dropped her off at the Forty-Seventh Street El station. After he drove away, she flagged a passing police cruiser and reported the attack.[63] Her detailed description of the man's car, including a partial license plate number and particulars about a continental spare tire kit mounted on its trunk, helped police find James Wilson, whom they subsequently arrested for rape.[64]

James Wilson told the court a different version of the events of that night. He admitted to having intercourse with Barber in his Pontiac but insisted that he knew her and that she had consented. He used to drive a cab and claimed to have met the victim a few months earlier, when he picked her up as a fare. He testified that he asked her out the first night they met, but that she told him she did not have time for dates. He also told the court that she said if he wanted to see her again he could give her a ride after work, which he did. According to Wilson, they continued to see each other, but that he could not go home with her because "she said that her husband might see her and she had respect for him." Nevertheless, Wilson alleged that they went out several more times and, when he kissed her and "fooled around" with her, she never said no. When Barber accused Wilson of rape, the defendant told the court that he gave her a ride like he often did and that their relationship had just progressed a bit further than was usual that night.[65]

The contradictory testimonies of this victim and this defendant are similar to current understandings of sexual violence: cases today are often characterized as misunderstood circumstances of she said / he said. James Wilson's defense attorney used a particular approach to convince the court that his client was innocent. He argued that the victim had consented, and he also cross-examined Barber about her financial circumstances. This established a context for Wilson's later testimony that he had loaned Barber money on several occasions and that it was only after she could not pay him when she accused him of rape.[66] In the cases under study in this book, only one defense attorney prior to the 1950s argued that the alleged victim had consented to a liaison with his client. In that case, the attorney asserted that he did not intend to attack the white victim's "immoral character" in order to defend his client (even though he did), but neither did he try to imply that she had solicited sex for money.[67] Although attorneys never directly accused alleged victims of prostitution in rape trials during the 1950s, they emphasized sexual misunderstandings that unfairly brought their clients into court.

The race of rape victims—and the myths about their sexuality that went along with their race—informed consent defense strategies during the 1950s. By the interwar period, prostitution was predominantly associated with African American women, especially in urban centers like Chicago. Although white women were also vulnerable to solicitation arrests, racial bias shaped the policing of prostitutes. So too did limited employment opportunities for black women, thus making them more likely than white women to enter the commercial sex trade.[68] Attorneys in the 1950s did not explicitly suggest that the rape accusations they defended against were tricks gone awry, but racial rape myths and the high levels of policing against African American women engaged in vice made it plausible to surmise as much from defense arguments. James Wilson testified that he offered Barber money, despite her insistence that she was not "a cheap tramp or something."[69] Although Wilson's attorney attempted to connect Barber more to blackmail than to prostitution by suggesting that her allegation "was an attempt on her part to get money from him," he also clung to the stereotype of the "bad" black woman, hoping that it would raise doubts about the rape charge.[70] When Bernice Briggs testified against Lawrence White, she insisted that he dragged her into an alley while she waited for a cab to pick her up and take her to her mother's house. White's attorney suggested that he did not "believe that she was out on the street at that time for that purpose."[71] In the State's closing arguments in the 1958 case against Leonard Pleasant, the prosecutor responded to defense insinuations by contending that if the victim were lying, "What is her motive? . . . Her character stands beyond reproach here. No one has come in and said she is a woman of the street."[72] No one said anything like that directly, but defense attorneys routinely used racial stereotypes to bring these sorts of allusions into courtrooms in an attempt to affect rape trial outcomes.

Conversely, white victims less often faced consent defense arguments at trial. When they did, attorneys usually argued that the State failed to prove force was involved, thus negating a rape charge. Prior to 1950, only one available rape trial transcript indicated a defense based on the white victim's consent. In this 1949 case, the public defender argued that his white client could not have forced the alleged victim to do anything, because if he had, there would have been evidence to prove it. According to the defense, the State failed to prove force because when the prosecutor presented the victim's underwear and garter belt as evidence of her resistance, which she claimed had been torn off during the attack, they were not ripped at all.[73] In his mind, the condition of the victim's undergarments proved that she had consented. Rape charges dropped or reduced, or white defendants acquitted because white women had allegedly consented, appeared only slightly more often in the newspaper than they were in the transcripts of convictions appealed. Prior to 1950, of the approximately thirty-five *Tribune* articles featuring these types of cases, only six either implied or clarified that the women involved had consented to sexual activities.[74] During the 1950s, white victims appeared less often in the available transcripts than they had in previous decades in general, and they continued to face rare consent defense arguments.[75] These defenses did not yet go so far as to harshly interrogate the sexual reputations of the women involved but rather emphasized their lack of resistance to the white defendants' actions.

Attorneys in trials involving white victims, whether they were intra- or interracial cases, did not imply prostitution in their consent defenses prior to the 1960s. Despite concerns about what the press sometimes called false "tavern rapes," a concept based on the myth that women lie about sexual violence in order to hide their shame over their own desires, accusing white victims of vice did not enter the public rhetoric during the 1950s.[76] Prostitution was illegal and was thus in keeping with mistaken assumptions that hypersexual black women were prone to lying and to engaging in crime and vice. These women were unlikely to be victimized by sexual violence, or so many white Americans believed. While it was a defense attorney's job to undermine the State's cases in any way possible, such tactics against black rape victims especially during this period created the kinds of obstacles to claiming justice that women found difficult to overcome. Nonetheless, as appellate records demonstrate, barriers to a culture of rights were not insurmountable for the many victims who appeared in court to seek legal recourse after being raped, no matter where or how those attacks may have happened.

When sex crimes occurred within racial minority neighborhoods in Chicago, defense attorneys tried to use geography to their advantage. Neighborhood, in their reasoning, might imply consent. If they suggested that African American women had been on particular streets at particular times, the plausibility that an alleged victim had really consented increased, which is what Wilson's attorney argued and White's attorney implied. Consent negated a rape charge, even if the law recognized that different levels of resistance could support indictments.[77] However, judicial precedent also allowed that consent "no matter how reluctantly yielded" still amounted to consent.[78] In 1955, Charlestine Mills testified in the rape trial of Osker Hill and told the court that Hill forced her into his car at gunpoint and drove her to a vacant lot in the lakefront Oakland community area, where he raped her.[79] In his closing statement, Hill's attorney wondered why Mills felt she could go out after dark, carrying money. He suggested, "There should be some doubt about why an eighteen-year-old girl would leave home . . . carrying eight dollars with her. Certainly, I would be afraid in that neighborhood to carry eight dollars at twelve o'clock in the daytime."[80] When Helen McMichael testified against George Mack Sawyer in 1959, his attorney asked her how she encountered the defendant. She told the court that she was standing outside of a tavern on a crowded street in the North Lawndale neighborhood one night when Sawyer grabbed her arm and dragged her into a car.[81] When he testified in his own defense, Sawyer insisted that he just "wanted to have a little fun" and that McMichael drove him to a secluded spot where she proceeded to take off her clothes "freely herself."[82] The defense attorney implied several points about the complaining witness in this case, based on recognizable facts about the location of the alleged rape. It was a busy neighborhood, so she should have been able to get away if someone tried to force her into a parked car. Moreover, several taverns, pool halls, and similar types of businesses were located there. According to community population studies, during the 1950s "whites fled North Lawndale in droves, many succumbing to racial fears which were easily manipulated by unscrupulous realtors."[83] In 1959, North Lawndale was known as a dangerous neighborhood that respectable people—unlike, presumably, the alleged victim in this case—avoided after dark.

African American leaders, in Chicago and across the nation, increasingly challenged institutionalized discrimination and racism as the postwar atmosphere of civil rights expanded. Although the city did not have official Jim Crow laws, de facto segregation caused severe problems as Chicago's minority population grew and strained against traditional neighborhood boundaries. White business leaders and politicians sought to relieve the pressures, but they did so in such a way that reinforced the segregation of minority residents. Ethnic whites strongly resisted community integration because of social fears about racial intermingling but also because limited space had created ghetto conditions in the city's existing black neighborhoods. Chicago historian Arnold R. Hirsch points out that "the conditions produced by real estate speculation and exploitation [after World War II] began to yield visible proof to those who believed that black 'invasion' meant slum creation."[84] Civil rights leaders tried to tackle the urban housing issue, along with agitating against unfair policing and discrimination against African Americans accused of crimes. What they did not pay attention to were criminal complaints from black women against black men. Doing so would have undermined arguments that Chicago's predominantly white police force unfairly targeted them. Admitting that some African American men may have been guilty of sexually attacking African American women also would have damaged claims that black men were not inherently criminal or sexually dangerous. Moreover, admitting intraracial sexual violence would have highlighted unequal gender relations among African Americans—an issue long hidden because of an emphasis on challenging racial discrimination coming from outside the black community.

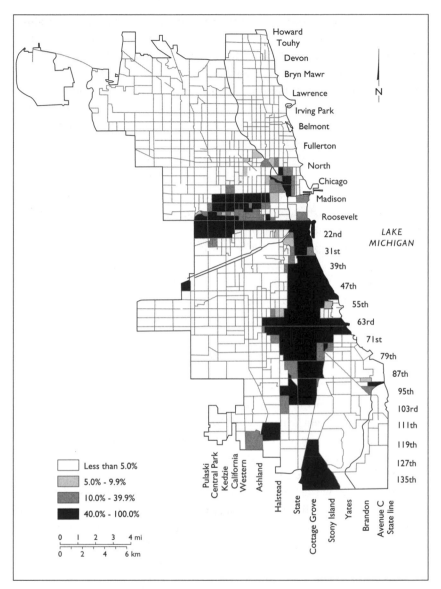

Howard
Touhy
Devon
Bryn Mawr
Lawrence
Irving Park
Belmont
Fullerton
North
Chicago
Madison
Roosevelt
22nd
31st
39th
47th
55th
63rd
71st
79th
87th
95th
103rd
111th
119th
127th
135th

N

LAKE
MICHIGAN

Pulaski
Central Park
Kedzie
California
Western
Ashland
Halstead
State
Cottage Grove
Stony Island
Yates
Brandon
Avenue C
State line

Less than 5.0%
5.0% - 9.9%
10.0% - 39.9%
40.0% - 100.0%

0   1   2   3   4 mi
0   2   4   6 km

Map 1. City of Chicago: Percentage of Black Population in Census Tracts, 1960.
Source: Arnold R. Hirsch, *Making the Second Ghetto: Race and Housing in Chicago,
1940–1960,* rev. ed. (Chicago: University of Chicago Press, 1998), p. 8. Information
taken from, U.S. Bureau of the Census, *Eighteenth Census of the United States,*
"Population and Housing Characteristics," 1960.

Emboldened by new attitudes regarding civil rights and facing the realities of residential overcrowding, many black Chicagoans sought to change their circumstances by moving beyond traditional neighborhood boundaries. In 1948, the Supreme Court declared unconstitutional the restricted housing covenant, a legal device that prevented the sale or rental of homes to both racial and religious minorities.[85] Cities like Chicago continued to enforce de facto segregation, in spite of black protests, even after the Court had mandated open housing in the private market. In the face of an expanding civil rights movement that targeted issues like restricted housing, Chicago's white ethnic population forgot their cultural differences and worked together to prevent neighborhood integration (see map 1).[86] Or they fled the city all together, basing many of their arguments about postwar changes on stereotypes of black criminality. Police statistics supported white fears, reflecting higher numbers of offenses in black and border areas than in historically white neighborhoods. Outside the downtown Loop, precinct maps show that south side districts including Wabash and Woodlawn had a high offense rate per 1,000 residents. So too did the west side areas of Monroe, Maxwell, and Warren, where Chicago's African American population expanded significantly during the 1950s as white residents moved out (see map 2).[87] The recorded crime rates in Chicago's growing south and west side ghettoes were due to more biased policing in minority communities, but the rates also reflected higher levels of crimes committed in economically poor areas.[88] White authorities considered African American men more dangerous than African American women. However, prejudicial beliefs about black women's criminal behavior or licentious sexuality made doubts about their rape accusations easier for defense attorneys to exploit in court. They connected alleged black victims to the slum neighborhoods and transitioning areas that many white Chicagoans feared. Defense attorneys questioned white victims about the circumstances of attacks that occurred at night in deserted lots and dark alleys as well. These inquiries did not, however, have the same racially charged impact that they did when presented to African American women during the postwar years of racial strife and housing riots in Chicago's neighborhood borderlands.

Defense attorneys exploited rape myths about black women, but they also used class bias to support their arguments in the courtroom. Despite ideological claims that the U.S. justice system is impartial, scholars have repeatedly shown how, in court, some individuals are more equal than others.[89] Although the prosecutors built the 1958 case against Lawrence White on important elements—including the victim's immediate complaint, a show of resistance, and her positive identification of the suspect—his attorney insisted

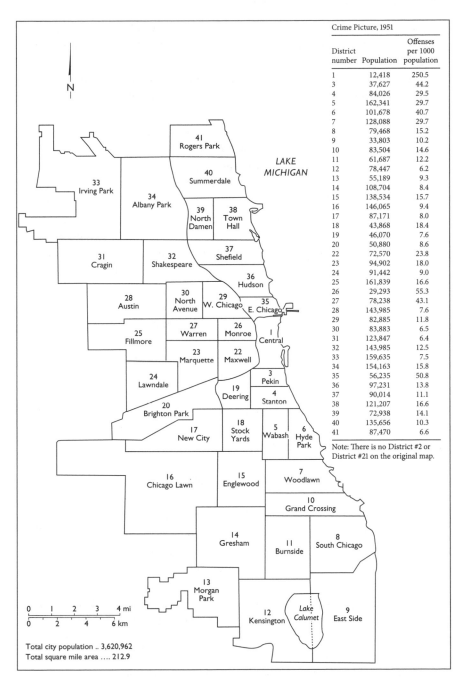

District number	Population	Offenses per 1000 population
1	12,418	250.5
3	37,627	44.2
4	84,026	29.5
5	162,341	29.7
6	101,678	40.7
7	128,088	29.7
8	79,468	15.2
9	33,803	10.2
10	83,504	14.6
11	61,687	12.2
12	78,447	6.2
13	55,189	9.3
14	108,704	8.4
15	138,534	15.7
16	146,065	9.4
17	87,171	8.0
18	43,868	18.4
19	46,070	7.6
20	50,880	8.6
22	72,570	23.8
23	94,902	18.0
24	91,442	9.0
25	161,839	16.6
26	29,293	55.3
27	78,238	43.1
28	143,985	7.6
29	82,885	11.8
30	83,883	6.5
31	123,847	6.4
32	143,985	12.5
33	159,635	7.5
34	154,163	15.8
35	56,235	50.8
36	97,231	13.8
37	90,014	11.1
38	121,207	16.6
39	72,938	14.1
40	135,656	10.3
41	87,470	6.6

Crime Picture, 1951

Note: There is no District #2 or District #21 on the original map.

Total city population .. 3,620,962
Total square mile area 212.9

Map 2. City of Chicago, Neighborhood Policing: Offenses per 1000 of Total Population, 1951. Source: Chicago Police Department, "Annual Report," 1951.

that the State failed to prove the defendant guilty. The defense challenged the prejudicial arrest of his client but saved the harshest criticisms for the victim, scrutinizing at trial both her activities and general character. He asked the victim, Bernice Briggs, several questions about her children, implying that she was a negligent mother because they did not live with her, even though she told the court that she provided money for them when she could. He later asked her if they were "three children of the same husband?"[90] In doing so he shifted his attention away from negligent maternity and toward promiscuous sexuality, both contrary to ideal feminine gender roles. After the State entered Briggs's knife as evidence in the case, the defense attorney questioned her about it. When he asked if she had "good leverage" to stab her attacker's head, as she had testified about earlier, she did not respond. This provoked him to ask, "You don't know what leverage is, do you?" He claimed that he could not figure out how to open the switchblade and asked her, "You practiced that a lot, didn't you? Answer me. You can do it pretty well, can't you?" He also asked Briggs how she knew that the Forty-Eighth Street police station (where she made her complaint) was in her district.[91] All of these exchanges demonstrated how defense attorneys implied that black victims, especially single-mother welfare recipients like Bernice Briggs, were familiar with crime, poverty, and the police, and thus likely lying about being raped.

As was his job, defense counsel portrayed Lawrence White in the best possible light. He questioned the defendant about his home, family, and education. White testified that he lived with his married sister and her family; was regularly employed as an apprentice at the Interlake Iron Corporation; was a graduate of Chicago's DuSable High School; and had attended Wilson Junior College before spending time in the Air Force.[92] While the victim and defendant in this case were the same race, their trial narratives indicated that they did not share the same socioeconomic status. The phrasing White used in court reflected his education and likely some coaching from his attorney as well. He tried to explain his presence at the hospital where the victim identified him, telling the court that he had been stopped earlier in the evening by what he thought were police and that "in order to prevent any misunderstanding between us, I yielded to the idea . . . that he was a police officer." According to his testimony, it turned out not to be the police who stopped him but instead the people who mugged and stabbed him that night. This was why his neighbor "proceeded to offer his service of taking me to the hospital" for treatment.[93] White's attorney also called other witnesses who supported his client's alibi and further emphasized his good character in court.[94]

Despite the defense's best efforts, the judge was not convinced of White's innocence. He found the defendant guilty and, "in view of his prior record," sentenced him to twenty years for the rape of Bernice Briggs.[95] White's attorney appealed the ruling, and in a hearing regarding alleged new evidence in the case, he told the judge that "this Briggs woman came in the hospital that morning intoxicated" and that "she lied about the situation."[96] He brought in witnesses from the hospital to testify that she had alcohol on her breath, and her eyes "were sort of bloodshot," and that "her speech was slurred . . . she sounded like a person who had been drinking. You know how you get when you have too much to drink." The defense attorney insisted that Briggs must have lied about the rape because she had also lied about her employment. He told the judge, "The woman has been on some kind of relief, ADC, relief at all times, and her word is good for nothing."[97] Bringing up the fact that Briggs was a welfare recipient was a way for the defense to capitalize on prejudicial beliefs that African American women were unworthy to receive State aid because they were often unwed mothers and not the unfortunate (white) widows the system had originally conceived of as the appropriate type of welfare recipient.[98] This evidence failed to convince the judge, who suggested that the defense should have presented it during the trial. He denied White's motion and allowed the original sentence to stand.[99]

Defense attorneys could also manipulate the language of African American rape victims' testimonies, using both racial and class prejudices to challenge the sincerity of their words. Geraldine Horton reported to the police that she was raped while on her way home from work after her 4 PM to midnight waitressing shift. She testified that she stopped to visit with friends at a local tavern before going home, when a man grabbed her, told her not to yell, and made her walk to a nearby park, where he ordered her, "Just act like I am your boyfriend."[100] When cross-examined, the defense attorney asked her about telling the court, "[The defendant] put his penis in your vagina" because the attorney wanted to know, "Who told you to say that?" and "[Have you] ever used that expression, vagina, before?" He further queried, "Are you acquainted with medical terms?" The prosecutor insisted that he did not know "if that [vagina] is a medical term. I thought it quite common in usage."[101] The defense attorney in this case implied that perhaps Horton received more witness coaching than was permissible, an argument made more plausible by her nonwhite and non–middle-class status. Similarly, when Audrey Thomas testified against Leonard Pleasant, she told the court that he raped her. As expected, the defense attorney objected to the conclusion, so the prosecutor had her clarify what she meant. She explained, "He put his penis in my vagina."[102] During his closing arguments, Pleasant's attorney argued that her narrative equaled "the trite statements that are made by any complaining witness who has been adequately schooled . . . they are words of law, legal phraseology, words of art, words that mean specific things that don't come naturally from the mouth of a lay person."[103] Whether victims' linguistic choices at trial were described as "medical terms" or as "legal phraseology," defense attorneys characterized them as words reserved for educated professionals, only suspiciously appropriated by working-class, black women.

As seen in these cases, arguments questioning the sincerity of African American women who accused men of rape did not work, but defense attorneys' contentions situated black victims in a particularly difficult position as complaining witnesses. Prosecutors tried to counter defense claims by objecting to their relevancy in court, but the strategies that defense counselors used and the questions they asked African American rape victims reveal how racial, class-based, and gendered prejudices were linked in the courtroom. The State nonetheless stood up for these women, believed them, and presented them as legitimate victims, despite persistent social beliefs about their sexual promiscuity. Prosecutors did not do this out of a sense of altruism necessarily, but because it was their job. They were charged with defending the interests of the State, upholding the law, and prosecuting criminals. For the first time in significant numbers during the 1950s, the interests of the State coincided with the interests of African American women who sought legal recourse against sexual violence. But black victims also had to face a system particularly hostile to the rights of racial minorities and did so under circumstances that were compounded by the suspicions historically lodged against most adult women, of any race, who accused men of rape.

Defense strategies that invoked racial stereotypes informed trial outcomes, as did the idea that criminal rehabilitation might successfully replace punitive sentencing. In 1951, the Illinois legislature funded a bipartisan fact-finding commission on sex offenders in the state. Representatives charged the commission with a number of duties. Among them was to analyze and coordinate their findings with results from similar commissions appointed in other states in order to "determine the best methods for the apprehension, prevention, treatment and cure" of sex offenders, and to "recommend any . . . modification of existing avenues of treatment."[104] Among their findings, issued in a 1952 report, was the idea that long prison terms were not useful in promoting rehabilitation; one expert equated sex offenders with the way many prison reformers already viewed drug addicts.[105] The commission recommended that rehabilitation be implemented more consistently for men convicted of sex crimes in order to help keep low and even further reduce existing rates of recidivism.[106] Whereas Chicago rape trials during the 1930s and 1940s that ended in convictions found prosecutors emphasizing the need to protect the community against dangerous sexual criminals, sentencing recommendations during the 1950s were increasingly shaped by defense pleas about rehabilitation.

Despite requests of leniency, however, judges often remained unconvinced about the prospects of rehabilitating sex offenders. Gerald Chatham's attorney argued that the court "cannot sentence an insane man." The judge insisted, "If he is insane, we will protect him on it," but he then sentenced Chatham to two consecutive sixty-year prison terms.[107] After A. C. Harvey was convicted, his attorney appealed to the judge that Harvey was "immature both intellectually and socially [and] he has not been given the social guidance that he needs." The judge was unmoved, saying he "would give great consideration to youth and lack of education except the testimony proved him to be worse than the others" involved in the gang rape of Hazel Morrison. He sentenced Harvey to ninety-nine years in prison, the same sentence as one of his co-defendants and considerably longer than the forty years assigned to the other.[108] Leonard Pleasant's attorney argued that "the purpose of the penitentiary sentence is rehabilitation" and that "a just sentence need not be a severe sentence," after his client was convicted of rape in 1958. Pleasant was nonetheless sentenced to twenty years for the rape of Audrey Thomas.[109]

Judges were more lenient in cases when defense attorneys clung to racial stereotypes of promiscuous black women and argued that they had consented to sexual liaisons. When Dale Barber testified against James Wilson, she indicated that he had threatened her with a gun, which was usually an aggravating circumstance in the sentencing of convicted rapists. However, the State never produced a weapon as evidence, and the defense argued that it was highly unlikely his client would feel he needed to use one, since he claimed that he and the victim had dated. Although the judge found Barber's narrative of rape more believable than Wilson's explanation of a sexual misunderstanding, he sentenced the defendant to only five years.[110] Similarly, the judge deciding the outcome of the case against Dennis Kane found that "the conduct and demeanor of the prosecuting witness on the stand" suggested she was telling the truth about being sexually attacked, in spite of defense arguments about her alleged consent. He sentenced Kane to only one to five years on the charge, however.[111] In cases like these, racial rape myths about criminal black men and promiscuous black women both influenced trial outcomes. Although newspaper articles regarding the conviction and sentencing of African American sex crime defendants during the 1950s usually did not detail the defense strategies used in cases that were not appealed, the sentences highlighted in the press ranged from one to two years for attempted rape or assault with intent to rape, to life (or longer) in prison for multiple counts of rape.[112] Such a wide range suggests that black

defendants encountered numerous different case circumstances, legal strategies, and courtroom personalities in all sex crime trials, whether or not they
pursued appeals. Prosecutors succeeded in gaining convictions of the African
American defendants analyzed here, but the lighter sentences assigned in
certain cases suggested that judges did not consider too severe the sex crimes
perpetrated against some African American women.

* * *

During the 1950s, the profile of a so-called winnable rape case in Chicago
had begun to change. The State had previously focused on trying cases that
primarily involved white victims testifying against black defendants, but during this decade, African American women increasingly sought legal recourse
after being raped. They, like white women, did so in an effort to claim their
own rights in a postwar context of asserting social equality while reject-
ing rape myths that questioned their respectability as women. Prosecutors
listened to their complaints and pursued cases based on their testimonies,
extending to black victims the kind of legal recourse for which the American
justice system was not historically known. While the majority of defendants
appearing in circuit court cases that were appealed during the 1950s continued to be African American, these cases were no longer almost exclusively
interracial. Many African American women in Chicago during the 1950s
turned to authorities after being raped by African American men, and they
did so with the support of friends, family, and neighbors. Although postwar
civil rights leaders appeared unconcerned about sexual violence against black
women (unless it was targeting white men so accused, who usually got away
with it), people who knew and cared about black rape victims stood up for
them and tried to help them when they could. Black women's presence in
Chicago courtrooms began to destabilize beliefs about their promiscuous
sexual nature. The convictions they helped the State pursue challenged the
idea that African American women did not suffer "real rapes."

African American women who entered the criminal justice system did so
in the face of that same system's historical discrimination toward racial minorities. Defense attorneys used racial prejudice and sexual myths to weaken
the effect of black victims' complaints, which reflects the particular difficulties that African American women encountered during trials. They attacked
black women's characters, questioned their actions, and interrogated their
testimonies on the basis of stereotypes about the marginal status of African
Americans. Because they may have been poor, or reported attacks that had
occurred in rough neighborhoods, black women, the defense attorneys insisted, lied about sexual violence. Defense attorneys did not all display the

same level of hostility toward the victims whose testimonies they tried to undermine, but most relied on racial rape myths and prejudicial beliefs about wanton black women to shape the strategies they used in court. Defense bias had little to do with the actual circumstances of attacks and much more to do with dominant perceptions regarding who, truthfully, could be raped. That they failed in their attempts to challenge the veracity of African American women's allegations suggests that entrenched ideas about the expected racial status of rape victims were beginning to break down during this period. It also demonstrates how steadfast black women were in their pursuit of respectability and rights during the postwar years, just as black men were when they challenged a system that they experienced as rooted in discrimination.

This did not mean, however, that black women who reported intraracial sexual attacks did not suffer internal conflicts about the complaints they made or were able to avoid racially charged hostility during postwar trials in Chicago. In these cases, they faced a choice: pursue judicial protections after suffering sexual attacks without knowing what kind of treatment they might have to endure from white authorities, or remain silent in order to help improve the social status of black communities that faced a hostile white society convinced of their inherently criminal nature. The civil rights movement's relative silence about intraracial sexual violence also made reporting attacks particularly taxing for African American victims.[113] By the 1960s such choices had taken a toll on the broader movement, which began to label black women who accused black men of sexual violence as traitors to their race.

The racial status of victims tempered defense arguments that disputed rape myths about black men. These defendants were not in court facing white women, so they could not invoke miscegenation hysteria in order to deflect criminal charges in the same way that they had tried when interracial rape cases dominated trial dockets. As a result, other defense strategies also emerged during this decade. Defense attorneys not only used sexist and racist stereotypes and class bias to undermine black women's claims of sexual violence, but they also attacked prosecutors' presentations of evidence. They increasingly claimed that crime-scene technology and medical evidence should help corroborate victims' complaints.[114] If these things were absent, defense attorneys wondered, what was the State trying to hide? Defense attorneys cast rape victims as unbelievable and rape investigations as untrustworthy, thus attempting to present a shadow of reasonable doubt about the guilt of their clients.

The combination of attacks against the character of black victims and arguments about faulty and insufficient criminal investigations continued into the 1960s, when such tactics became more pronounced. This shift reflects how the system intensified its distrust of already suspect women and complicated the prosecution of felonies during a time when public attention increasingly focused on the rights of the accused. The State sought more and more corroboration for women's allegations of sexual violence, moving the legal category of rape closer to how prosecutors approached other violent crimes that required extensive evidentiary support in modern trials. The experiences of the African American women and men who testified during rape trials in Chicago during the 1950s, and attorneys who employed distinct legal strategies, helped produce a new courtroom atmosphere that protected the rights of defendants while simultaneously denigrating female victims of sexual attacks. Advocates of defendants' rights applauded the altered structure of the 1960s rape trial, even while a burgeoning women's liberation movement vehemently opposed the increased abuse of victims' rights and personal privacy in the courtroom.

4. Order in the Court

During the 1960s the United States Supreme Court, under the leadership of Chief Justice Earl Warren, handed down a series of opinions that altered the structure of criminal trials across the country. Following legal trends of the postwar era, the high court standardized how authorities treated criminal suspects. Although the U.S. Constitution had insured many rights of the accused for over a century, these protections were applied inconsistently.[1] The Fourteenth Amendment began to change the application of federal protections to defendants tried in local courts, but prior to the 1960s, the Supreme Court had resisted applying rights defined in federal amendments at the state level. The Warren Court, however, changed the interpretation of the rights of the accused. In 1963, it handed down a decision in *Gideon v. Wainright*, which mandated that every criminal defendant at every level of prosecution had the right to legal representation in court.[2] Other decisions that further expanded constitutional protections for the accused soon followed. *Escabedo v. Illinois* (1964) guaranteed suspects the right to have legal counsel present while the police questioned them and in 1966, the Court handed down *Miranda v. Arizona,* which required officers to read suspects their rights, including the right to legal representation and the right to "remain silent" upon arrest.[3]

At the local level, decisions about defendants' rights dramatically changed the structure of criminal trials and introduced new complexities at the circuit level. While defendants in Chicago had enjoyed representation in court for decades prior to *Gideon,* the formal expansion of the rights of the accused during the 1960s created different legal points for defense attorneys to exploit at trial.[4] They combined new strategies with already well-established assertions of police prejudice, especially on behalf of black defendants who continued to be arrested and tried more often for rape than were white men. African Americans have, historically, been more heavily policed for all types of violent crimes in the United States, and this was especially true for sexual violence in light of racial myths about the beast rapist.[5] Decisions that reorganized the trial process in order to protect defendants' rights required prosecutors to support cases with expert testimony and thorough explanations of exhibits before they could be admitted as evidence. Judges also had to adhere carefully to newly standardized directives. They decided which testimony and evidence would be admitted during trials, but they also had to be cognizant of higher court opinions. It was possible the decisions that local judges had been making for years might not conform to new federal mandates, thus giving convicts legitimate grounds for appeals. The protection of the rights of the accused did not proceed without bias at the circuit level, but the emergence of new trial testimonies and altered legal tactics reveal the steady push for equality in Chicago courtrooms. A culture of rights, the expansion of constitutional protections, and an increase in the number of practicing attorneys in the United States encouraged more criminal appeals during the 1960s, even if higher courts continued to affirm most circuit-level convictions.

At the same time, trial examinations of rape victims intensified. Judges, taking greater care to protect the rights of defendants, allowed a kind of testimonial latitude that they had prohibited in the past. Defense attorneys interrogated victims about their sexuality and, using a new approach, they also accused some women of being prostitutes who lied to get back at customers who refused to pay. In the story told by defense counsel, the alleged female victim was both sexually immoral and, potentially, a criminal herself. Why should the court, already historically suspicious of women lying about matters of sexuality, believe her when she cried rape? As defendants' rights thus expanded, victims' power contracted. Although a direct causal connection between these trends is unclear, what is evident is that, working simultaneously, they produced an increasingly hostile trial atmosphere for rape victims. As victims' testimonies throughout the mid-twentieth century have demonstrated, talking about private sexual traumas in a formal judicial setting was never easy for women. In the rape trials of the 1960s, it became even more difficult for them to be heard. Additional witnesses called to corroborate victims' accusations contributed to the complexity of the new rape trial—a complexity that drowned out almost completely the voices of women, as attorneys debated subtle points of law, and defendants made familiar claims about police brutality. Women continued to demand justice as they always had, but in the altered trial of the 1960s they faced obstacles

Table 2. Rape Statistics in Chicago: Report and Arrest Rates compared to National Average, 1960–1969

Year	Forcible Rapes Investigated	Cleared by Arrest (% of Reports)	National Average, Cleared by Arrest
1960	880	504 (57.3%)	72.5%
1961	1479	720 (48.7%)	72.6%
1962	1621	631 (38.9%)	66.0%
1963	1134	713 (62.9%)	69.0%
1964	1188	842 (70.9%)	66.9%
1965	1223	773 (63.2%)	64.0%
1966	1236	860 (69.6%)	62.0%
1967	1403	1016 (72.4%)	60.9%
1968	1226	743 (60.6%)	55.0%
1969	1334	*	56.0%

Sources: Virgil Peterson, comp. *A Report on Chicago Crime* (Chicago: Chicago Crime Commission, 1960–1968). Federal Bureau of Investigation, comp. *Uniform Crime Report* (Washington D.C.: Government Printing Office, 1960–69); Kenneth Block, comp. *A Report on Chicago Crime* (Chicago: Chicago Crime Commission, 1969), 8. Averages tabulated by author.

* Data unavailable.

informed by a gendered culture of rights that emphasized masculine privilege despite the rhetoric of equality.

Urban crime and violence, as well as social activism and an emphasis on equality, expanded in Chicago and across the nation during the 1960s. At this time, Chicago police investigated thousands of reports of forcible rape and cleared (with arrests) on average around 60 percent of these, which was slightly lower than the national average but comparable with the risk and arrest rates in other urban jurisdictions during this period (see table 2).[6] While the vast majority of the arrests ended in guilty pleas, often for lesser offenses, the number of sex-crime cases that were heard by the First District Appellate Court of Illinois fully tripled in the 1960s. A sample of one-third, or thirty-three transcripts of convictions, appealed between 1960 and 1969 are analyzed in this chapter.[7] Over half involved African American victims who testified against African American defendants. In the remaining fifteen cases, white women testified against black men only slightly more often than they did against white men.[8] During these years, defense attorneys more readily attacked the characters of women who did not conform to rape myth expectations, but they also began to scrutinize more closely victims who did as well. As the transcripts from earlier decades demonstrate, African American and working-class women were easier defense targets in court than sexually chaste, middle-class white women. During the 1960s, however, arguments that questioned women's sexuality, regardless of race, class, or marital status, also emerged in the trials analyzed here. Challenging the investigations of even the most traditionally believable of circumstances surrounding sexual attacks—such as a chaste (white) woman attacked by the proverbial (black) stranger jumping out of an alleyway—also began to appear regularly in Chicago courts during this period. Such defense strategies produced an intimidating atmosphere for the victims who reported sex crimes and cooperated with authorities throughout these years.

Revelations about the Chicago Police Department also intensified the scrutiny of criminal investigations, once cases made it to trial. While defense attorneys had been questioning the actions of the Chicago police throughout the postwar years, by the mid-1950s their courtroom arguments resonated more profoundly. Justice officials and jury pools were members of the Chicagoland community, and citywide scandals had begun to expose some of the failings of the urban machine during this period. Daley's Chicago may have been, in many ways, the "city that worked" at the time, but it was becoming clear that it did not work well for everyone. Residents increasingly began to doubt the abilities of investigators, especially after a series of child murders in 1955 remained unsolved.[9] The *Chicago Defender* published a two-part exposé on racially motivated police brutality in March 1958, contributing to mounting skepticism of local law enforcement.[10] Historically infamous for corruption within the ranks, even cynics were scandalized by the disclosure in 1959 of a burglary ring run from inside a north side precinct.[11] That same year, Anthony "Big Tuna" Accardo retired as the head of Chicago's organized crime syndicate. He went on an extended European vacation, taking Police Lieutenant Anthony DeGrazio with him. Upon their return, DeGrazio was suspended for violating departmental codes against fraternizing with a known criminal, further undermining local faith in the police department.[12]

Although solidly entrenched as head of Chicago's political machine and enjoying nearly total support among the city's voters, the publicity surrounding the scandals put Mayor Richard J. Daley's authority on the line. According to former Chicago police officer Bernard James Ward, Daley had to take "swift and decisive action of an extraordinary nature" in order to re-inspire the public's faith and to save his political career.[13] He did so by hiring a committed police reformer, Orlando W. Wilson, as the department's new superintendent in 1960. Wilson was a disciple of a new type of law enforcement: the "college cop." Adopting the innovations of his mentor, Berkeley (California) Police Chief August Vollmer, Wilson advocated the use of technologies, such as polygraphs and two-way radio contact with patrol cars, in police work.[14] He was devoted to rigorous training and had proven himself a savvy administrator who was above corruption during his eleven-year tenure as chief of the Wichita (Kansas) Police Department.[15] His charge was to uproot police corruption and put an end to political patronage within Chicago's many neighborhood districts.

Wilson got to work immediately, reforming procedures and standardizing the presentation of crime statistics throughout the city. He used internal searches to expose dishonesty and had trusted officers violate laws in neighborhoods outside their own precincts in an effort to discover who was prone to accepting bribes. Police who did were promptly dismissed. Chicago detectives who kept their jobs or who were hired and promoted under Wilson had to have training, preferably a college degree, or had to otherwise prove that they were not patronage appointments.[16] Trust in the Chicago police was not entirely reaffirmed during Wilson's years as superintendent, however, as his directives were applied inconsistently on the street. After he retired in 1967, it quickly became clear that police corruption and brutality, as well as racism both within the force and as directed against African American residents, were hardly eliminated in Chicago. One need only consider how patrols carried out Daley's infamous "shoot to kill, shoot to maim" command to keep order following Martin Luther King's assassination in 1968, or the deadly raid against the local chapter of the Black Panther Party in 1969, to understand why the Chicago Police Department's poor reputation persisted, in spite of the reforms implemented during this decade.[17]

Legislative and judicial developments nonetheless changed how rapes were prosecuted in Chicago during this period. A few years prior to the main defendants' rights decisions handed down in the 1960s, the Illinois Supreme Court declared that anyone had the right to appeal their convictions and that, when necessary, the State was responsible for providing funds to produce copies of the transcripts used in appeals.[18] This decision allowed more defendants to pursue appeals, and prosecutors faced pressures to adhere more carefully to national guidelines in an effort to avoid having their convictions overturned. In 1962, Illinois's First District Court of Appeals clarified that rape cases especially "demand exercise of extreme care in excluding evidence that might deprive defendants of a fair and impartial trial."[19] The nature of this ruling and the higher numbers of defendants appealing their sex crime convictions during the 1960s profoundly affected prosecutorial strategies in the courtroom. Whereas they had once depended on women's trial narratives and had manipulated expectations about believable victims and likely perpetrators, prosecutors in the 1960s had more trouble countering rape myths that doubted the claims of women and upheld the authority of accused men. The result was a rape trial dominated by experts, investigators, and judicial arguments, which also involved some women too. While these changes brought the prosecution of sexual violence closer to that of other felony crimes during a time when the protection of the rights of the accused had become paramount, such reform had additional consequences for women. While they continued to demand the right to be heard when they reported sexual attacks, changes in trials during this period made women's narratives less central to successful prosecutions. Their personal lives and characters were thus less vitally safeguarded against exposure and courtroom attacks.

Experts on Trial

Throughout the mid-twentieth century, prosecutors made use of different witnesses to help them prove rape. The number of State witnesses varied in each case, but the victim and at least one police officer always testified about the attack and about the details of an investigation and arrest, respectively. Less often, prosecutors called a victim's family members or friends whom she had told about the rape to help substantiate her claims. Medical experts also sometimes testified about their findings after conducting forensic examinations if a victim went to the hospital following an attack. These supplementary witnesses were not necessary to prove rape, though, as judicial precedents allowed that a victim's "clear and convincing" testimony was enough to prosecute sexual violence.[20] However, the emphasis on protecting defendants' rights informed legal revisions in this area.

Prosecutors began to rely more heavily on several witnesses to help them build cases against defendants during the 1960s. Indeed, additional witnesses and courtroom debates on points of law and procedure came to dominate rape trials, overshadowing the centrality of women's testimonies. Although a victim's testimony was all that was legally required for a conviction, by the early part of the decade judicial decisions had changed expectations about what constituted a "clear and convincing" rape narrative. Higher courts overturned numerous circuit-level convictions appealed during this period, concluding that uncorroborated testimony was "insufficient evidence when the defense's evidence conflicts in a convincing manner with the victim's story."[21] To avoid this potential point of appeal, prosecutors had to proceed differently to prove rape.

As a response to new precedents, Chicago prosecutors almost always supported women's testimonies with a variety of expert witnesses, whom defense attorneys regularly challenged. Judges typically sustained objections if prosecutors failed to connect expert testimony to what women had to say. Or they disregarded the portions of women's narratives unconfirmed by experts. Victims still claimed their right to justice during the 1960s, but these claims required more extensive kinds of support than they had before. Providing corroboration became mandatory and more standardized in rape trials during this period, as opposed to being offered only on behalf of victims who were unlikely to be believed, according to rape myth expectations. Such procedural developments had a complicated effect on women's courtroom experiences. Similar to the victims of other types of violent crimes, rape victims' allegations were taken seriously and substantiated with respected evidence. Conversely, their trial narratives were disrupted and impersonalized, giving their accusations less judicial credence and thus reasserting the myth that women lied about sexual matters and could not be trusted when they cried rape.

As courts became more rigorous in protecting defendants' rights, prosecutors, accordingly, had to be more precise about what they offered as evidence. In order to abide by the new standards, judges adhered to strict regulations governing exhibits' chain of possession. Chain of possession refers to the "movement and location of real evidence from the time it is obtained to the time it is presented in court."[22] This legal requirement, enforced more stringently during a new era of protecting the rights of the accused, called into question the veracity of women testifying in rape trials. It also potentially exposed the blunders of the police. In spite of publicity about evolving forensic technologies and the efficacy of the Chicago Crime Lab, the newspaper was also filled with articles about the mistakes investigators made allowing for the release of suspects.[23] More precise expectations about criminal evidence had the potential to lead to more trial acquittals if prosecutors were not careful. A victim's identification of her own clothing or police testimony about the reports officers collected no longer provided sufficient bases for accepting into evidence laboratory findings during sex crime trials that took place during this period.

This procedural change reflected timely concerns about police incompetence, but also reinforced rape myths about lying women. In the 1968 rape and deviate sexual assault trial of Frank Bruno, the State offered as evidence a torn nightgown that the victim recognized as her own, worn the night she was attacked. The defense attorney objected, arguing, "no chain is proved, there are many unanswered questions. We don't know who had it, kept it, examined it, none of these things."[24] Despite the State's insistence on its validity, the judge sided with the defense. He indicated, "If there were an officer that indicated he took it from the complaining witness and saw it torn at that time, this would be one thing" but since no officer testified as such, the judge excluded the nightgown.[25] When Francis Oldsby stood trial for the attempted rape and deviate sexual assault of Leone O'Berendt in 1966, the State attempted to corroborate the victim's accusation. The prosecutor asked the arresting officer if "anybody took any of [Oldsby's] clothing" when the defendant was identified at the scene of the alleged attack. He answered that the suspect's "shorts were taken, yes sir. They were sent to the police crime laboratory for examination."[26] When asked, "What were the findings there?" the judge sustained the defense's objection and ended that line of inquiry.[27] Because that officer had not conducted the exam or written the report, the judge would not let him testify about it. He represented one link in the chain of possession and could only testify about his involvement in that particular link.

The expansion of defendants' rights altered how prosecutors offered expert medical testimony as well. As earlier trials have shown, physicians did not regularly testify in rape cases that took place prior to the 1960s. When they did, they told the court about their findings and offered opinions about consent, potentially providing strong support for victims' claims of sexual violence.[28] As evidentiary rules became more precise, however, the implications of medical testimony began to change. The physician who examined Patricia Danner after she was raped in 1968 testified that he found areas of redness in and around her vagina. It was his "medical opinion that these were bruises . . . probably a result of unnatural copulation."[29] While the witness never admitted that his opinion was not based on medical facts, he was also never able to assert that his findings amounted to anything more than just an opinion. In the 1965 deviate sexual assault trial of Bernard Bendig, the State and defense stipulated to the medical evidence offered. The report included information about the bruising of the victim, but that the examining physician "would be unable to testify as to the cause," or whether her bruises were a result of a sexual attack.[30] The prosecutor and public defender in the rape case against Ernest Hayes also stipulated to the medical findings of the physician who examined the victim after she was attacked in 1965. The report described signs of intercourse, but specifically mentioned "no signs of trauma."[31] Defense attorneys regularly challenged the State's presentation of medical evidence, suggesting that physicians' reports proved nothing except that intercourse, which was not a crime, had taken place.

In order to track the movement of physical evidence, a new series of expert witnesses began appearing in rape trials during the 1960s. Although both sides stipulated to the findings of the physician who examined Nancy Marie Aderman, the prosecutor called several other witnesses in this 1966 rape trial in order to verify the lab samples mentioned in the medical report. A police officer testified that he picked up the samples from the hospital. The State then called the mobile crime laboratory technician who transported them to another lab, staffed by the technician whom the prosecutor called to testify next. After establishing his qualifications, this witness finally told the court that his microscopic examination "revealed the presence of spermatozoa on these exhibits."[32] Each witness testified about his or her connection to disparate links in the chain of possession.

In an effort to corroborate women's rape allegations with medical evidence, prosecutors introduced to trials a series of experts whose testimonies were detached from victims' experiences of sexual violence. Their contributions to the trials analyzed here suggest that the State took seriously the demands of prosecuting sexual violence while upholding the rule of law. But the aloof nature of expert testimony also compounded the alienation women had long experienced in the courtroom, in spite of their efforts to claim judicial protections. By making expert witnesses necessary for successful rape prosecutions, the myth of lying women, which both victims and prosecutors had worked to destabilize throughout the years surrounding World War II, reasserted itself during 1960s trials. Not all experts were equally trustworthy, though. Their testimonies also provided defense attorneys with new issues to raise in support of their clients' innocence.

By the 1960s, defense attorneys routinely exploited medical testimony, whether or not it was presented in sex crime trials. They used a negative (for sperm) medical test to refute criminal charges, even though the law did not require "an emission" to prove rape.[33] Guarzee Gray's attorney willingly stipulated to the medical evidence offered in the 1966 rape case against his client. The report read that a "vaginal smear was obtained and no sperm was seen . . . there were no signs of any violence."[34] Similarly, during Herbie Wright's trial for a rape he allegedly committed in 1969, the defense attorney challenged the victim's testimony that she thought her attacker "had a climax" by pointing out that the results of her hospital "smear test" were negative.[35] In the 1965 rape trial of W. Q. Thompson, his attorney called the examining physician to testify after the prosecutor did not offer any medical evidence. The doctor described his examination and testified that, "there was no injury, nothing."[36] The State did not include a medical report to support an accusation of rape against Whitson West in 1964, prompting his attorney to argue, "There is not a scintilla of evidence, other than from the prosecutrix herself, that something took place as far as rape is concerned."[37] Prosecutors countered with their own arguments about what medical findings, or the lack thereof, did or did not mean in their cases and both medical testimony and bodily forensic evidence soon became a mandatory part of Chicago rape trials.

As a result of the introduction of myriad new witnesses in these cases that proved rape, women's testimonies became only one element of a complicated felony prosecution. Whereas in past decades women had been the centerpieces of the State's cases, their status declined during the 1960s. Their testimonies were, of course, still necessary for successful prosecutions, but during this period rarely were victims' voices as "clear and convincing" as many once had been. The changes in rape trials had the related effects, for women, of making them less often safeguarded against character attacks in the courtroom and making their narratives appear less reliable than those of the experts who testified. This reinforced the kinds of rape myths that victims had long been challenging on the witness stand, even as successful rape prosecutions had begun to resemble more closely those of other violent crimes.

Police on Trial

During the 1960s, defense attorneys intensified arguments about police corruption and brutality in an effort to refute the charges leveled against their clients. The Chicago police had long been targets of urban reform, with a formal organization to address corruption within the department's ranks first emerging in 1929.[38] Even before but certainly in the years immediately following World War II, an expanded civil rights movement increased its scrutiny of racial prejudice and brutality in policing. Despite the new superintendent's efforts to reform the Chicago Police Department, many of the city's black residents—who constituted the majority of defendants analyzed in this book—remained skeptical about the honesty and authority of local officers.[39] The emphasis on protecting the rights of the accused easily lent itself to familiar defense strategies about investigative discrimination, and these arguments took on a new tone in the trials that occurred within a context of expanding rights and radical social activism.

Defense arguments about racial discrimination and police brutality during this period incorporated the spirit of civil rights activism that had captured the nation's attention. By the late 1960s, civil rights activists began to target issues beyond Southern disenfranchisement and Jim Crow segregation. Increasingly, they combated poverty, challenged labor and housing discrimination, and focused public attention on judicial prejudice and police brutality throughout the nation. Indeed, Chicago's militant black power leaders warned local residents that the police would "fail to respect the law in order to destroy us."[40] They referred here to numerous police shootings of alleged black criminal suspects on local streets and especially the murders of Black Panther leaders Fred Hampton and Mark Clark by Chicago officers in 1969.[41]

Failure to respect the law is exactly what many African American rape defendants accused the police of doing. Kenny McCarroll, a black man charged with rape and deviate sexual assault against a white college student, testified in 1969 that an officer "hit me in my testicles with his revolver . . . I did not flinch or bat an eye. I took the lick. I wouldn't grab them. I hadn't did anything, but I didn't know why I was getting hit."[42] Roy Young was an African American defendant on trial for the attempted rape of white beauty school student Pamela Campisano in 1969. He told the court he was in the neighborhood where Campisano was attacked because he was out with friends. He ran when a police car stopped because, he explained to the court, he was underage and had a bottle of wine in his pocket. Young testified that he heard a gunshot and "all of a sudden I was on the ground. There was this policeman standing over me, calling me all sorts of dirty names and kicking me in the stomach."[43] The arresting officer in this case told the court a different story: he cornered the defendant in a courtyard when the suspect yelled, "Come in and get me," and that he fired his gun because Young came at him with a knife.[44] The State offered the knife as evidence in this case but the defense attorney dismissed it and suggested instead, "I think the police officer saw someone running . . . he may have said halt, he may not have, and he shot. And, as an after thought, which is common practice on the south side these days, you have to justify shooting someone. So you have what is called a drop-knife."[45] Both of these black defendants, accused of sexually attacking white women, presented defenses of mistaken identity tied to the history of the brutality and prejudice of the Chicago police and shaped by the militant activism of the times.

Defense attorneys argued that racial discrimination also surfaced in black suspect identifications during the 1960s, as it had in the past. Herman Burks, an African American man, was on trial in 1966 for raping Louella Winston, who was also African American. Winston identified Burks at the police station, telling the court, "[The police] showed me pictures. They said, 'Do you know this man?' I said he is the man that attacked me."[46] Rather than put Burks, who was already at the police station, into a lineup for Winston to view, officers instead showed her an array of photographs. The pictures, taken at a prior arrest, depicted the defendant as a criminal even before he was formally charged with Winston's rape. During closing arguments, Burks's attorney claimed that Louella Winston was victimized not by his client but "by a system that is concerned with records and how well they do rather than the justice that they are supposed to be concerned with."[47] When Police Superintendant Wilson standardized how criminal statistics were reported upon assuming his post in 1960, the numbers went up. The newspaper published reassurances that the statistical increase in crime was merely a "paper crime wave," which is precisely the point counsel hoped to exploit in challenging the defendant's identification.[48] When Eddie James Virgin stood trial for rape, his attorney cross-examined the police about the suspect's identification at the victim's apartment in 1967.[49] In a telling exchange, the public defender asked if the white police officers brought "other people that she could look at that weren't police officers that weren't dressed up in uniforms?" He then summarized the situation by asking additional questions about how the victim came to identify the defendant: "So you were two white officers with one Negro man standing between you by Mrs. Smith's house, is that right?" and he then moved to suppress the identification as "tainted with suggestion."[50] Questioning suspect identifications was not a new defense strategy in the 1960s, but the expanded culture of defendants' rights during this period supported close scrutiny of these procedures.

Defense attorneys probed all aspects of Chicago police investigations and implied that general incompetence, in addition to racial prejudice, undermined the rights of the accused. Herman Burks's attorney wanted to know if it was "customary for various police officers to handle various parts of an investigation, sort of piecemeal?" implying that evidence and information likely got lost in the process.[51] Eddie James Virgin's attorney also questioned the arresting officer about his experience in dealing with rape cases and about his familiarity with Chicago's crime lab. In closing arguments that responded to the victim's earlier testimony, the defense attorney rhetorically asked the jury, "If the crime lab analyzed her underwear and they were positive [for sperm], why aren't they in evidence? And if they took hers, why not his for analysis?"[52] Defense attorneys hoped that accusing the police of incompetence, especially in cases involving black defendants like Burks and Virgin, might plant seeds of doubt about the State's cases in the minds of jurors and judges alike. In the wake of scandals that necessitated the department's overhaul during this period, the credibility of the Chicago Police Department was particularly vulnerable to such attacks.

Although racial bias provided one possible explanation for the potentially unconstitutional mistakes of white Chicago officers, sloppiness provided another. Forensic science and standards of collecting and testing evidence rose during the decades following World War II and, by the 1960s, crime scene investigators and laboratory technicians became new targets at which attorneys could take aim. When the State offered a stained bed sheet as evidence in the case against white defendant Ernest Hayes, his public defender objected. The witness testified that he identified both blood and semen on the sheet, but that he did not "make any determination as to the blood type," nor was he asked to find anything else that might connect the exhibit to the defendant in the case.[53] The attorney for George Hankins, who was charged with the intraracial rape of white victim Donna Marie Bowling, questioned Bowling about the investigation of her 1965 attack. She explained that an investigator was at her house "outside dusting over fingerprints [and] was inside checking everything in my bedroom." The public defender asked if anyone examined her bed sheet as well? Bowling told the court no, even though she had mentioned earlier that her attacker had had "a climax."[54] In his closing remarks, the defense wondered about this. If crime scene technicians were called in when the alleged victim reported the rape, they "would be duty bound to collect the evidence so that it would be presented to a court, preserved for evidence. This did not occur."[55] In the same way that defense attorneys questioned the expertise of medical witnesses during this period, they also challenged the actions of crime scene investigators, which they cast as incomplete or even incompetent, and not just in the cases involving black defendants.

Prosecutors responded to attacks against the presentations of their cases by defending the actions of the police. They appealed to judges and juries, acknowledging that while residents might fairly scrutinize the actions of local officers, this did not justify acquitting guilty rapists. In the State's closing arguments during the Burks trial, the prosecutor pointed out to the jury that the defense was trying to put the police department on trial: "They are counting on the fact all of you are going to say they don't know what they are doing. They are counting on the fact sometime or other you have been stopped, got a ticket by a policeman. Nobody loves policemen."[56] In responding to the defense presented in the Virgin case, the prosecutor suggested, "He did what all good defense lawyers do. Let's take the spotlight off my defendant and put it on the poor guy in blue. Let's . . . get up here and say, oh this police investigation was horrible."[57] Prosecutors countered investigative skepticism by successfully encouraging judges and juries to honor police authority, which they ultimately did in the cases analyzed here.[58] However, at a time when the media repeatedly informed the public about corrupt patrolmen and failed criminal investigations, defense attempts to highlight such issues made sense.

Defense attorneys explained their strategies in court by insisting that no one, not even members of the Chicago Police Department, was above the law. The lawyer defending Osborn Fortson in his 1967 rape trial wondered how the defendant came to be arrested. The victim in this case, Lottie Blair, testified that she told investigators, "He had a nice face and pretty hair and he looked young." Based on that vague description, two officers took her to Fortson's home where she recognized him as her alleged attacker.[59] In a motion to suppress the identification, the defense attorney argued, "The method by which they went about this identification and apprehending this defendant was sophistry, chicanery, trickery, and . . . against a patent violation of his constitutional rights."[60] In his closing arguments to the jury, Kenny McCarroll's attorney outlined, point by point, the numerous mistakes the police had made in their investigation. He ended by asserting, "Some of my best friends are policemen. But I know when they got a job to do, sometimes they get a little overzealous and I tell them about it. And they thank me because I keep them out of trouble."[61] One wonders if the Chicago police ever thanked defense attorneys for keeping them "out of trouble"? By the time the 1968 charge against McCarroll reached a courtroom one year later, however, events like the riot outside the Democratic National Convention made the city's residents quite aware of instances of extreme police violence.[62] Chicagoans had different opinions about the actions of the police patrolling a city caught up in the social upheavals of the day, but no one at the time was unaware of the potential for violence in the streets.

The opinion handed down in *Miranda v. Arizona* in 1966 created an important change in defense arguments about the illegal arrest and detention of, especially, black suspects in Chicago. This and other court decisions about the rights of the accused, including mandates about how long a suspect might be held in custody before being charged or released, generated much publicity and debate when they began to affect policing at the local level.[63] Chicago defendants, either from personal knowledge and experience or, more likely, because their attorneys strategically prepared them to do so, testified about how the police denied them their rights. Kenny McCarroll told the court that when the police arrested him, he "did not hear anyone tell me of my constitutional rights."[64] In 1967, Frank Evans testified about his arrest for attempted rape the previous year. When his public defender asked him if the police told him he "had a right to remain silent" the defendant answered, "He didn't say no such thing, not to my recollection." When asked if "he told you that you have a right to have an attorney," Evans replied, "He did not say that." Although it was unclear exactly what this African American defendant understood about his rights, he evidently understood something because he also testified, "I told them [the police] I wouldn't say anything till I seen my lawyer."[65] Defense attorneys in cases involving white men also focused on police incompetence to be sure, but those defending black men forcefully incorporated the rights arguments of the period, reflecting the significance of the movement for racial equality on all fronts.

Although defense arguments regularly condemned the bias of police, trial decisions also reflected how Chicago judges attempted to adhere to mandates protecting the rights of the accused. When African American teenager

Eugene Hawkins was tried for rape two years after his 1968 arrest, an officer specifically testified that he read the defendant his rights.[66] The defense attorney objected, and the judge heard arguments on the issue. The defendant's father told the court that after he arrived at the precinct and was informed that his son had been arrested for rape, "I just looked at him. I said, boy I know you didn't do that. . . . And the officer got up there and said he don't have to talk. He advised me of my son's rights."[67] Hawkins testified that no one told him anything when he got to the police station, nor was he allowed to call his parents. He claimed that officers eventually told him he was being held for rape, which was when, according to the defendant, the police "wanted to advise me of my constitutional rights."[68] Despite State arguments to the contrary, the court ruled, "A sixteen-year-old being held does not know what waiving his rights is all about." The judge excluded from evidence anything the defendant said to the police before his parents arrived at the station.[69] Rules governing criminal investigations had existed prior to this period, but after *Miranda,* defense attorneys in Chicago developed arguments explicitly related to this mandate. And judges listened to them, even when the defendants involved embodied myths about black sexual predators.

Defense attorneys also contributed to the growing complexity of trials by making numerous objections to the State's cases. The judge had to rule on each one. This usually meant a brief response in court—either "overruled" or "sustained"—but it sometimes also necessitated an "in camera hearing" to be sure that a particular ruling was allowed.[70] The hostility that rape victims came to face during trials in the 1960s sometimes extended to exchanges between legal authorities in the courtroom as well. As attorneys debated which investigative documents the defense was allowed to see in the case against Bernard Bendig, the prosecutor insisted he had turned over everything the law required.[71] The public defender disagreed, prompting the prosecutor to tell him, "Oh, shut up."[72] The defense immediately objected, "insisting on either an apology or a mistrial in this case."[73] He got neither. Osborn Fortson's attorney objected many times as the prosecutors presented their case. The judge overruled most of them, prompting further defense protests. When one prosecutor asked, "How many motions for mistrial are you going to make?" defense counsel responded, "I think about forty if necessary."[74] The legal complexities of the felony cases analyzed here constructed violent attacks in an impersonal way, making it easier for authorities to separate the actions of the individuals involved from the crimes about which they were in court to testify. Although this had the potential to positively affect rape defendants, the majority of whom were black men struggling against myths that defined their personal and sexual lives as inherently criminal, it had different consequences for victims. Whereas once prosecutors and judges had an easier time shielding many women from rhetorical attacks in the courtroom, during the 1960s rape victims found themselves more consistently enduring the type of accusations that accompanied rape myth expectations. Nowhere was the suspicion of lying women more obvious than when some judges began to question sex crime victims themselves.

Victims on Trial

Judges were aware that their decisions could be scrutinized, closely and more often, because of expanded opportunities for those convicted to pursue appeals during this time. Their knowledge of the law and procedure were put to the test during the increasingly complicated trials of the 1960s. In order to clarify legal points and reduce the likelihood of reversals from a higher court, circuit-level judges occasionally examined witnesses themselves. When they did, the questions they directed toward rape victims reveal a stark change from earlier trials, when judges often silenced particular implications against prosecuting witnesses in court. The Chicago judges who interrogated victims about their sexuality during this period still presided over cases that ended with convictions, but the context in which sexual attacks took place had changed.

The 1960s saw a profound transformation in the American public's attitudes toward sexuality, even if some changes in thinking had begun years earlier. An explicit campaign against venereal disease during World War II, as well as the celebrated publication of the postwar Kinsey Reports on human sexuality, encouraged a frank discussion of sexual matters to enter the public sphere during the 1940s and early 1950s.[75] At the same time, Hollywood's postwar creation of glamorous and sexually provocative starlets like Marilyn Monroe translated public titillation onto the silver screen and began to challenge the accepted parameters of a rigid film ratings system. In 1953, Illinois journalist Hugh Hefner founded *Playboy* magazine in order to espouse a philosophy of carefree sexuality that rejected the strict gender role expectations of masculine breadwinner and feminine homemaker; *Playboy's* first nude centerfold featured Monroe herself.[76] In 1960, the Food and Drug Administration approved a new oral contraceptive that forever changed especially female sexuality by more conveniently and reliably separating intercourse and reproduction for married women. In 1965, a landmark case on rights and privacy struck down laws prohibiting the prescription of "the pill," expanding its access to unmarried women.[77] None of these or myriad other issues pushing a more open sexual discourse developed without corresponding social critiques, but they nonetheless influenced the public's opinions about appropriate and inappropriate sexual behaviors.

One major change in Chicago trials that was linked to the social atmosphere of this period involved judges who were increasingly comfortable pressing victims to testify about their sexuality, and not just about the attacks they alleged. These examinations rarely happened during earlier trials, when judges preferred to let the attorneys establish their adversarial cases while guarding victims against tangential interrogations. The shift toward judges' interventions reflected, in part, the concerns they had about violating defendants' rights—in this case, the right to fully face their accusers—as defined in the Constitution.[78] As the U.S. legal system allows appeals on the basis of technical flaws alone, only judicial rulings provide the grounds for overturning circuit-level convictions. No judge wanted convictions based on his decisions about evidence in rape trials reversed on appeal.[79] The culture of rights that had been expanding nationally throughout the mid-twentieth century filtered into circuit courts during the 1960s, where local judges altered their behaviors.

Judges' examinations also demonstrated how attitudes of privilege, which permeated the male-dominated sphere of the courtroom, affected rape trial proceedings. Judges who questioned victims felt justified in asking them about sexual matters that were not directly related to allegations of sexual violence because the law allowed it and because the victims who appeared in the transcripts under study here were often working-class women, and over half of them were racial minorities.[80] Although some ideas about sexual morality were beginning to change during the 1960s, class and race intervened with rape myths in such a way as to make working-class and African American women's sexuality easier for white male judges to interrogate. The simultaneous processes of safeguarding defendants' rights, the persistence of rape myths about lying women, and the context of a more sexually permissive society and all of the potential dangers that it invoked created an acutely severe trial atmosphere for victims to endure.

Some judges were not as concerned with protecting a victim's right to privacy at this time, as many had been in prior years. They specifically questioned women about personal life circumstances unrelated to the rape allegations that they had made. In 1967, African American defendant Ben Murphy was charged with the intraracial rape of Ethel Thomas. The defendant insisted that Thomas had consented. After she had finished testifying, she faced further examination by the court. The judge asked if she was employed and was she a "Miss or Mrs.?" She replied that she was not working, that her husband did not live with her and, when asked, the thirty-year-old victim indicated that she had two teenaged children. The judge also wanted to know if her estranged husband was the father. After finding out that he was not and the father—to whom the victim had never been married—lived in Mississippi, the judge asked, "But you had his babies?"[81] Neither the State nor the defense brought up any of these points when questioning Thomas about the rape she was in court to testify about, but the judge felt that clarifying her marital and employment status was relevant to include in the court record. Prior statute revisions did not require strict scrutiny of a rape victim's general character and placed the burden of proving her to be "unchaste" on the defense, but this courtroom exchange effectively demonstrates how legal standards had changed since the 1930s.[82] The prosecutor objected but the judge overruled him, oddly insisting that "no specific acts of immorality were pried into by this court regarding this woman."[83] It is easy to doubt the sincerity of that statement, however, because the judge's questions positioned Thomas as a single mother with an estranged husband who was not the father of her children, living on State aid. Such a characterization was indeed specific and implied a great deal of immorality, given the defendant's arguments about her consent.

Judges' examinations allowed defense attorneys to exploit details about victims that were otherwise off limits. After the judge questioned Thomas about details of her personal life, Murphy's attorney capitalized on this testimonial opening in his closing arguments. He reminded the court that she was an unmarried mother and attempted to redirect attention away from his client who, as a blues musician known to frequent south side taverns, also had a questionable reputation.[84] When the public defender for black defendant Isaac Griggs cross-examined the black victim, Georgia Karellas, in a 1969 rape case, he wanted to know if she "invited him in to talk about some marijuana."[85] The defendant insisted that he and Karellas used drugs together, and that because she had no money to pay him, she offered intercourse instead. The judge interrupted to find out if it was the "first time you [Karellas] had intercourse . . . with anybody?" The seventeen-year-old answered that it was not her first time, but that she had intercourse before "with boys my age."[86] Although she denied using drugs and also denied consenting to intercourse with Griggs, the judge's questions about the victim's sexuality made the defendant's version of events seem more plausible. As detailed earlier, authorities tended to weigh a woman's sexual chastity in evaluating the veracity of her rape allegation. Karellas admitted she was not a virgin prior to being raped, so had she perhaps really consented to Griggs's advances?

By the mid-1960s, a sexual revolution was in full swing in the United States, and one of its unintended consequences was what appeared to be an almost cavalier attitude toward the victims and perpetrators of sexual violence. The judges hearing the cases against black rape defendants like Murphy and Griggs, who argued that the women accusing them of rape had actually consented to intercourse, intensely scrutinized the sexuality of the alleged victims. Both of these men were convicted, but the court sentenced them to an average of only four years each.[87] Their sentences were very different from the twenty-six years to life in prison that African American men convicted of rape averaged in the years leading up to 1960 and were also significantly less severe than the fifteen to seventeen years assigned to men who were convicted, despite their claims about consent, prior to this period.[88] Rape myths were at work here in favor of even those defendants who were ultimately convicted. Women who "asked for it" were interrogated in Chicago courts, and men who could not control themselves or who somehow misunderstood female sexual "signals" were not punished too severely for their transgressions within this altered trial context.

Assessments of female sexuality during trials in the 1960s were increasingly unaffected by a victim's race, even though this had previously been a factor enhancing women's believability. During the 1930s and 1940s, judges usually stopped defense attorneys from questioning white victims, especially, about their sexual histories, even though case law allowed that a woman's general reputation could be considered in determining the validity of a rape allegation.[89] In the 1950s, defense attorneys expanded a strategy of female sexual interrogation by examining predominantly African American victims—who were the majority of those testifying in rape cases appealed during that period—more comprehensively about their sexual pasts. They did not question white victims at that time in the same manner because, as we have seen, judges usually shut them down when they tried. During the 1960s, however, concerns about protecting the rights of the accused and changing social attitudes about sexual openness came together to place victims of any race in the difficult position of publicly defending any, and potentially all, of their actions prior to a sexual attack. Coupled with the addition of corroborating witnesses that reinforced myths about lying women, rape victims' sexuality became a key target of defense attorneys. They also attempted to take advantage of another profoundly disturbing rape myth: that all women really wanted to be sexually ravished.

Although this myth was first popularized during the 1930s by Freudian disciple Helene Deutsch, defense attorneys did not regularly take it up in court until the 1960s, when Americans were examining sexuality in different ways. This myth was related both to white hysteria over interracial rape and to the sexual double standard. White women were expected to be sexually chaste and reject all erotic advances except those related to procreation within marriage, and certainly they would reject any interracial propositions. If they did not, they could predictably be expected to lie about their proclivities in order to protect assumptions about their sexual innocence and to confirm the legitimacy of a racially divided social order.[90] Defense tactics in the 1960s increasingly began to suggest that alleged rape victims, of any race, were likely to lie in order to preserve their reputations, which were already questionable or they would not have encountered even the potential for sexual violence in the first place. Or, they would lie in order to seek revenge against men who grieved them.

Defense arguments about a woman's consent, or her lack thereof, came to dominate rape cases that were appealed during the 1960s. In the thirty-four sex crime cases appealed between 1937 and 1959, eight (23.5 percent) used consent defenses. The sampled thirty-three transcripts that were appealed during the 1960s revealed seventeen (51.5 percent) that relied on arguments of consent.[91] Some judges permitted more latitude to question in this area than others, allowing defense attorneys to pursue aggressively inquiries about women's sexual histories and providing some convicted men with viable points of appeal.

In trials when defendants argued consent, rape victims could expect to have their sexuality closely examined. Women's responses to invasive courtroom examinations defied traditional beliefs about female sexual purity and consistently challenged questions about their integrity. By doing this, victims in the 1960s found themselves in the awkward position of having to justify innumerable aspects of their personal lives while seeking legal recourse after being sexually attacked. Consent defense strategies had always been difficult for prosecuting witnesses, but during this period judicial suspicion turned into outright hostility toward women, such as that which rape victim Patricia Eason faced in 1964. Acting on a tip, a police patrol stopped in the Woodlawn neighborhood on Chicago's south side, shined a light into an alley, and discovered two people: the woman screamed and the police yelled, "Stop." According to the victim, "I told the police he raped me and . . . [then] he threw the gun over in the vacant lot." The police found a gun nearby and arrested Alexander Griffin.[92]

Having been caught in the act, the defendant claimed that Eason had consented, and his attorney questioned her about that, and about her sexual past more broadly. The prosecutor objected, but defense counsel claimed he would prove that "she had been having sexual intercourse with strange men for a period of at least three years prior to the time that she had this intercourse."[93] In his closing arguments, which are worth quoting at length, Griffin's attorney summarized his opinion of the victim. He argued,

> Here is a woman who not only had sexual intercourse before but she had a child born by somebody she was not married to. She had to have sexual intercourse with somebody in order to have this child, and the possibility is that she had sexual intercourse with several people. We have no explanation on the part of the prosecuting witness of this relationship. Now, the prosecuting witness did deny that she ever knew this man before. It is her word against his. Now, here is a man who has been working ever since he came to Chicago. Here is a woman who has never worked in her life and she is pregnant again at this time. It is evident that she is a woman of loose character. It is evident that she has extramarital relationships and there is good evidence that she probably gave her consent to this sexual intercourse . . . She was evidently enjoying it just as much as he was.[94]

This attorney implied a shameful, yet not criminal, characterization of the victim opposite a respectful, albeit brief, portrayal of his employed client—the man who was actually charged with a crime. Defense counsel claimed that he did not "want to hold it against this girl if she did have [intercourse]."[95] Yet his courtroom depiction belied any empathy he may or may not have felt about sexually active women and instead maliciously attacked the victim while attempting to direct suspicion away from his client.

The victim in the case against Alexander Griffin was African American, but white women faced intense scrutiny of their sexuality during the 1960s as well. The defense attorney for John Milton Kepler argued that his client, a white businessman, encountered the alleged victim, Linda Linn, when he saw her on the street one day in 1965 and asked her for directions. Linn testified that she gave Kepler her telephone number because he said he might have a job for her, and she "just wanted a better paying job" than the one she already had.[96] According to Linn, the promise of employment encouraged her to accept a date with the defendant. In an exchange later made well known by feminists who articulated the need for revolution in rape courtrooms, the defense attorney questioned her about what she wore the night they went out. He wanted to know, "The type of slacks you were wearing, could those be characterized as . . . real tight-fitting slacks?"[97] Linn said no, "They weren't tight fitting, they were stretch pants." The judge interrupted, indicating that he was "thoroughly familiar with them. I have three daughters and they wear stretch pants. They're tight."[98] Defense counsel's questions and the judge's intervention underscored the plausibility of Kepler's narrative about a date that ended with consensual intercourse over Linn's allegation of rape. The judge in the case against Bernard Bendig allowed Bendig's attorney to ask the white victim, Patricia Vermillion, numerous times, "[Did he engage] in conversations about you being a virgin?" referring to the few separate occasions when the defendant walked her home.[99] The State objected, but Vermillion had to admit, "It was mentioned. It wasn't a long conversation."[100] In what would today be called instances of date rape, these women faced difficult interrogations of their truthfulness and morality because they wore certain clothes or knew, however remotely, the men they accused of sexual violence.

Defense attorneys who argued consent sometimes also suggested women had, themselves, committed crimes. Specifically, they charged some rape victims with being guilty of prostitution.[101] By accusing them of actual illegal acts rather than (subjectively determined) sexual immorality, defense attorneys attempted to crystallize doubt about women's motives in court. Their point was that any woman who was already a criminal would have little trouble lying about sexual violence in order to get back at customers who had not paid. None of the attorneys who argued consent in the cases appealed prior to 1960 directly mentioned prostitution at trial, although they occasionally let such an implication hang over the proceedings. In the seventeen consent defenses sampled during the 1960s, seven involved specific accusations of sexual solicitation. Accusing rape victims of prostitution was also more credible when the complainant fit the racial profile of a sexually promiscuous woman. African American women or white women who frequented de facto segregated bars or lived in historically black neighborhoods in Chicago during this period were those most likely to face solicitation defenses.[102] The shift from hopeful inference to direct accusation is an important one. Defense attorneys were uncertain if merely accusing victims of immorality, or surmising as much from their life circumstances, would inspire rape acquittals during the more sexually open decade of the 1960s. Consequently, they searched for new ways to attack the credibility of women.

A typical solicitation defense during a rape trial attempted to reverse the roles of the female victim and male criminal. George Strong's attorney claimed that the African American victim, Victoria Speight, was inherently suspicious because of her third-shift employment at a cheap south side hotel where an alleged rape took place in 1966. When the defendant testified, he told the court that he had met Speight several weeks earlier; he said, "She looked like a nice prospect, so I wanted to make out."[103] According to Strong, his "rap" was successful and they had intercourse. He indicated that he had promised to "set her straight," which he explained meant that he would reimburse her for sex, but he also told the court that he "was jiving" about that. It was only after a third sexual encounter at the hotel when he refused to give her money that, he claimed, she threatened to get even with him as she stormed out of the room.[104] While he was waiting for her to return, the police came instead.

Prosecutors who faced this type of defense attempted to undermine solicitation arguments. During cross-examination, Strong admitted that he never actually paid Speight for intercourse. In his closing arguments, the prosecutor contended that no one could deduce from the defendant's testimony that the victim in the case was a prostitute, since there was never any remuneration involved.[105] The State presented Victoria Speight as a "capable, deliberate witness . . . she did not have the slang, jive vocabulary [that Strong did] and comes on as a refined woman."[106] Roosevelt Flournoy Jr. indicated that he saw the African American woman who accused him of rape outside a tavern in 1969. He testified, "When she said she needed money, she just put her arm on mine, you know."[107] The prosecutor questioned him about this, wanting to know, "Did you agree on a price at this time?" When the defendant answered no, the prosecutor followed up by inquiring, "She didn't ask for any money?"[108] Embedded in these exchanges were middle-class attorneys' wary assumptions about black and working-class sexuality. In spite of the changes in sociosexual attitudes permeating American society during the 1960s, bias in the courtroom remained.

Attorneys who mounted solicitation defenses against white women attempted to associate them with prejudicial beliefs about sexual promiscuity based on class and racial bias. In 1966, Leone O'Berendt was on her way to a neighborhood El stop when Francis Oldsby forced her into an alley, fondled her, and attempted to rape her. When he was not able to complete the act, O'Berendt told police that she invited him back to her apartment building, under the auspices that he might be more comfortable there, but where she was also sure she could effectively get away from him. When they got to her building, she gestured to the front desk clerk, who grabbed Oldsby and kept him in the lobby until the police arrived and arrested him.[109] Conversely, the defendant testified that he had given O'Berendt ten dollars and that they were on their way to complete their sexual transaction when the police interrupted.[110] Although it was unusual to find a black defendant arguing consent when accused of rape by a white woman, Oldsby's attorney had little choice. Since his client was held at the victim's place of residence after allegedly attacking her in a nearby alley, he could not viably argue that the police had arrested the wrong man.

Historical beliefs about the links between race, sexuality, and violence informed the presentation of rape cases in Chicago. By the 1960s, defense attorneys had developed numerous strategies that attempted to connect these

issues in their favor. In trying to diffuse doubts about a white woman's possible consent to interracial intercourse, Oldsby's attorney questioned the
victim about where she lived. O'Berendt acknowledged that she had few white
neighbors, since the area she lived in was considered a "colored" neighborhood.[111] Located just south of the University of Chicago, Woodlawn, where the
victim lived and where the attempted rape occurred, was around 90 percent
African American.[112] O'Berendt told the court that just before Oldsby attacked
her, a police car drove by, ignoring the man in the alley. She accused the police
of thinking he was "just another drunk," which was why they did not stop to
investigate.[113] Throughout the 1960s, the notoriety of Woodlawn increased
as residential confrontations with the university became more frequent. As
administrators looked to expand the campus, unemployment escalated, and
the growth of a neighborhood gang and the violence associated with their
activities surged. This was a neighborhood where police responded to, but
also ignored, a lot of crime.[114] In his closing arguments the defense attorney
accused the victim of being a prostitute who ran a scam where she "collected
ten dollar bills, running into the hotel and hollering help help . . . victim-
izing people like Francis Oldsby."[115] It was not as if, he pointed out, his client
was in a white neighborhood looking to attack a white woman; rather, "He's
in his environment, and she's a white girl with flirtatious eyes at five o'clock
in the morning."[116] These telling arguments played on social prejudices that
Chicagoans struggled to reconcile as the modern city continued to change.

Familiar with white ethnic protests over neighborhood racial integration
at that time, the prosecutor responded with his own closing remarks. In them
he also talked about crime and urban geography:

> We are told constantly, from day to day, that a man, or a woman for that mat-
> ter, regardless of their race, [has] a right to live wherever they may see fit . . . it
> is a two-way street and when a white person chooses, lawfully, to live in what
> has been described here as a predominantly Negro neighborhood, that white
> person is exercising the same rights as a colored person, in an opposite situa-
> tion, claims to have.[117]

The conflicting trial narratives that emerged in this case demonstrate how
far Chicago jurists in this decade had drifted away from rape myth expectations about chaste white women and criminal black men. While constrained
by the circumstances of his client's arrest, the times had changed enough so
that Oldsby's attorney felt it was possible to argue successfully that a white
woman had consented to sexual relations with the black defendant rather
than agree to a plea and avoid a trial. But times had not changed completely.
While the victim had to endure a pointed interrogation about where she lived

and what she may have done for a living, Oldsby was still convicted for this interracial attempted rape and deviate sexual assault.

Even when they did not face consent or solicitation defenses, prosecutors in the 1960s continued to defend against implications about a victim's potentially suspect sexuality. They did so by attempting to justify women's actions based on the liberal social attitudes more prevalent throughout the United States during this period. Although Bernard Bendig's public defender questioned the victim's sexuality, the prosecutor countered with his own assessment of her actions. During closing arguments, he summarized: "This is the twentieth century and there is nothing . . . unusual about a young lady going to a man's apartment, or to his room. Certainly in the old days, perhaps it might have been frowned upon, but not today."[118] The prosecutor trying John Milton Kepler for rape argued to the court, "It's a sad, sad case, your honor, because I think it demonstrates that a young lady who I think I can characterize as gullible can get into a situation like this, and what can happen from it."[119] He did not suggest that the victim might have been complicit in the attack because she chose to go on a date with the defendant or because she wore enticing clothing when they went out. Instead, he insisted that she was young, "gullible," and was, in fact, raped. He reiterated testimony that revealed how the victim's and defendant's intentions about the evening may have been different, but only his were criminal.

Prosecutors undermined defense strategies by redirecting the court's attention to actual criminal charges, which only the defendants faced. The prosecutor in the case against Alexander Griffin argued that it was a rape case, not a paternity suit, hence the victim need not "talk about who the father of her child was."[120] After a grueling cross-examination of Lottie Blair, the State attempted to refocus the jury's attention to the indictment at hand. With arguments that mirrored what anti-rape activists would later come to use with great effect to lobby for legal reform, the prosecutor asserted, "The defense suggested that the title of this case should be the People versus Lottie Blair. We are trying the wrong person here. I tell you this is the People versus Osborn Fortson. Osborn Fortson is on trial, not Lottie Blair. She is the victim. Please don't forget that."[121] Although prosecutors were initially successful in all of the cases analyzed here, defense implications about women's licentious pasts sometimes caused appellate courts to reconsider circuit-level convictions.

The bases for overturned rape convictions, while rare, reveal that wariness toward victims had become vital to defense attorneys preparing appeals. While such skepticism was not new to the 1960s, in the cases that were appealed before that decade, appellate opinions rarely mentioned victims

or their actions. Those cases instead focused on trial decisions and procedural errors that, almost exclusively, involved defendants and constitutional
guarantees.[122] In most appeals made before 1960, however, convictions were
upheld or the cases summarily dismissed, thereby confirming the original
court's decision.[123] In contrast, during the 1960s the appellate court elected
to hear arguments about the majority of appeals and summarily dismissed
only four of the thirty-three sampled cases.[124] The numbers, 88 percent of
this sample, suggest that the expansion of federally mandated protections
during the 1960s encouraged higher courts to consider appellate arguments
carefully, even though reversed convictions remained rare.[125]

In all of the cases sampled during the 1960s that were reversed on appeal, the higher court cited the victim's behavior as a basis for overturning
rape convictions. In the 1968 opinion handed down in *People v. Hayes,* the
appellate court doubted the veracity of the victim's accusation because she
did not promptly report the attack. According to the opinion, the victim
"claims she was too afraid of the defendant to call for help while he was there
. . . [and] although her attacker had been in and around the building after
the attack, the prosecutrix felt no compulsion to leave the building to get
away from this dangerous individual or to have him arrested."[126] The court
of appeals found Josephine Johnson's 1966 testimony against Frank Evans
"unbelievable" as well. In this case, the victim indicated that she left her four
children, ages eight to fourteen, at home around midnight to go to the corner
store to buy cigarettes. According to her testimony, the store did not have
her preferred brand, so she went to a nearby tavern to buy them. This was
where she encountered the defendant, who followed her home and tried to
rape her.[127] A higher court agreed with John Milton Kepler's assertion that
his rape conviction was actually a consensual sexual encounter with Linda
Linn, and the court supported its reversal with the opinion that since her
stretch pants were not torn and because she made a later date with him she
did not resist, and therefore was not raped.[128] Frank Bruno's rape and deviate
sexual assault convictions were reversed because the victim let Bruno, the
husband of an acquaintance, into her apartment late at night and did not
immediately call the police after he left.[129] The opinion also cited a lack of
medical corroboration, despite her testimony that she went to the hospital
after she was sexually attacked.[130]

Testimony about hospital visits and forensic examinations provide compelling evidence that rape investigations, and not just sexual attacks, were also
traumatic for victims. Prior to this time, women did not always testify about
medical treatment, preferring not to speak publicly about the intimate bodily
intrusions they faced in Chicago's emergency rooms, or because they avoided

visiting the hospital altogether for the same reason. Because defense attorneys made medical evidence—either the presence or lack of it—an essential element of rape trials throughout the 1960s, prosecutors asked women about their experiences in this regard. Their testimonies reveal some important concerns that contemporary feminists continue to educate the public about today. Connie Smith testified that the first thing she did after calling the police and telling her husband and son she had been raped was to go into the bathroom where she "took soap and water and washed my vagina."[131] Diana Williams testified that after she was raped, she went to her parents' house: "I tried to explain to her [Williams's mother] what had happened. And my clothes was so filthy and so was I. She took my clothes off and gave me a bath."[132] When asked why she did not go to the hospital immediately after reporting a rape to the police, Verdie Mae Johnson told the court that before leaving her house she "washed up" because she "didn't know what kind of disease he had."[133] This type of testimony provides some clues that reveal the difficulties a victim faced after a sexual attack was over, but the investigation of it had just begun. Such insights are best summarized by the testimony of Vera Young, who told the court that after she was raped in 1968, she "was afraid to walk the street even in the daytime. I was afraid to sleep at night without someone near to me and I often had nightmares about it."[134]

*   *   *

In August 1967, leaders in the New Left organized in Chicago a National Conference for New Politics (NCWP), in an attempt to unify increasingly disparate strands of radical youth activism. Women who took part in the conference encountered ridicule when they demanded rights and inclusion in the movement on an equal basis with activist men.[135] The following week, many of the same women who had been dismissed at the NCWP met independently. According to historian Sara Evans, Chicago women took seriously "the admonition to look to your own oppression" and wrote a hopeful manifesto outlining their concerns to "make women more aware and organized in their own movement through which a concept of free womanhood will emerge."[136] This "second wave" of feminism spread quickly throughout the United States, and many women, active in civil rights, antiwar, and other New Left political movements, began to focus their efforts on battling gender oppression exclusively. The issue of sexual violence gained their immediate attention. They began to challenge a system, shaped by rape myths, which encouraged women to remain silent about sexual violence. They pointed to the "re-victimization" of women by police and legal authorities and cited the harsh environment of the rape trial as proof that society devalued women by upholding ideals of aggressive masculinity and oppressive patriarchal authority.[137] The rape trials they encountered certainly reflected such an atmosphere at the end of the 1960s, but as this research demonstrates, they were conducted during a particular historical moment when a variety of social and legal forces converged, resulting in the pronounced mistreatment of adult female rape victims.

The expanded emphasis on protecting the rights of the accused, supported by judicial decisions standardizing investigative procedures, affected the treatment of both rape victims and defendants in Chicago trials during the 1960s. Women's narratives, once a principal element of the State's cases against rape defendants, became background voices in a spectacle dominated by expert testimonies, legal debates, and corroborative evidence. Without a victim there could be no crime, but defense attorneys increasingly challenged women's rape allegations by deflecting blame away from their clients and, in effect, putting other courtroom witnesses on trial. These strategies produced a particularly intimidating atmosphere for women to endure. The rape may have been over, but their difficulties with men were not.

In Chicago, the police faced defense attorneys who questioned their investigations in ways similar to the challenges posed to victims. The police, however, fell on the side of male privilege and authority rather than on the side of skepticism that most raped women automatically faced. Chicago defense attorneys had tried to avert convictions by questioning the motives of the police and by accusing them of brutality and racial discrimination for years following World War II. During the 1960s, however, legal trends and a militant civil rights movement provided more support for such strategies and defense counsel enthusiastically pursued them. Their arguments in court were not entirely convincing, but their efforts to illuminate unlawful investigations were taken seriously, as evidenced by the increased complexity of the 1960s rape trial. Prosecutors had to present evidence and exhibits to corroborate sex crime charges, and if they tried to do so without considering the shifting parameters of admissibility, defense attorneys objected and judges sustained those objections.

During the 1960s, defense attorneys focused the court's attention on rape victims by interrogating women's actions and sexual reputations in ways that judges rarely permitted before. Racial stereotypes about women's sexual promiscuity continued to influence this strategy, although white victims were not immune from character attacks. Defense attorneys and sometimes judges questioned women's sexuality and attempted to undermine their reputations, no matter the circumstances of a case. When defendants argued that the women testifying against them had consented, defense attorneys treated victims even worse. They implied that issues unrelated to a sexual attack, such as a woman's employment or marital status, informed the likelihood that she consented to a brutal violation of her body. They also linked defense arguments about consent to explicit accusations of prostitution. In these cases, it was not the defendants' actions that were against the law, but those of the prostitutes (not victims) who sought revenge over being cheated. Although having one's reputation dissected in court was never easy for victims, accusing women themselves of sexual crimes resonated differently during trials and provided a new type of foundation for establishing reasonable doubt.

Case law precedents and an expanded culture of rights encouraged more convicted rapists to pursue appeals during the 1960s. While most convictions were affirmed or summarily dismissed, some were reversed. Higher courts based these reversals on women's actions prior to, or following, an alleged rape. Familiar suspicions about "an accusation easily to be made and hard to be proved" found intensified support in the sex crime trials during this period, as defense attorneys used both new legal provisions and historical beliefs about women's complicity in sexual attacks to defend their clients. Although prosecutors worked hard to expose "the dual-pronged attack" against a woman's body and against "besmirching her character in the court room," there was not much else they could do except proceed in an attempt to gain convictions when they could.[138] It was up to feminists outside the courtroom to lobby for legal reform and create victim advocacy services and educational programs to help women better deal with the aftermath of sexual violence.

5. Second-Wave Feminists (Re)Discover Rape

On a summer day in 1975, real estate agent Lori Grisco met James Dvornik, her former neighbor, about a potential sale. They had been friendly before Dvornik got divorced and moved from the neighborhood, so she agreed to discuss the details of her company's listings over a late lunch. While at the restaurant, Dvornik excused himself to make a phone call. After several minutes, he returned and asked if she would mind taking him to the VIP Lounge where they could meet his girlfriend, who would bring a down payment there after she went to the bank. Thinking he had spent so much time on the phone making these arrangements, and excited about the prospects of the sale, Grisco agreed. They arrived at the lounge around dinnertime and ordered drinks while they waited. By close to 8 PM, Dvornik's girlfriend had not arrived, and Grisco thought she was not coming. She told her client that they could meet the next day to finalize the paperwork, and he mentioned that he would like to get things started as soon as possible. Could she drop him off at a hotel close to the realty and he would come in early the next morning to close the deal? As she drove, he pointed a gun at her head, ordered her to pull into a secluded parking lot, and said, "I am going to fuck you, bitch." Astonished at this turn of events, Grisco wondered if he was kidding: he was not. After forcing her at gunpoint to park behind an auto dealership, he raped her. Not satisfied, he decided to drive to a nearby hotel, and when he went to rent a room, Grisco escaped. She ran to the first home she saw and pleaded, "Please let me in, I have just been raped." The residents called the police, who arrived quickly. After she told them what had happened and who had done it, she asked if they would take her to the hospital. An emergency room physician at the Christ Community Hospital examined her and "told [her] about rape counseling."[1]

On their drive to the hospital, Grisco pointed out the parking lot where she had been attacked, and the hotel where she had fled her car. Since she knew Dvornik, it did not take long for investigators to find him. The circumstances of this crime were quite different than a more familiar rape scenario informed by myths about strangers jumping out of the bushes to attack unsuspecting, chaste women. Grisco, a divorced mother, volunteered to accompany Dvornik to a tavern and had drinks with him (on the pretense of a business deal) before he threatened her and raped her. The State brought criminal charges against him, and her trial testimony reflected the long ordeal that she had endured two years earlier but also highlighted important changes affecting public responses to rape victims after they reported sexual attacks.

Many victimized women throughout the mid-twentieth century had demanded the right to be heard in court, in spite of public doubts about their sincerity and historical reservations about prosecuting false reports of rape. By the 1970s, the State consistently recognized that the circumstances of sexual violence usually differed from the portrait painted by rape myth expectations. Prosecutors pursued criminal charges in these types of cases more often than they had in earlier decades, defending the rights of unexpected victims by indicting unexpected defendants. Authorities who dealt with rape victims also began to pay attention to advocacy services that went beyond those formerly provided only by criminal investigators and medical personnel. The context of law, activism, and American society during this period reveals how both the legal and social understandings of sexual violence were undergoing important transformations by the 1970s. These changes worked to destabilize rape myths on a scale broader than earlier efforts put forth most often only by those individuals directly engaged in the justice system.

Calling attention to the realities of sexual violence was an important part of urban reform activism in the United States throughout the twentieth century, but with the emergence of second-wave feminism in the late 1960s, attention to it took different forms. Feminists began publicly challenging rape myths in a more systematic fashion, exposing the contradictions inherent within them. Women did not secretly want to be raped, nor were they vindictive liars about men's propensity to sexual violence. Although victims and prosecutors had been asserting this during rape trials for years, feminists outside the courtroom voiced their concerns about a patriarchal system that upheld male privilege at the expense of all women, not just those directly victimized by sexual attacks. They targeted a justice system that, by categorizing rape as legally similar to other violent crimes, ignored how differently it was treated. They pointed out, for example, that male victims of assault were not questioned about the expensive clothes they wore that prompted muggings, nor were murder victims typically blamed for getting themselves killed. Indeed, the nicely dressed, blameless male victim of a mugging became a standard feminist critique of the period, exposing by comparison the poor treatment female victims encountered when they reported sexual attacks.[2]

Feminist critiques disclosed the uncomfortable fit of rape into the successful prosecution of violent crimes. They argued that the system was set up to defend men against false accusations, rather than to provide women access to legal recourse following attacks.[3] Often, they were right. By the time activists began mounting campaigns to reform the legal and social treatment of rape victims, a number of things had changed in Chicago courtrooms. These changes were encouraged, in part, by postwar civil rights activism and by a growing emphasis on protecting the rights of the accused that was reaffirmed by the Warren Court. A focus on equality and activism, however, reinforced masculine privilege, as women struggled to make their voices heard in the complicated rape trials that took place during the 1960s. Trials provided women with a way to assert their rights as citizens, deserving of State protection in court. What many found, however, was that their narratives of sexual violence were often overshadowed by a dominant culture rooted in rape myths that doubted women.

In spite of their cooperation with authorities and in spite of prosecutorial efforts to overcome suspicions directed toward victims, a culture of rights that increasingly benefited the accused did not incorporate similar protections for women who reported rapes. The hostilities that victims faced, both inside and outside the courtroom, convinced many second-wave feminists to work toward transforming an unequal system. As the cases analyzed here suggest, protecting the rights of both victims and defendants of sexual attacks in Chicago was complicated by a number of rape myths that were challenged in various ways by the 1970s. Criminal trials did not operate solely within the vacuum of the courtroom space but were indeed profoundly shaped by social activism outside it. How women and men negotiated the system, and the support they found in doing so, demonstrates new ways in which both victims and the accused rejected the rape myths that restrained them, as they demanded respect, citizenship rights, and judicial protections.

In 1971, the women's liberation group known as the New York Radical Feminists (NYRF) held the first public "speak-out" on rape. Twelve women who helped coordinate the event planned to talk about their rape experiences, and twenty-eight more spontaneously addressed a Manhattan crowd of more than three hundred.[4] Following the speak-out, the group organized a conference to raise consciousness about sexual violence and to call into question the myths associated with it. Similar events spread throughout the nation, and many women began to insist that rape was a feminist, as well as a feminine, issue. As a member of the NYRF, Susan Brownmiller was deeply affected by these events and by membership in a radical organization that defined manhood itself as the primary root of women's oppression. While some critics questioned that assertion as ahistorical, Brownmiller—and many other feminists—pointed out the seemingly "timeless" quality of gender oppression manifested in myriad social issues, including biased thinking about sexual violence.[5] Brownmiller began researching and writing a book about the history of sexual violence informed by feminist theories about patriarchal oppression. As she commented at the time, her "purpose in this book has been to give rape its history. Now we must deny it a future."[6] Feminists eagerly awaited the book's publication, while they worked to undermine rape myths and lobbied for legal reforms.

The response to Brownmiller's research was widespread. Reviews of *Against Our Will: Men, Women and Rape* appeared in dozens of popular magazines and newspapers, as well as in a few academic journals.[7] Being hailed as an immediate "feminist classic" and promoted as November's National Book-of-the-Month Club selection in 1975 ensured its wide readership.[8] Many reviewers applauded Brownmiller's efforts, even if they did not always like her writing style—panned as "repetitive" and "overkill" among other invectives—or necessarily agree with her broad premise that rape is "a conscious process of intimidation by which *all men* keep *all women* in a state of fear."[9] Many also agreed that *Against Our Will* was the most comprehensive study of rape ever published, giving history to a long-dismissed issue, and that her political analysis of rape was "provocative" and would force people to rethink their assumptions about sexual violence.[10]

Not all reviews were positive, however, and not all reviewers balanced their comments with critique and praise. Some dismissed Brownmiller's scholarship as "fighting words from a feisty woman" or posed the question, "How is this undifferentiated hatred of a whole sex different from that which drives the rapist?"[11] Jean Stafford of *Esquire* magazine wondered how to "*begin* to measure the swath of that declaration that sweeps everything off the map but male chauvinism?" Stafford accused Brownmiller of being "bossy" because the "our" in the title "stands for the unstated word 'sisterhood,' a society I flatly refuse to join."[12] In the *Chicago Tribune*, reviewer Andrew Greeley called Brownmiller a self-righteous "heretic" and characterized *Against Our Will* as "a vile, evil, vicious, sick book."[13] Other critics pointed out the racial bias in the book, as Brownmiller dismissed how white Americans had often used the excuse of interracial rape to justify extreme mob violence against black men.[14] Whether lauded or panned, *Against Our Will* altered the public discourse about sexual violence as feminists pushed anti-rape activism to the forefront of their political agenda.

In Chicago, feminists in the 1970s joined national efforts to provide immediate victim advocacy services and, more broadly, attempted to revolutionize society's attitudes about rape. They worked to staff emergency crisis hotlines, which women could call to get information about what to do after being attacked. Many radical feminists were neutral about whether or not a woman should report rapes to the authorities. They recognized that invasive questioning, suspicious attitudes, and the "voyeurism of the police" dissuaded victims from reporting. But they also recognized that not calling the police meant that "men can rape with the full knowledge that nothing will happen to them."[15] They were correct on both counts. Chicago crime data revealed an increase in the number of rapes reported and investigated every year since the end of World War II, as well as a higher rate of "unfounded" reports of rape than of other violent crimes throughout the mid-twentieth century.[16] By the 1970s, the number of forcible rapes investigated in Chicago exceeded fifteen hundred per year.[17] These data suggest that rape was a growing criminal problem, even if some investigators did not always take it as seriously as other violent crimes. Feminists thus approached anti-rape activism from many angles, seeking to revolutionize social attitudes about sexual violence even while they worked to reform investigative practices and the law.

Reform or Revolution?

During the 1970s, anti-rape activists worked to keep women informed about the law, rape myths, and social response trends, respecting victims' right to choose for themselves whether or not to report. Chicago's rape crisis hotlines were available for anyone to use but especially served victims who had nowhere else to turn: women living alone, those without family in the city, or those who were reluctant to admit they had been attacked. Prior to the first hotline, established in November 1972, some women had only the police to turn to for help, which was not always forthcoming, given the "unfounded" rate for reported rapes.[18] This new type of advocacy service provided much-needed support for Chicago women victimized by sexual violence. A feminist organization called Chicago Legal Action for Women (CLAW) worked to expand advocacy services for rape victims as it quickly became evident that crisis hotlines were not enough to serve all of the city's sexually victimized women.[19]

As a result of women's overwhelming response to hotlines on both the north and south sides, CLAW worked with other local feminist groups to establish a more extensive victim advocacy program in the city. Rape crisis staffers also worked with Chicago's Abortion Task Force in an effort to eliminate prohibitive abortion laws based, in part, on the argument that conceptions resulting from sexual violence were particularly cruel to force women to endure.[20] Their cooperation on this front recognized rape as a feminist women's health issue, not just a criminal problem. Early rape crisis centers also provided reproductive health services for women, legal advice clinics, and staffed hotlines.[21] Advocates offered "both legal advice and emotional support for rape victims throughout the legal process" in an attempt to counteract rape myths about lying women.[22] While women continued to depend on family, friends, and neighbors for support after being raped as they had in the past, the establishment of lay advocacy programs offered informed and consistent support for any victim who turned to them.

Victim advocacy efforts departed somewhat from a radical feminist agenda, which advocated a social revolution to eradicate rape. Rather, lay advocacy programs dealt with the ongoing problem of sexual violence and hoped to diminish the suspicions victims faced after suffering attacks, even if advocates could not guarantee women's safety on the streets or even in their own homes. Of course, lay advocates hoped that someday rape would be a crime of the past, but in the meantime they dealt with the realities of the present. Some radical feminists were also ambivalent about the type of "professionalism" that lay advocacy programs seemed to promote. They felt that an emphasis on professionalized advocates providing help for rape victims maintained "class distinctions in this society."[23] They favored a more grassroots approach to advocacy, preferring the support offered by everyday women, many of whom had been victims of sexual violence themselves. Their preference reflected a radical agenda that rejected hierarchies as inherently oppressive. Many radical feminists believed that they, and not formal lay advocates, were in the best position to safeguard the interests of rape victims. Disagreement over standards of professionalism exposed the internal conflicts of the second-wave feminist movement more broadly, as women struggled to organize against patriarchal oppression without replicating the kinds of hierarchal structures best suited to affect change.[24] In spite of these ideological differences, lay advocates in Chicago worked to support rape victims and helped them endure the public aftermath of being attacked, whether or not they chose to report.

Feminist efforts to support rape victims throughout the legal process represented a response to the particularly hostile atmosphere that had developed in Chicago courtrooms throughout the 1960s. Lay advocates were trained as legal experts, although they did not have to be attorneys, and were available to accompany victimized women to the hospital. They advised women not to wash after being raped, no matter how much they may have wanted to, because washing could eliminate physical evidence of an attack—a fact that defense attorneys regularly exploited in seeking rape acquittals. They suggested victims contact the police immediately or go to the hospital with a friend, relative, or rape crisis center volunteer, and to save their clothing as evidence for a future legal case.[25] Advocates were familiar with courtroom proceedings in order to ensure that victims "received as fair treatment as the defendant."[26] As the transcripts analyzed here have demonstrated, judges during this period were particularly concerned about violating the rights of the accused. They allowed defense counsel to attack the corruption, incompetence, and prejudices of the Chicago police and to closely interrogate the actions of women, whom defendants and their attorneys pointedly accused of lying. Victim advocates hoped that their efforts might counterbalance this legal trend.

Feminists were determined to offset judicial bias with advocacy services that also protected the rights of victims who reported sexual attacks. They encouraged the Chicago City Council to implement changes in the investigation and prosecution of sexual violence because, as one newspaper headline put it, "The Men Have Failed: Let Women Punish Rapists."[27] Groups like CLAW pressured the Cook County State's Attorney, Bernard Carey, to assign rape cases to women. They believed that female attorneys would be less likely to doubt rape allegations and more rigorous in their attempts to prosecute them.[28] In keeping with the radicalism of the times, and much to Carey's dismay, CLAW occupied his office in 1974 to demand action.[29] In response, he appointed five women to a prosecutorial task force and created a citizens' advisory panel that included representatives from local feminist groups as well as the Chicago branch of the American Civil Liberties Union.[30] After initially appointing a man to oversee the office's rape prosecutions, Carey promoted one of the task force's original female attorneys to take over. Edna Epstein promised to work with local feminist groups in reorganizing and increasing the prosecution of sex crime cases in Chicago.[31]

Another program that enjoyed success in changing public responses to rape victims included intervention in the hospital examination process. "Code R" was a program initiated at the University of Chicago's hospitals and clinics in March 1972. When a rape victim entered one of the participating emergency rooms, the hospital chaplain was immediately summoned. He stayed with the victim, helped comfort her, and remained available for post-visit counseling.[32]

Like women in previous decades who called their parish priests for support, this program gave victims the opportunity to have a sympathetic presence stay with them as they endured invasive exams and questions. According to its supporters, "Code R" was also "successful in changing the attitudes of the police," who were forced to censor themselves; they were unwilling to yell "'We got a rape for you!'" to emergency room workers while in the presence of a chaplain.[33] The program provided a model for feminists not necessarily associated with the university's medical centers, who continued to lobby for reform outside the courtroom. The Chicago Hospital Council, the governing board for all of the city's medical institutions, recognized victim advocacy reform in its annual procedural recommendations. Acknowledging that patient-victims "will be suffering from emotional trauma," the council advised that "she be treated promptly, carefully, and sympathetically . . . and that possible rape cases be referred to by a *code* so that comments by hospital personnel such as 'Where's the rape?' are avoided. For example, one hospital refers to such cases as 'Code R' cases."[34] Victimized women still had to endure uncomfortable examinations and potential skepticism from medical and police personnel, but those difficulties were tempered by recommendations that all of the city's hospitals eventually adopted.

Some feminists also worked with civic authorities in an effort to reform investigative procedures involving rape victims. Convened in 1974, the Chicago Citizens Advisory Committee on Rape hoped to align the city's investigative practices and laws with a feminist analysis of rape that challenged myths about sexual violence. Medical reform was a primary part of the committee's agenda leading to its formation of a hospital subcommittee under the leadership of Pauline Bart, who was then affiliated with the University of Illinois-Chicago's Abraham Lincoln School of Medicine. Other members of the subcommittee included ad-hoc representatives from the broader advisory panel, women's health service personnel, feminist academics, and representatives from various medical institutions in the city. They included regular medical schools (University of Illinois-Chicago, Northwestern University), feminist health centers (Emma Goldman Women's Health Center, Loop YWCA), and victim advocacy programs (Rape Victim Advocacy Program at St. Luke's Presbyterian Hospital, University of Illinois-Chicago Circle Women's Caucus).[35] The subcommittee issued a report based on the premise that "there should be a recognition by all medical personnel that some medical treatment may feel like another rape. The victim needs respect, validation and privacy."[36] Their efforts strayed far from the radical feminist agenda. Instead of attacking the problem of rape as a representation of violent maleness and sexual oppression in an effort to subvert entirely this criminal act, both the broader committee and its hospital subcommittee recognized that sexual violence was unlikely to be soon eradicated in the United States. Although everyone agreed that abolishing rape was a worthy goal, the group made concrete recommendations to improve the immediate treatment of patient-victims in the aftermath of rape.

The hospital subcommittee's report recognized the legal needs required of medical examinations while simultaneously proposing suggestions embedded in feminist ideals about rights, equality, and respect. It recommended that women be allowed to have a friend or advocate with them at all times while at the hospital and that she should be kept in a separate examining room rather than in the general waiting area, not to be left alone unless she wished. The report advised emergency room workers to call advocates immediately when a victim entered the hospital (even if she came in with someone), not to rush a woman to talk about what had happened, and to explain fully all medical procedures before performing them. It also recommended that no police should be allowed into the exam room unless the victim wanted to make a statement right away, and that photographs could be taken only with the victim's permission—preferably by a woman photographer using Polaroid film.[37] In contrast to exams in earlier decades when witness testimonies underscored women's emergency room isolation, these proposals emphasized sympathetic, respectful treatment of victims in the hope of eliminating what many feminists argued was, in essence, a "second rape" at the hospital.[38]

The hospital subcommittee also directed its attention to the forensic rape examination itself. Many of its recommendations mirrored procedures already in place, such as testing for venereal diseases, observing general trauma, and recording marks on the body "even if not medically serious," as they provided potential proof of a woman's resistance, which was legally necessary for rape convictions.[39] Other recommendations were embedded within feminist discourse about sexual violence. Defense attorneys in the 1960s had routinely made medical examinations, either their inclusion or absence, an important element of rape trials. By the 1970s, the subcommittee made it clear that a victim had the right to refuse anything at the hospital, although they suggested that an advocate could help convince her of the usefulness of a complete exam for her case. They advised that a woman be told about the importance of evidence collected by combing pubic hair, for example, and proposed that she be allowed to do this herself to counteract any discomfort she might have about such procedures.[40]

The report also reflected legal concerns that emerged as courts sought to protect defendants' rights. It emphasized that a minimum number of personnel should handle evidence and that everything collected must show "the date, time and name of person receiving the items, and from whom they were received" in order to avoid legal problems with evidentiary chains of possession.[41] The recommendations combined feminist concerns about the sympathetic treatment of victimized women with judicial mandates about admissible evidence. For example, the report recommended that speculums used in pelvic examinations on rape victims be lubricated only with warm water, as many commercial lubricants immobilized sperm, a potentially corroborative piece of evidence.[42] Those involved in promoting this set of medical recommendations recognized the inherent contradiction between respecting women's bodies and privacy while simultaneously putting these same things on public display, which successful rape prosecutions necessitated. Strategies to prosecute, and to defend against, sexual violence were constantly evolving in Chicago's courtrooms, and feminists were determined to shape these changes in ways that would benefit women. The subcommittee helped standardize hospital procedures, and the Chicago Hospital Council approved a series of guidelines that mirrored its recommendations shortly after they were released.[43]

Although it is difficult to know how consistently these policies were followed, publicity about medical reform encouraged local hospitals to adopt new procedural standards. Although some feminists were leery about mandating designated rape units only at certain medical sites, believing this would allow others to shirk their responsibility to adopt similar reforms, change in this area spread quickly.[44] Several witnesses in the cases analyzed here testified about hospital procedures that reflected feminist-inspired reforms during the 1970s. Medical evidence regarding Barbara Robinson, in court to testify about being raped by Roosevelt Bridges in 1972, revealed that before being examined at the University of Chicago's Billings Hospital, a female nurse conducted the initial interview, took vaginal swabs, and stayed with Robinson while the male physician performed a pelvic exam.[45] When Sandra Stith testified against the men who gang raped her in 1974, attorneys' questions indicated that a nurse at the Michael Reese Medical Center took the lead during this patient-victim's hospital experience by conducting the initial interview and staying with her while she was examined by the male doctor on call in the emergency room that night.[46] The physician who examined Diane Syrett at the Henrotin Hospital after she was raped in 1976 also mentioned in court that the head nurse remained with the patient-victim throughout her time there, serving as a "chaperone" during the exam.[47] Given the history of strained relations between caregivers in American hospitals, a male physician describing a female nurse as a "chaperone" to any medical procedure is powerful evidence of an altered approach to the medical treatment of rape victims.[48] They had not come to the hospital for routine checkups, after all, but deserved sensitive treatment that attempted to respect women's privacy in the face of traumatic circumstances.

Rape victims felt the impact of the medical reforms that were implemented in Chicago during the 1970s and both they, and expert witnesses, talked about them in court. Lori Grisco was not only told about rape counseling, she also testified that a female nurse stayed with her throughout her Christ Hospital emergency examination when forensic evidence was (uncomfortably) collected.[49] The physician who testified in this case later indicated that referring patient-victims to rape counseling following an attack was "part of [their] routine."[50] Similarly, the physician who examined rape victim Christine Brown at the Ravenswood Hospital in 1974 told the court that he "referred her to a crisis worker" after he was finished.[51] When Frankie Gage testified against George Jeffers, she indicated that two nurses remained with her while she was examined at the Loretto Hospital Emergency Room after being raped in 1976, and that she also "talked to a lady there" about the attack itself.[52] It was unclear in her testimony if that "lady" was a female police officer or perhaps a victim advocate, but she was significant enough for Gage to mention, suggesting that she represented to her a comforting presence.

For decades, rape victims told Chicago courts about the gendered support they received from family members or friends and neighbors following an attack. Many especially appreciated the sympathetic presence of other women, who often accompanied rape victims to the hospital if they went. Female nurses and victim advocates also offered women gendered support during the 1970s. Their presence helped alleviate some of the discomfort and alienation patient-victims felt when being examined following a sexual attack. Reflective of the impact of the University of Chicago Hospitals' successful "Code R" program, the cases analyzed here demonstrate how medical policies, and not just individual physicians' attitudes, had begun to change. Women were no longer so isolated in claiming State protections against sexual violence and were supported in doing so by medical institutions with a history of reservations about rape victims.

Hospitals throughout Chicago were clearly making an effort to adhere to new guidelines regarding the medical treatment of patient-victims. Importantly, the different facilities wherein raped women sought treatment represented facilities serving a broad demographic of patient populations. Southwest suburban Christ Community Hospital and the Ravenswood Hospital on Chicago's north side primarily saw white patients from different socioeconomic backgrounds.[53] The Michael Reese Hospital was one of Chicago's oldest, opened in 1881. Its south side location and policy of indigent patient care transitioned Michael Reese into a medical center that served a predominantly African American patient population by the mid-twentieth century.[54] Although the University of Chicago's Billings Hospital had a contentious history of racial segregation throughout much of the twentieth century, by the 1970s Billings not only cared for a diverse patient population but employed a racially integrated staff as well.[55] Loretto Hospital, a not-for-profit health care institution that opened on Chicago's west side in 1939, was partnered with the Austin Community Organization, a neighborhood association located in Chicago's de facto segregated "second ghetto."[56]

During the 1970s, diverse hospital staffs and feminists in Chicago forged an uneasy relationship in an attempt to address the health needs of rape victims of all races, while trying to minimize some of the racial tensions that had long plagued the city. African American nurses revitalized their professional organization with the creation of the National Black Nurses Association (NBNA) in 1971.[57] The NBNA, influenced by both second wave feminism and radical black activism, stated its purpose as "a response to concerns regarding the growing inequities in health care for African Americans and the lack of a voice from black nurses on their issues."[58] Although interracial and cross-class conflicts sometimes stalled the efficacy of second-wave feminist organizations, medical reform and anti-rape activism represented arenas for cooperation as sexual violence affected a broad spectrum of women. Black nurses in Chicago were able to draw on the support provided by their own professional organization, as well as the broader anti-rape movement, and took such sensibilities into their workplaces where they increasingly encountered and promoted the use of feminist-influenced procedures on patient-victims.

As civil rights moved in a more militant direction by the late 1960s, many male activists carried their reservations about voicing black violence in a new direction. At the core of black nationalism was, for many, the belief that black women should inspire black men to lead; supporters accused powerful and outspoken African American women of being too controlling or even emasculating.[59] Black nationalist men asserted that charges of intraracial rape amounted to a betrayal of the race, even though many black Chicago women viewed silence about sexual violence at the hands of black men as a betrayal of black sisterhood.[60] Many African American women rejected chauvinist civil rights rhetoric and practices, preferring instead to forge their own activist paths as early members of predominantly white feminist groups or founders of their own organizations.[61] The Chicago Citizens Advisory Committee on Rape included representatives from the Loop YWCA, which had a long and celebrated history of interracial programming and services, and whose organizers worked to bridge the demographic boundaries that divided women.[62] The Loop YWCA also served as the meeting place for the Chicago branch of the National Alliance of Black Feminists, a short-lived group that attempted to combine feminist consciousness-raising, rape crisis intervention, and radical black activism as a counterbalance against white exclusivity within second-wave feminism.[63]

Other organizations also attempted to alleviate racial and class differences among feminists while working to expose the historic prejudices of the criminal justice system. Groups like the League of Black Women worked with Chicago authorities to enforce egalitarian standards toward both black rape victims and sex crime defendants, to educate the community about intraracial sexual violence, and to encourage black leadership in attempting to eradicate it.[64] The Hospital Subcommittee of the Citizens Advisory Committee on Rape was chaired by a researcher who investigated and analyzed the unique concerns and distinct survival strategies of a number of demographic communities in the city. Throughout the 1970s, Pauline Bart and her research partner, Patricia O'Brien, collected data on surviving rape. Their research specifically outlined the experiences of African American women who refused to keep silent about rape, in spite of the broader civil rights movement's reticence in recognizing the realities of intraracial sexual violence.[65] While interracial cooperation among victim advocates, medical personnel, and feminists had its limits, many Chicago women were willing to try to ease social divisions for the sake of anti-rape activism.

Changing Practices, Evolving Courtrooms, Reforming the Law

While feminists worked to implement procedural changes in Chicago hospitals and volunteer services throughout the 1970s, they also tackled the issue of reforming rape laws. Some of their efforts continued to focus on issues relating to women's health and bodies. Illinois House Bills 278 and 279, introduced in 1975, included provisions about extending health insurance coverage to forensic rape examinations and mandating State payment of them for the uninsured.[66] Effective January 1, 1976, the new law addressed a familiar problem that pitted the growing costs of healthcare in the United States against an increased reliance on physical evidence to corroborate women's testimonies about sexual violence.[67] The Chicago City Council also applied for additional federal funds to cover the expense of rape counseling services for victims, especially for those "who live in poverty and are unaware of the programs available to them."[68] While a lack of medical insurance prevented many women in the past from seeking treatment after sexual attacks, many others also went directly to emergency rooms after being raped, where they encountered sometimes suspicious and less-than-sensitive medical personnel. After the adoption of the Chicago Hospital Board's new guidelines in 1974, forensic rape examinations evolved into the more familiar "rape kit" processes that are used in emergency rooms today.

The standardization of the rape kit recognized that this unique type of procedure required attention paid to the medical and psychological needs of patient-victims, as well as to the legal needs of the court. Although medical staffs were charged with providing the best care possible in all situations, rape kit provisions outlined techniques for the proper collection of medico-legal evidence in cases of sexual violence. Rape kit mandates also, importantly, directed the professional and moral responsibilities of hospital personnel in attending to the emotional needs of women under their care.[69] In recognizing that victimized women had undergone a "dehumanizing, emotionally shattering experience," rape kit manuals directed emergency room workers to find, whenever possible, a private room for patient-victims and that female nurses should remain present throughout the exam and "act as [an] advocate throughout the entire examination and treatment."[70] Rape kit procedures mirrored many medical practices from earlier decades, but their standardization helped to counter the pervasive effects of rape myths. Dubious physicians conducting rape kits risked their own professional reputations by ignoring any steps, or failing to adhere to agreed-upon guidelines and state law, especially since defense attorneys routinely attacked the presentation of medical evidence during trials and questioned the professionalism of attending physicians.[71] Every rape kit ideally contained a variety of supplies including glass slides, blood tubes, swabs, labels, and forms so that the evidentiary chain of possession was protected.[72] Directing hospitals to keep supplies organized in this fashion helped ensure proper adherence to legal mandates about the collection of bodily forensic evidence in rape cases.

Other legal reforms that feminists lobbied for during the 1970s reflected their concerns about investigative methods and trial strategies used both to defend against and to prosecute rape. In addition to advocating for procedural reforms in Chicago hospitals, CLAW also targeted the police and male attorneys, whom second-wave feminists accused of being callous toward rape victims.[73] Although initially suspicious that police would dismiss their ideas, increasingly, both feminists and criminal authorities recognized the need for cooperation between their ranks. Anti-rape activists, who were at one time reluctant to work with police bureaucracies, soon realized that "keeping the lines of communication open" benefited all parties engaged in the system.[74]

CLAW recommended that female police officers be assigned to investigate rape complaints, in an effort to undermine historical suspicions and victim mistreatment rooted in gendered assumptions about lying women.[75] The belief that women were less likely to doubt other women's accusations of rape is difficult to prove, given the variety of individual responses to sexual violence throughout history. However, the lieutenant who managed a new sex crimes unit staffed by policewomen in New York City reported to the Chicago City Council's Police Committee in 1973 that rape arrests were up and the unfounded report rate had dropped significantly under this initiative.[76] Inspired by urban reform elsewhere, and responding to local feminist demands, the Chicago Police Department instituted a similar training program for female officers in 1974.[77] Although its uneven implementation was criticized by groups like CLAW, who argued that the Daley administration purposefully understaffed the unit in order to save money and to make women working in nontraditional occupations look bad, the context of the times demanded a change in policing.[78] The Chicago Police Department had a long history of gender bias among its ranks, but by the 1970s policewomen patrolled the streets just as their male counterparts did, where they were regularly called to investigate reported rapes.[79]

Police reform was reflected in a number of cases successfully prosecuted in Chicago during this period. A detective testifying in the 1975 trial against Roberto Leyva informed the court that both Pamela Dougherty of the Homicide/Sex Division, as well as Jana West from the Ravenswood Health Clinic, were present when the victim was questioned about being raped.[80] When Pamela Gains testified in 1974, she indicated, "I told a policewoman" about the attack when officers arrived to investigate her complaint.[81] When police were called to investigate a 1975 rape in a vacant lot on Chicago's south side, the victim in this case testified that two female officers arrived and took her to the Roseland Hospital, where they waited to take her statement until after she received treatment.[82] The mere presence of a policewoman taking a victim's statement or accompanying her to the hospital did not, of course, guarantee sympathetic treatment. However, multiple references to female officers during rape trials in the 1970s—references absent in earlier testimonies that featured male police exclusively—suggested more policewomen were now working in Chicago, which was something feminists encouraged.

In contrast to their effect outside the courtroom, few second-wave feminists worked as Cook County prosecutors, and so they found it more difficult to directly shape the trial atmosphere that rape victims faced during the 1970s. Defense attorneys continued to interrogate victims' personal lives, reinforcing rape myths that doubted their sincerity, and probed how their actions undermined proper feminine ideals of chastity and sobriety. The attorney defending James Dvornik, convicted of raping Lori Grisco after pretending to be interested in her real estate services, spent a great deal of time cross-examining the victim about her drinking habits.[83] The repeated questions implied that perhaps she was too drunk to remember exactly what had happened when she accused the defendant of rape. The inference against her, however, was that she went out drinking with this man and did not try to get away from him when he first indicated his allegedly violent intentions, and thus she was not really raped at all. The defense attorney who questioned teenager Christine Jakubczak, in court to testify about being raped by Karl Plewka and Reginald Blakemore at a party in 1972, managed to convince the court that his clients were not guilty of rape, although the judge in this bench trial convicted the defendants on the lesser charges of indecent liberties and contributing to the delinquency of a minor.[84] The defense's successful acquittal strategy here highlighted the drinking and drug use of the young partygoers, who had skipped school the day of the alleged attack, as well as emphasizing a lack of force apparent in the case. Jakubczak claimed she had struggled with the defendants, but the medical report submitted as corroborative evidence showed no bruising on her body. Moreover, her clothes, also offered as evidence in support of the victim's allegations, were undamaged. The defense attorney wondered, "[How it was possible that] she puts up a fight to such an extent, she wasn't injured, nor were her clothes ripped?"[85] Newspaper articles about sex crime acquittals or charges dropped during the 1970s similarly suggested that women's contradictory actions led to such results.[86]

As opposed to the methods of defense attorneys, strategies to prosecute rape during the 1970s revealed an awareness of second-wave efforts to reform both the law and social attitudes about victims. In his closing arguments in the 1971 rape trial of Sidney Robinson, the prosecutor acknowledged feminist complaints about the exclusion of marital rape from the criminal code. He appealed to the jury, "Whatever you think of that Statute, that's what it says."[87] The law still defined rape as forced sexual intercourse by a man of a woman "not his wife," a restriction rooted in the historical definition of rape as a crime against male property that was no longer relevant in the modern age.[88] Other prosecutors adopted language in the courtroom that echoed feminist analyses of sexual violence, such as the Assistant State's Attorney in the case against Albert and Calvert Faezell. While questioning the victim, who had been brutally raped and left for dead by the Faezell brothers in 1975, he prompted her testimony by asking, "After the first man finished using you, tell us what happened."[89] In constructing his central question this way, the prosecutor rejected the assumption that rape was a crime of sexual passion and cast it instead as one of power and control that had little, if anything, to do with men's "uncontrolled" sexual urges.[90] Not all attorneys were equally enlightened, however. In his closing arguments of a 1974 rape trial, the prosecutor suggested to the jury that if they chose to acquit the defendant, they were sending a message to the "Don Juans of Lake and Wood Street" that sexual violence was not so bad.[91] Reference to the familiar romantic character here suggests that this attorney conflated issues of power, violence, and sexual passion, ignoring feminist arguments to the contrary even while he tried to secure a conviction.

Feminists worked to undermine bias in American rape law, specifically addressing doubts about victims' resistance. Although legal precedents had long recognized that a lack of resistance did not automatically preclude the possibility of sexual violence, they also conceded that consent, no matter how reluctantly given, negated a rape charge.[92] As feminists increasingly took up the anti-rape cause, they challenged this idea. They lobbied for investigators to recognize that just because some victims could not successfully resist sexual attacks did not mean that they had consented to them. They pointed to the advice regularly offered by the police, which instructed women not to fervently resist a sexual attack in order to avoid serious injuries or even death.[93] Information about self-defense classes and "whistle stop" campaigns, where women could pick up free whistles to scare off would-be rapists, advised that physical resistance was potentially dangerous for women and that they might be better off making a lot of noise to thwart sexual attacks.[94] In publicizing these issues, feminists exposed a profound contradiction between rape law and personal safety advice: women needed to protect themselves from injuries however they could if facing an attack, but the law required clear resistance in order for them to help successfully prosecute sexual violence.

Arguments about a rape victim's resistance, or lack thereof, made their way into trials in new ways during this period, reflecting the impact of feminism activism outside the courtroom. When Roberto Leyva's public defender addressed the jury hearing his 1974 rape case, he suggested that the victim failed to resist his client's sexual advances in any significant way. Because the victim was attacked in the hallway of her building before being pushed inside her apartment and "no one heard her yelling," the defense attorney asked the jury to consider what that silence really meant.[95] Had she really consented to a liaison that she, perhaps, later regretted? The prosecutor responded to this characterization with his own insistence that "she doesn't have to die . . . women in our day and age don't have to fight to the death to prove they have been raped."[96] The State's closing arguments here echoed those that feminists used to push for legal reform.

Courtroom strategies from both State and defense attorneys shifted as juries began to hear sex crime trials during this period more often than in earlier decades. While judges alone continued to try the majority of cases throughout the mid-twentieth century, growing numbers of Chicago rape defendants in the 1970s declined to waive their right to jury trials. While defendants who opted for bench trials in earlier years tended to be African American as opposed to white men in the cases analyzed here, by the late 1960s and 1970s the opposite was true.[97] African American men on trial for rape in the cases sampled during the 1970s were increasingly reluctant to trust only judges to determine their guilt, undoubtedly influenced by well-known charges of corruption among Chicago's political and criminal authorities.

Radical civil rights organizations fought against justice discrimination and police brutality in Chicago throughout the late 1960s and 1970s. Their efforts were broadly publicized, especially in the wake of the 1969 police murders of two Black Panthers. An early morning raid at Fred Hampton's west side apartment resulted in a shootout (or, massacre) that killed Hampton and fellow Panther Mark Clark. Evidence at the scene contradicted what police claimed had happened and proved that only one of the nearly one hundred shots fired came from inside the apartment, where several Black Panthers were staying at the time.[98] None of the officers involved was charged with any crime, in spite of local outcry against their actions.[99] However, the contradictory evidence proved more damning in the civil suit that Panther representatives filed against the city, and the families of Hampton and Clark were ultimately awarded a financial settlement.[100] Under the militant leadership of Renault Robinson, members of the Afro-American Patrolmen's League, founded by black Chicago officers in 1967, openly criticized discrimination faced by the local black community as well as the prejudices they encountered on the job.[101] The AAPL filed an injunction against the city in 1971, which froze federal law enforcement funds until discriminatory issues were more systematically addressed.[102] While newspapers like the *Chicago Defender* had long protested in print racial prejudice, by the 1970s even the politically conservative *Chicago Tribune* highlighted such bias. Several articles published during this period criticized criminal racial profiling, abusive policing in black Chicago neighborhoods, and prejudicial court decisions.[103] Judges were an integral part of what the militant activists of the day insisted was a discriminatory system, which they worked to expose. So instead of being skeptical of everyday people's judgment of sexual violence as they had been in the past, black rape defendants in the 1970s more often preferred to defend themselves before Chicago juries, where rape myths were most profoundly negotiated.

Feminist challenges to rape myth assumptions in Chicago courts during the 1970s were apparent in the jury trials analyzed here. Chicago prosecutors were mindful of the difficulties that publicly reporting sexual attacks could present for women. They clarified to juries the extensive process women faced when they pursued State protections against sexual violence, in essence lamenting the ordeal of the "second rape" and suggesting that no woman would willingly go through that unless she were telling the truth. Recalling defense skepticism about Lori Grisco's allegations against James Dvornik, the prosecutor in this case challenged the jury to consider the events that preceded her testimony before rendering their verdict. In his closing arguments he reminded jurors that,

> a lot of women are terrified at the very idea of coming to talk to people like me, to prosecutors. If you're raped you have got to talk to people like myself before you're put on a witness stand . . . you have to go to a preliminary hearing and testify there . . . you have to testify also in front of a grand jury. And, of course, you have to be examined at the hospital. You have to be examined by a number of police departments. You have to get a warrant, then they have a lineup. You have to view the lineup . . . then eventually if they finally ever get him into custody in the first place, you may have an opportunity to testify against him at a jury trial.[104]

By outlining in such detail the many times Grisco had to repeat herself, and how authorities must have believed her at every stage or they would not all be in court (again) a few years later, the prosecutor hoped to undermine any doubts the jury might have had about the circumstances surrounding this attack. The prosecutor trying the 1976 rape case against George Jeffers reminded jurors that, "despite current pleas for equality," they needed to acknowledge that physical size difference often mattered more in rape cases than did ideological adherence to gender parity.[105] Men and women were, on paper, equal as American citizens, but this prosecutor also agreed with feminists that it was still difficult for many women to fight off the unwanted criminal intentions of many men. For this, women should not be blamed, nor should they be held responsible for getting raped, in spite of myths about how women who truly wanted to resist sexual violence should effectively be able to do so.

Feminists also tried to combat rape by lobbying against laws that contained embedded elements that assumed women's sexual complicity. Proposed legal reform during the 1970s specifically took on defense strategies that had, in the past, been used to undermine women's accusations by interrogating their personal backgrounds and activities unrelated to the charges about which they were in court to testify. At the urging of the local feminist lobby and following national trends, Illinois legislators took up the issue of victims' privacy.[106] Introduced in 1975, Illinois House Bill 274 proposed, among other things, amendments regarding the admissibility of a woman's past sexual conduct in court.[107] Elements of the original proposal, subsumed under the revisions eventually passed by Illinois lawmakers, included provisions that mandated police sensitivity training and forbade the use of a prostitution defense in rape cases.[108] Accusations of criminal solicitation in rape cases, which first appeared in 1960s trials, thus presented feminists and lawmakers with tangible statements to which they could point in order to legitimate the need for protection against this type of slander. These protections, feminists hoped, would be extended into other areas of personal conduct as well. They argued that a woman's sexual behavior in her everyday life was irrelevant to the question of consent, upon which a rape indictment turned.

Authorities in Chicago met the proposed revisions with mixed results. Many judges respected the eventual changes, but the recommendations also allowed latitude within which courtroom officials could maneuver. While researchers concluded that Illinois's reforms were stronger than those implemented in many other jurisdictions, the particular setup of Chicago's criminal courts sometimes undermined the strength of the proposed changes.[109] The structure of the court system here assigned particular prosecutors and public defenders to particular courtrooms, and thus to the same judge, often for years. These courtroom "workgroups" were sometimes more likely to trust each other than they were to consider the finer points of the revised law.[110] Public defenders were less likely to ask inadmissible questions in front of judges whom they knew to be exceptionally strict in their trial rulings. Similarly, Chicago judges were less likely to question the motives or tactics of familiar defense attorneys. Put another way, women's sexual histories were sometimes admitted as evidence in rape cases when, legally, judges should not have allowed it.

Rape shield laws, as these types of revisions have become known, inspired controversy from their outset. As a reflection of a public discourse that recognized feminist arguments about rape, many Americans hailed them as a triumph for women. Praise for the reform and criticism of its opponents filled the local press while legislators debated the issue in 1975.[111] Concerned civil libertarians, however, questioned their value in terms of how such reforms could undermine the rights of the accused. Rape shield controversy involves what some believe to be fundamental legal conflicts. One attorney summarizes it as "the right to confront one's accuser versus the victim's right to privacy and the State's interest in obtaining justified convictions."[112] Suspect advocates posit that a woman's past sexual conduct is indeed relevant to whether or not she consented to intercourse with the accused—exactly the issue that feminists continue to challenge today. According to shield critics, Sixth Amendment protections that ensure the right to face one's accuser, to question witnesses, and to develop a full defense are at stake.[113]

Even before rape shield provisions made their way into the Illinois Revised Statutes, Chicago prosecutors asserted their relevance in court. When cross-examining Pamela Gaines, the defendant's attorney repeatedly questioned her about her relationships with other men. Gaines had been attacked in the home of a man she had been living with in 1974; she testified that they were not married, so she did not share his last name. Defense counsel wanted to know if she had "sexual intercourse during the time she was with" her former boyfriend (they broke up shortly after she was raped). The prosecutor objected to the inquiries as "irrelevant," and the judge agreed.[114] Asking the victim about her past sexual relationships with anyone other than the defendant was increasingly off-limits in Chicago courts during the 1970s, anticipating the legal reforms that were then being debated in Illinois and throughout the nation.

Even when defense attorneys tried to interrogate victims about sexual activities that they may have been involved in with rape defendants, prosecutors recognized feminist arguments about the contingency of consent. Some cases involving victims and defendants who had known each other and who may have had prior consensual relationships found their way into Chicago courtrooms during this period, where they were successfully prosecuted. These cases hardly mirrored expectations about victims who were believed only when they were virginal white women attacked by predatory black strangers in the middle of the day. Expanded prosecutions of rapes involving circumstances that diverged from such myths made clear that the cooperation between victims and the State, which had begun to take seriously the rights of women long before modern feminists challenged authorities to do so, had benefited from the activism of the times.

The indictments in these cases still turned on the issue of force, even if a victim may have consented to some, but not all, sexual activity with the accused. Edward Reed's attorney was stymied in his efforts to obtain a directed verdict in the rape and deviate sexual assault trial of his client.[115] A directed verdict is a legal maneuver whereby defense counsel claims the State did not prove its prima facie case and thus a not guilty finding should be automatically awarded when prosecutors rest. The motion assumes no defense is necessary for acquittal.[116] As a basis for the motion in Reed's case, the defendant claimed that the alleged victim had voluntarily agreed to go to his apartment for a "nude massage," and what did she expect was going to happen? The State countered that the victim also testified how she had believed that Reed was a physician when he "lured" her to his home. The prosecutor acknowledged that she was "extremely naïve," but that did not mean she consented to being attacked.[117] In support, he cited case law, which held that even if a complaining witness had consented to intercourse with a defendant in the past it did not mean that she automatically conceded all future sexual engagement with him.[118] Although strategies questioning the sexual motives of men and the sexual immaturity of women were familiar in Chicago courtrooms by the 1970s, the influence of feminist activism and legal reform altered their presentation. Legislative debates about issues of consent and character lent weight to the arguments about sexual violence and women's rights that victims and prosecutors had been presenting in Chicago courtrooms for years.

As in Chicago rape trials that took place throughout the mid-twentieth century, sentences assigned to those convicted during the 1970s varied. The legal reforms encouraged by feminists and sympathetic lawmakers encouraged prosecutors to pursue the kinds of cases that had not typically been seen in earlier years. The "real rape" of past decades—a stranger jumping out of an alley and raping a woman on her way home from church—rarely occurred, and the trials analyzed here reflect that. They present a broad array of sexual violence narratives, some involving victims and defendants known to each other or circumstances that reflected consensual activities up to a point, such as in cases involving Edward Reed and James Dvornik. Both of these intraracial cases involving a white defendant and a black defendant (respectively) ended with convictions, although both men received relatively minor sentences for their crimes.[119] The average sentence for rape and other sex crime convictions during the 1970s was six to thirteen years.[120] This average was slightly lower than the eight and a half to fifteen years assigned during cases sampled during the 1960s, and significantly less than the average minimum of thirty years that convicted men, of any race, received prior to then.[121]

In contrast, some rape cases during the 1970s involved extreme violence, and those that did saw long sentences imposed upon convicted defendants. The Faezell twins, African American men who were convicted of vicious attacks against an African American woman in 1975, each received twenty- to forty-year sentences on several counts of rape, attempted murder, and kidnapping.[122] Delbert Scott, a black defendant brought to trial after raping, beating, and leaving for dead a black woman on a south side rooftop in 1973, received a twenty-five- to fifty-year sentence on merged counts of rape and aggravated kidnapping, and an additional twenty-five to fifty years on two counts of robbery.[123] Unlike in years past, sentencing outcomes during the 1970s appeared to have more to do with the level of violence of a sexual attack than with the race of the victims or perpetrators involved. Nonetheless, given the long history of biased policing of minority communities in the United States, as well as (mistaken) assumptions about violent black criminality, it is also not surprising that the most brutal cases appearing in this sample involved African American defendants.

By the 1960s and 1970s, newspaper reports no longer automatically clarified the race of individuals who pleaded guilty or who were convicted of sex crimes that they did not appeal, although sometimes articles included pictures or other details from which race might be inferred. Predictably, the average sentences assigned in most cases involving African American men as covered in the press were quite severe. During the 1960s, the *Tribune* published around sixty articles outlining the sentences for sex crime defendants. While three were sentenced to life, the average sentence that convicted black men received ranged from almost thirty to thirty-six years, according to the (admittedly limited) press coverage of sex crime sentencing during that decade.[124] Still fewer reports were published in the 1970s, approximately thirty in total for the years under study here, and the sentences assigned averaged twelve and a half to twenty-eight years.[125] Reporting trends during this period reflected broader social changes, including a demand to know that authorities at least attempted to deal with public safety concerns, as national data demonstrated ever-rising rates of violent crime, especially in urban areas.[126] As well, contemporary critics of ongoing trends in journalism suggest that increased media competition today demands more sensational coverage, especially when it corresponds with familiar beliefs about the inherent criminality of black men. In other words, "if it bleeds it leads," with African American men playing a starring role in incomplete and superficial reports of violent crime.[127]

Not all convicted rapists were punished so harshly, however, and convictions appealed during the 1970s sometimes resulted in sentence reductions or even verdict reversals. This change was almost entirely absent from the cases that appeared before the Illinois First District Court of Appeals in earlier years. After considering the appeal of Kenneth Dalton and Samuel Ames, two African American men convicted of the rape and attempted rape of two white victims, the higher court affirmed the men's convictions but reduced their sentences. The women had accused Dalton and Ames of attacking them after they left a Rush Street tavern in downtown Chicago on a September night in 1970. Both defendants denied the attacks but were nonetheless convicted and received prison terms of ten to twenty years for rape (Dalton) and eight to fourteen years for attempted rape (Ames).[128] The appellate court reduced the sentences by more than half in recognition of new guidelines that went into effect in the time that passed between their December convictions and their January sentencing hearing.[129] Timing was also an issue in the case of Ricky Vanderbilt, a black man convicted of intraracial rape and deviate sexual assault in 1973. Vanderbilt was arrested the day after his brother's girlfriend accused him of attacking her.[130] After his arrest, he faced a court-ordered psychiatric evaluation, which concluded that he was competent to stand trial in spite of opinions about his "antisocial personality."[131] The trial was delayed, and before it began, his term expired. Criminal courts have a set period of 120 days to try defendants after indictments are brought, although various legal motions and court orders usually extend that limit. In Vanderbilt's case, his term began after the psychiatric evaluation was presented to the court in February yet the trial did not come before the bench until June 21, 1973, five days too late.[132] The appellate court thus reversed the conviction and released Vanderbilt from custody.[133] Delays and statute revisions potentially affected the prosecution of all felonies, and the issues in these cases demonstrate the legal similarities between rape and other violent crimes, even if there remained significant social differences among them.

Some of the cases analyzed here ended in rape acquittals even while the same defendants were convicted of lesser charges, which also affected sentencing. Although Karl Plewka, Reginald Blakemore, and Paul Watts were all convicted of some sex crime charges in two separate trials in 1972, all three defendants were acquitted of rape, despite the allegations made against them by the teenage victims in these cases.[134] Moreover, their original sentences were reduced upon appeal. The decision for Watts acknowledged a lack of violence in the case and declared his sentence unduly harsh, given the evidence presented at trial. The appellate court affirmed his conviction for indecent liberties and contributing to the sexual delinquency of a minor, but it modified the sentence, making Watts eligible for parole two years earlier than he otherwise would have been.[135] When the court of appeals heard arguments in Plewka's and Blakemore's case, it reduced the charges against them and vacated the original sentences. The court asserted that the indecent liberties statue was designed to protect "innocent children from the sexual advances of older persons," but that the evidence presented during this trial "supports the conclusion that she [the victim] was anything but immature in sexual experience."[136] The appellate decision recommended

sentences in line with the revised criminal code, which allowed a maximum
punishment of one year in prison for contributing to the sexual delinquency
of a minor.[137] When Roosevelt Bridges stood trial for the alleged rape and
robbery of Barbara Robinson in 1972, the judge convicted him of robbery
and sentenced him to one to three years for it but acquitted him on the rape
charge in light of the victim's inconsistent testimony.[138] The appellate court
agreed, declaring the victim's testimony "improbable, unconvincing and
contrary to human experience."[139]

While circuit-level acquittals and appellate decisions to vacate or reduce
sentences or even to overturn convictions were not common in the cases
analyzed here, they reflect changes in judicial responses to sexual violence
during the 1970s. In the cases appealed during the decades prior to 1970, the
higher court summarily dismissed or upheld the original convictions in 90
percent of them.[140] In the transcripts sampled after 1970, over 25 percent of
them had modifications imposed by the appellate court (see Appendix).[141] This
trend can be analyzed in different ways. The successful prosecution of different
kinds of cases suggests that more victims were willing to report rapes and that
authorities were willing to proceed to trial, even when the circumstances of
an attack defied rape myth expectations. Conversely, the lighter sentences and
occasional acquittals or reversals demonstrate that sexual violence remained a
challenging crime to prove, in spite of the legal and procedural reforms being
debated and implemented during the same period.

* * *

When expansive rape law reform went into effect in Illinois in 1978, politicians, feminists, and social activists had been debating the need for, and how
to execute, legal revisions for several years. Prosecutors and rape victims
within the courtroom had been disrupting traditional beliefs about sexual
violence for even longer. Rape shield legislation in Illinois codified challenges to historical rape myths, and while these reforms did not proceed
without disputes at both the constitutional and practical levels, the influence
of second-wave feminism here was evident. Shield critics tried to subvert
the intent of the law, arguing that a woman's sexual character and actions
were vital to understanding her resistance, or lack thereof, in alleged cases
of sexual violence. Feminists nonetheless continued pushing legislators to
further reform the law—to eliminate the "resistance requirement," thus placing the onus on the rape defendant to prove consent rather than placing the
burden on the victim to prove resistance.[142]

Legal reform was an important part of the anti-rape agenda, but it did not
constitute feminists' only attempt to transform American society during the

1970s. Second-wave efforts to shape a discourse on sexual violence began to challenge rape myth expectations, and this rhetorical defiance spurred changes in the practical treatment of victims outside the courtroom. Feminists recognized the difficulties women faced in reporting rape and sought to alleviate suspicions against them, even if victims ultimately refused to go to the police. They organized lay advocacy programs to provide legal advice and emotional support for women who had been raped and convinced them of the need for medical attention—both for their own health and for the possibility of pursuing criminal charges against sexually violent men. Procedural reforms in Chicago hospitals incorporated many feminist demands, even while they continued to adhere to the demands of the law. Respect for, rather than suspicion of, rape victims shaped medical practice during the 1970s, which saw the evolution of a uniform system to treat patient-victims (as far as it was ever possible to treat different individuals uniformly), whether or not they chose to report sexual attacks. The standardized rape kit remained an intimidating prospect for victims, but it nonetheless incorporated elements designed to lessen their emotional and physical distress while in the emergency room.

Anti-rape activism represented a potential arena for interracial and cross-class feminist cooperation, something that proved challenging during the identity politics of the era. Many white women had difficulty understanding how the legacy of racial discrimination affected biased prosecutions of sexual violence and could not comprehend why black feminists were sometimes reluctant to join the imagined bonds of universal sisterhood. Nor did they always appreciate how racists had long used the specter of interracial sexual violence as an excuse for the lynching of black men. In spite of chauvinistic demands from some African American men to ignore the realities of intraracial violence, many African American women refused to keep silent about it. They looked for ways to protect black womanhood, even while they continued to fight for equal rights and for black manhood as well. Women from different socioeconomic and racial backgrounds all faced the possibility of sexual violence, and many feminists recognized the need to work together in order to improve the treatment of victimized women in the name of equality. While this type of cooperation had its limits, anti-rape activists shared the goal of eventually eradicating sexual violence and, in many cases, collaborated with each other in order to achieve it.

While they lobbied to reform the law, second-wave feminists also hoped that challenging rape myths would affect strategies to prosecute sexual violence successfully. They encouraged the Chicago Police Department to hire more women and to implement sensitivity training for male officers so that more victims might be willing to come forward to report sexual attacks rather than fear that they would be doubted or dismissed by investigators. Feminist arguments found their way into Chicago courtrooms during the 1970s as well, where juries increasingly confronted their own personal beliefs as they considered the evidence presented in cases that did not always mirror stereotypical expectations about sexual violence. Often, prosecutors helped them in their deliberations by incorporating into their trial strategies the social arguments of the day. In doing so they demonstrated how the law still applied, even in the purportedly atypical rape scenario. Defense attorneys continued to use tactics designed to undermine the veracity of women's narratives and to call into question the investigative abilities of the police. The results of this varied, as reflected in the wide range of sentences assigned in the cases analyzed here.

When Susan Brownmiller researched rape's past with an eye toward "denying [its] future," she publicized a social revolution that many Americans had been engaged in for some time. The experiences of women during the 1970s in demanding State protections against rape—even if they had not been protected from actual violent attacks—were not unlike the experiences of women in Chicago trials during earlier decades, but neither were they exactly the same. Their attempts to assert themselves as deserving of judicial rights remained difficult to negotiate in male-dominated courtrooms, especially since prosecutors consistently added evidentiary support for their claims. Although necessary to prove rape, additional trial witnesses and extensive testimony beyond the narratives of victims and the police had the potential to reinforce suspicions about lying women rather than to aid victims in their pursuit of justice. Defense attorneys continued to exploit rape myths in order to push for acquittals, even though their efforts were generally unsuccessful in the cases analyzed here. However, a culture of rights that had been informed by civil rights activism and legal reforms designed to protect the accused was also increasingly shaped by second-wave feminists who demanded that rights be applied equally to women as well. Activism outside the courtroom thus shaped the narratives presented inside it, as prosecuting witnesses testified about what had happened to them and about both the obstacles and support they encountered from authorities and advocates following sexual attacks. The anti-rape revolution remained incomplete, but the impact of feminist-inspired reforms helped to change the treatment of many victims of sexual violence in Chicago during the 1970s.

Conclusion

Ripped from the Headlines

During the spring of 1989, a horrifying story appeared in the New York City media before capturing the nation's attention with its appalling yet arguably familiar tone. For weeks, newspapers reported on the vicious beating and rape of a white woman, a twenty-eight-year-old investment banker at Salomon Brothers who was a graduate of Wellesley College and Yale University. Press headlines referred to the alleged attackers, a group of African American and Latino youths, as a "wolf pack" and coined a new term to describe their criminal violence: "wilding."[1] There had been several reports about a group of teenagers engaged in numerous assaults in Central Park that evening, but none were so closely scrutinized as the attack on an unidentified woman who had been out jogging when she apparently encountered the gang. Police arrested several possible suspects the night of her attack and five young men of color all eventually confessed, after several hours of interrogation. Although the District Attorney's office had little physical evidence connecting the suspects to the attack on the jogger, and none of the other victims of the "pack's" alleged "wilding" activities that night were able to positively identify them, prosecutor Linda Fairstein relied on their videotaped confessions to gain quick convictions in the jogger case.[2]

That same spring, New York City was fraught with racial tensions. Incumbent mayor Ed Koch had lost the Democratic primary election to African American candidate David Dinkins, who was then engaged in a bitter campaign against Republican Rudy Giuliani. Giuliani had not exactly concealed his disdain for black leadership in the city during this contentious mayoral race. As well, outspoken civil rights advocate Reverend Al Sharpton at this time remained vocal in his support of Tawana Brawley; Brawley was an African American teenager who alleged a racially motivated sexual attack at the hands of several white suspects, including local police officers, in nearby Wappinger Falls a few years earlier. Sharpton continued protesting racial violence when he targeted white residents in Bensonhurst, a Brooklyn neighborhood, while the Central Park case was still in the news. In August 1989, four African American teenagers had been beaten by a large group of white Bensonhurst youths, which resulted in the shooting death of sixteen-year-old Yusef Hawkins. Sharpton led a protest march through this largely white neighborhood shortly after Hawkins's death, where marchers were greeted with jeers, racial epithets, and local residents carrying watermelons to mock the demonstration.[3] Around the same time, real estate developer and local celebrity Donald Trump spent thousands of dollars to take out full-page ads in the city's main daily newspapers, describing how he hated the accused in the Central Park case and that "they should be forced to suffer . . . I want them to be afraid."[4] It was against this backdrop that New Yorkers confronted the crimes in Central Park and debated the wisdom of the woman's decision to jog there alone at night, even while they condemned the brutality with which she was attacked.

Ongoing controversies surrounding this case suggest that the connections between sexual and racial violence are still salient in American society, as is the pervasiveness of certain rape myths. A 2002 confession from convicted murderer Matias Reyes along with DNA evidence exonerated the men originally convicted of the attack on the Central Park jogger. A New York Appellate Court has since vacated their convictions, though only after all had been released after serving out their sentences. Fairstein, who originally prosecuted the five young men, nonetheless maintains that the suspects she tried were involved in some kind of criminal activity in the park that night, even if they had not attacked the jogger.[5] This may or may not have been true, but her obstinacy reflects the difficulties that justice officials have abandoning beliefs about racial rape myths. The immediate sensationalism over this story mixed public sympathies and outrage with a hint of suspicion toward the victim's actions.[6] Whatever else can be said about the case, and much has been, it mirrored assumptions about what constituted a "real rape": the persistent belief that true sexual violence is committed only against middle-class white women by savage black men unknown to them, even though statistics consistently show this to be untrue.[7] The victim in Central Park, after all, was highly educated with a successful career, and she was white. She was attacked by a black stranger or strangers, who probably *had* jumped out of the bushes while she jogged in the park. The victim eventually came forward to reveal her identity and to tell her story. Fourteen years after the rape, she told television journalist Katie Couric, "I am proud to tell you that my name is Trisha Meili. To be able to say this represents an important breakthrough in my healing."[8] Meili's decision to come forward is indeed a brave one, but it is also very telling that even under the most supportive of public circumstances, she was compelled to wait for many years before she (re)opened herself to suspicions about the circumstances of her attack.

Given contemporary speculations about the number of sex crimes that go unreported, it seems particularly relevant that discussions about rape recognize its prejudiced legacies. Many women of all races remain reluctant to admit publicly that they have been raped for fear of the hostility and skepticism they might encounter if their assaults do not conform to public expectations about sexual violence. Yet women in modern Chicago regularly came forward to demand their right to be heard and protected, in spite of the difficulties they faced. And they did so for many years before second-wave feminists pushed to reform rape laws and create advocacy services for victims. Black and indigent men are prosecuted for all types of violent crimes at higher levels than middle-class white men, but the former's convictions for sex crimes come with a long history of discrimination informed by racial rape myths. Black rape defendants in Chicago throughout the mid-twentieth century regularly confronted authorities over the mistreatment they faced at the hands of a biased justice system, a system historically shaped by white beliefs about their inherent criminality. Even when they were unsuccessful in gaining acquittals, as they were in the cases analyzed here, the strategies that they and their attorneys used during rape trials highlight a little understood aspect of the modern civil rights movement. Activists and everyday people have, for decades, mounted many challenges to rape myths, even if these myths persist in trials and in media coverage of sexual violence today.[9]

Yet the myths themselves do not reflect the legal requirements of prosecuting sex crimes. Sir Matthew Hale's cautionary tale against an overzealous condemnation of rape did little to affect the language of the law over time. While provisions varied slightly from state to state, the Illinois criminal code at the state's founding in 1818 reflected almost precisely the wording of its rape statue in the late twentieth century. Prior to revisions that eliminated the category of rape and replaced it with gender-neutral degrees of sexual assault in 1984, the law defined rape as "sexual intercourse with a female other than a man's wife by force or threat of force against her will and without her consent."[10] This language masked the complicated strategies employed in prosecutions of sexual violence and the personal difficulties victims encountered during criminal investigations and rape trials. Moreover, rape myths long informed by Hale's seventeenth-century admonition shaped defenses against the crime in the mid-twentieth century as well. Attorneys, judges, and defendants liberally interpreted the degree of force necessary to complete this violent act and whether a lack of consent was unclear under any given set of circumstances. Debates about consent revolved around well-established myths, which assumed that a woman's sexuality and her word were inherently suspect and that she would lie in order to protect her reputation.

Before corroboration standards became more precise during the 1960s, women were usually the first to testify at trial and provided the bulk of evidence for the State's rape cases. The victims analyzed here represented diverse class, racial, and marital backgrounds and were of different ages: there was no single type of rape victim, in spite of dominant expectations to the contrary. They had different religious affiliations and lived in different Chicago neighborhoods. The only things they had in common were gender and the attacks that they brought to the system's attention. Reflecting some common rape myth expectations, the transcripts analyzed here reveal that rapes successfully convicted often included high levels of violence, usually involved victims and perpetrators unknown to each other, and happened throughout Chicago—in the city's alleys and dark vacant lots, as well as inside homes, stairwells, or parked cars. Prosecutors sometimes called other witnesses to support women's allegations, but victims were at the center of these cases, and their role in the courtroom reflected their importance to rape investigations. Due to their centrality, judicial protections could no longer be awarded to only the select few but rather had to be more systematically applied as different women claimed their rights during sex crime trials that ended with convictions, which were appealed during the decades surrounding World War II.

The rules of the adversarial system limited how witnesses could testify, but rape victims pushed against those restrictions as they repeated their stories in ways that made sense to themselves. They insisted that they had been raped and that they were not complicit in their attacks, as mythic expectations about sexual violence often suggested they were. Defense attorneys interrogated the veracity of their allegations, but judges and prosecutors tried to protect them from severe personal attacks in the courtroom, thus destabilizing expectations about lying women. While the majority of the women who cooperated in the trials under study here successfully worked within a framework that did not always overtly challenge entrenched ideas about rape, contemporary feminists have overlooked their efforts and experiences when criticizing the system's dismissive treatment of sexual violence.

Feminists active in the anti-rape movement seek to disrupt a patriarchal structure that defines only some women as "real rape" victims because, as they point out, it is inherently unjust. That the court sometimes helped victims who did not easily fit into the real rape paradigm does not automatically negate feminist arguments about a power imbalance in the modern justice system. However, this research demonstrates the importance of no longer ignoring or downplaying the reality that different kinds of victims in the past demanded judicial rights and found support from local authorities and community institutions alike. Rather, contemporary legislators and activists could benefit from a broader understanding of how women laid claim to a criminal justice system that, historically, denigrated their allegations of sexual violence. This research offers a new way to view the agency of rape victims in the past who rejected suspicions directed toward them, cooperated with authorities rather than avoiding them, and who continued to push for public recognition of their rights as American citizens deserving of judicial protection. There may have been far more women who never reported sexual attacks at all or who were unable to help the State prove rape, but the ones who did reveal a shift away from a common law awarding of protection to only some and a move toward a broader claiming of rights than previously recognized.

It was, in part, the exceptionally harsh trial atmosphere that developed during the late 1950s and 1960s that second-wave feminists responded to with demands to reform social attitudes, investigative practices, and rape law. At a time when local courts were pointedly concerned with safeguarding the rights of defendants, rape trials evolved into a spectacle of judicial debates and gendered interrogations within which women's narratives got lost; so, too, did their authority as the centerpiece of the State's cases. Feminists in the late 1960s and 1970s promoted an anti-rape agenda that began to change the way sexual violence was investigated and prosecuted in Chicago. Procedural reform in hospitals was especially pronounced during this period, as activists encouraged emergency room personnel to change their treatment of, and attitude toward, patient-victims. Following the lead of the feminist lobby, lawmakers also defined new ways in which the rights and privacy of rape victims, as well as rape defendants, could be protected during criminal prosecutions.

While myths about sexually promiscuous or lying women conflicted with rape shield provisions articulated in the law, racial rape myths also clashed with provisions designed to protect the rights of defendants. White misperceptions about criminal black male sexuality informed the majority of rape cases that were successfully prosecuted in modern Chicago, but such myths did not go unchallenged in the courtroom. African American men and their attorneys compared the criminal justice system in Cook County with lynch-mob violence and discriminatory practices that were predominantly associated with the South. They publicly challenged police brutality during rape trials, arguing that the treatment they received from Chicago authorities was little better than how racist white Southerners, who sought to maintain social dominance through intimidation and violence, treated African American men under the rule of Jim Crow. They used the rhetoric of rights and fatherly protection in an attempt to undermine judicial prejudices. Civil rights leaders during the 1940s and 1950s began to pay closer attention to the prosecution of African American men when it could be shown that racial discrimination informed their indictments. As activists began to expose corruption among Chicago justice officials, African American defendants also shifted their trust to juries to exonerate them during the 1960s and 1970s rather than rely on judges whom they had previously preferred to consider their cases. Throughout the mid-twentieth century, black rape defendants fought against myths that defined them as sexually dangerous and argued that the system in which they were enmeshed was inherently discriminatory.

All of the defendants in the trials under study here failed to convince judges and juries of their innocence, but the sentences assigned to men convicted of rape reveal a pattern of racial discrimination informed by gendered prejudices. In accordance with historical expectations about sexual violence, white men were typically given far lighter sentences than African American men found guilty of rape, especially if the latter were accused by white women. Newspaper articles about the sentencing of men who did not appeal their rape convictions confirm this pattern. Arguments about criminal rehabilitation began to inform sentencing recommendations during the 1950s. While there remained a prominent racial distinction between the sentences men found guilty of rape received, defense attorneys presented pleas for rehabilitative sentencing in cases with defendants of any race in an attempt to assert equal treatment under the law. By the late 1950s defense attorneys employed new strategies in the courtroom that questioned both the validity of investigations and how women's sexual histories viably undermined the truthfulness of their allegations. Eventually, these strategies affected trial outcomes insofar as the typical sentence assigned to African American men convicted of rape in the 1960s and 1970s averaged significantly less than it had prior to and immediately following World War II in all but the most violent of cases.

By the 1960s, judicial precedents affected the prosecution of all types of criminals, which shaped rape trials in a particularly gendered way. Extensive expert testimony, increasingly required to corroborate women's allegations during this period of safeguarding the rights of the accused, introduced a level of complexity into trials that overshadowed victims' narratives. Greater reliance on male witnesses undermined the importance of women's testimonies.

Although the requirements to legally prove rape became more standardized during this period, widespread corroboration reinforced myths that doubted women's honesty in matters of sexual violence. Defense attorneys exploited this opening, especially when they cross-examined victims who did not fit stereotypes of believability. Judges contributed to the changed trial atmosphere by allowing attorneys more latitude to interrogate women's sexual histories, something that they had limited in the past. More women were coming forward to demand judicial rights, and prosecutors were bringing forward more cases, whether or not they fit the expected standards of a "real rape" during these years. The paradox here meant that while more women were being heard by investigators during the 1960s and 1970s, they were also increasingly disregarded when they spoke in the courtroom.

A belief that most women lied about rape was evident in the reasons cited for overturning circuit-level convictions during this period. To appeal a criminal conviction was a long process, and in most cases higher courts upheld the original decision. When cases prior to 1960 were reversed, appellate judges did so exclusively on the basis of constitutional improprieties and mistakes made by circuit-level judges who admitted testimony and evidence they should have thrown out. This process itself was problematic, given the supposed "color-blind" nature of the law, which dismissed how racial prejudice may have intervened in the decisions judges made during criminal trials.[11] Appellate opinions during the 1960s and beyond, however, began to cite women's actions as contrary to their accusations, and reversed convictions because of them. Although reversals on appeal remained rare throughout the period under study here, this major shift reflected the hostility that rape victims increasingly faced by the 1960s. The sexual revolution may have liberalized public understandings of appropriate sexual behavior in many ways, but it did not always help the women who came forward to report sexual attacks. Anti-rape feminists in the 1970s tried to help victims while simultaneously promoting freer standards of female sexuality, but their efforts did not always prevent the kinds of character attacks and defense strategies that invoked the power of rape myths during trials. The lasting influence of stereotypical expectations about sexual violence was evident in many appellate decisions handed down during the 1970s that reduced or vacated sentencing recommendations, as well as in the rare acquittal for rape, even while the same defendants were convicted for lesser offenses.

Racial rape myths continue to have a significant effect on the ways that Americans think about sexual violence today. Even more recently than the revelation of the erroneous prosecutions in the Central Park Jogger case has been the media attention surrounding accusations of interracial violence involving members of the almost exclusively white Duke University lacrosse team and the African American women hired to dance at the team's spring break party in 2006. The facts of the alleged incident are unclear but what all parties agreed upon was that members of the lacrosse team at Duke University, an elite, private institution in Durham, North Carolina, hired two African American women to perform as exotic dancers at a party hosted in a house located off campus. One of the women, a student at North Carolina Central University—a historically black public college also located in Durham—alleged that she was sexually assaulted by at least three team members at this party. Members of the team denied the allegations.[12] The other dancer told police she did not see any assault, but she also admitted that the two women were separated for several minutes and that a tense atmosphere in the house convinced them to end their performance after only a few minutes. The tension she described involved the use of racial epithets and talk about aggressive sexual activities, including one man indicating that he wanted to use a "broomstick in a sexual manner" on the women.[13] The district attorney in the case moved quickly to indict the suspects in the light of public outrage about interracial violence and class privilege in this historically divided Southern community.

And things did move quickly. The party took place on March 13, and the police were called to investigate complaints shortly after midnight on March 14. The alleged victim visited the hospital that morning, where sexual assault specialists examined her and noted her condition. Their findings included a description of vaginal swelling and rectal tenderness but "no abrasions, tearing or bleeding."[14] Such details follow rape kit examination standards, for which specialists are trained not to make definitive conclusions in their medical reports, a practice that has evolved since the mid-twentieth century. The female medical personnel who examined the woman later told the police that her behavior was consistent with that of women who have been raped.[15] When the events of this night were made public to the Durham community ten days later, pressure to respond grew. Duke University's president held a press conference to address the investigation on the same day, March 28, that Durham police executed a search warrant for the house where the party took place. The investigation revealed inconsistent evidence, including several different versions of events as recalled by the alleged victim, and a lack of DNA evidence conclusively tying the suspects to the assault. These types of inconsistencies are not unusual in rape cases and the district attorney, who was in the middle of a reelection campaign in 2006, pursued indictments against several team members. The rest of the lacrosse season was cancelled for Duke's team, and the coach was forced to resign on April 7. On April 15

the grand jury handed down indictments for sexual assault and related offenses against two team members, and a third set of indictments was filed
one month later. The investigation continued for the next several months, and
defense attorneys in the case issued several statements denying the violent
allegations. Eventually, inconsistencies with the evidence proved too great to
counter effectively, and prosecutors dropped the rape charges in December
2006. All other charges against the men were dropped the following April,
and the Durham district attorney originally assigned to the case was investigated for conduct improprieties. He resigned in June 2007.[16]

The significance of the Duke lacrosse rape case embodies the cliché that the
more things change, the more they stay the same. What had changed when
this case was brought forward in spring 2006 was that the black victim was
initially believed and her white attackers were quickly indicted. Rather than
uphold traditional class and racial privileges, Durham residents, of all races,
pressured an investigation of the type of interracial sexual violence that had
long been ignored by white Americans. That this occurred in a jurisdiction
in the South profoundly speaks to an evolution in thinking about interracial sexual violence, at least at first. Although perhaps politically motivated,
the district attorney's aggressive pursuit of the suspects and his decision to
indict were not unreasonable, despite the questions and controversies that
they have since inspired. The circumstances of this case are not unlike other
rape indictments, the prosecutions of which are often based on inconsistent
or inconclusive evidence. Unlike other violent crimes, forced intercourse is
mired in a legacy of myths connected to biased assumptions about women's
and men's acceptable sexual behaviors.

What had not changed, however, was how the tone of the Duke story
shifted as investigative inconsistencies came to light. The African American
victim's troubled personal background, including a prior short-term marriage
and a similar assault she had reported in another jurisdiction that was never
brought to indictment, increased the public scrutiny of her allegations in
Durham.[17] Media reports also made much of her part-time work as an exotic
dancer, which reinforced historic misperceptions about promiscuous and
dishonest black women. The social privilege of the lacrosse team members
who hosted the party was evident. Details provided by the second dancer
made clear an expectation of interracial sexual access, by force if necessary,
which some of these young men held. Yet before the charges against the
indicted (white) men were dropped, never were they referred to in media
reports in the same way that the alleged (black and Latino) Central Park attackers had been several years earlier. No discussions of "wilding" or of the
"pack mentality" of the alleged lacrosse team gang rapists appeared in press

coverage of the case throughout its entire meteoric rise and fall between March 2006 and April 2007. Moreover, publications about this case since it made national headlines reflect how rape myths about lying women continue to inform the public's thinking about sexual violence. Their titles emphasize "political correctness" and "injustice," but the books ignore the injustices that rape victims regularly endure when they publicly report sexual violence, especially if their racial and socioeconomic position is not as privileged as that of their attackers.[18] A single publication from another perspective, that of the alleged victim Crystal Mangum, inspired the opposite reaction: outrage against a "drunk and high stripper" who only wanted to make money off of the "sordid mess" that she created with her lies.[19] As this book goes to press, Mangum is back in the news, facing a murder indictment after allegedly stabbing her boyfriend. Media coverage of this new case emphasizes her record of misdemeanor convictions and the "false charges" she made against the Duke lacrosse players, reinforcing the portrait of a disturbed, lying woman.[20]

The treatment of rape victims in Chicago, and throughout the United States, remains imperfect today. Although there are legal provisions in place that should cover medical expenses for forensic examinations, rape victims themselves are often left responsible for the costs of expensive emergency room treatments that are not consistently covered by medical insurance. The American Medical Association (AMA) endorses the concept of a Crime Victim Compensation Program to cover expenses incurred as a result of forensic medical examinations and encourages states to adopt such plans.[21] In spite of this effort to help offset costs incurred as a result of pursuing forensic medical treatment following a rape, these types of programs are usually limited to patient-victims with access to no other forms of public or private insurance coverage. Moreover, the application for such benefits is extensive and confusing, not unlike other medical claims forms in the U.S. healthcare system, and does not guarantee full compensation for all patient-victims.[22]

A lack of insurance or other funds to cover medical costs has the potential to deter rape victims from seeking expensive emergency room care, in spite of the importance of medical exams for both women's health and criminal prosecutions. The AMA estimates that the cost of conducting a rape kit— including examining vital signs, taking a health history, collecting bodily evidence, and medical photography—averages a minimum of $260 for a fifteen- to forty-five-minute exam, and close to $500 for an exam that takes 120 minutes or longer.[23] These averages do not include the additional costs of processing laboratory results, which can be extensive. Criticism of former Alaska Governor and 2008 Republican Vice-Presidential candidate Sarah Palin's policies while she served as mayor of Wasilla helped expose this issue.

Her critics incredulously pointed to Wasilla's policy of making rape victims pay for their own rape kits as evidence that Palin's politics are anti-woman, in spite of her gender. In 2000, the Alaska legislature passed a bill to stop this practice when it "got their attention," but only after Palin had already served four years as the city's mayor.[24] Although the *Associated Press* indicates that Wasilla was unique in this practice within Alaska, such a policy is not unknown in many jurisdictions throughout the United States today.

Published guidelines acknowledge the high cost of forensic rape examinations and have looked for ways to deal with it. Some health care reformers have suggested that samples sent to State crime labs for analysis are usually not charged to the patient (while in-house tests are), but there has developed an investigative backlog, especially in urban areas.[25] In an attempt to eliminate at least some of the vast accumulation of forensic evidence sitting untested on police shelves throughout the city, Chicago feminists began raising money to have rape kits privately tested. The Women's DNA Initiative, founded in 2003, inspired broader legislative attention to this ongoing problem.[26] After promising to increase laboratory resources, in July 2010 Illinois Governor Pat Quinn signed the nation's first law mandating new rape kit testing procedures.[27] The Sexual Assault Evidence Submission Act instructs police to send all rape kits to State labs within ten days, that all kits must be tested within six months, and that police must develop a timeline for dealing with the investigative backlog, which remains significant.[28] The law does not, however, designate funding for its provisions, causing critics to question its potential impact especially in the face of overwhelmed labs and constant budgetary constraints.[29] But even in nations where cost is not a deterrent to personal medical care, such as in Canada, the medical experiences of rape victims and the long waits they regularly face in urban hospitals reflect the often low-priority position of women's health services within the broader spectrum of national health care.[30]

In spite of the high costs of health care in the United States, the standardized rape kit has been important in shaping the prosecution of sex crimes. Procedural changes have also helped undermine the kinds of skepticism directed toward patient-victims that was often evident in medico-legal literature and among women's rape trial narratives prior to such reform. This is not to suggest, however, that contemporary rape kit procedures are simple or easy for women to endure. The process involves specific and complex rules about gathering a variety of evidence, including hair, saliva, and semen samples from a woman's clothes and body. While emergency room physicians are supposed to be trained to treat patient-victims with sensitivity and they are not supposed to be kept waiting in a general area, emergency rooms are busy places, often without extra available space. In addition, hospitals may be staffed with some personnel unwilling to use that space for victims of sexual violence, reflecting the legacy of doubt that raped women continue to confront in public spaces. Victims who are not at immediate health risk usually have to wait, as triage procedures dictate who gets treated first. Although advocates are routinely present during examinations, they cannot always influence the sometimes-impatient treatment of traumatized women at the hands of overworked doctors who need to move on to the next case.

Beginning in the late 1970s, some hospitals have since been experimenting with programs that would allow specially trained registered nurses (RN) to collect evidence in sexual assault cases. Advocates of this type of reform argue that the higher percentage of female nurses might alleviate patient-victims' discomfort at being treated by emergency room physicians, who are still predominantly male. RNs would also be able to take more time to conduct the rape kit, helping victims through the process without having to rush and more fully attending to their emotional as well as physical needs. Moreover, supporters believe, their growing familiarity with forensic rape exams could make RNs better qualified to testify in court than emergency room physicians, who do not regularly perform rape kits.[31] As such, their findings could not be so easily dismissed by defense attorneys seeking to undermine medical evidence or call into question the procedures surrounding its collection. Today, the Sexual Assault Nurse Examiner (SANE) program offers RNs specialized training on a regular basis. The Illinois legislature funded a SANE pilot project in 2000, and elected officials continue to support the program, growing the number of trained nurse specialists who conduct rape kits throughout the state.[32] While some emergency room personnel have always reacted more sympathetically than others toward patient-victims throughout the period under study here, the importance of second-wave feminism and its influences on hospital procedures involving victims of sexual violence cannot be overlooked in the twenty-first century.

Feminist activism has also had an important effect on contemporary legal reforms in the United States. Although controversial from its outset, the effect of rape shield legislation on criminal trials has proved significant. Examining the effects of Illinois's "strong" shield laws after their implementation in 1978, researchers Spohn and Horney observed important changes in how judicial authorities interpreted the circumstances surrounding hypothetical rape scenarios. When asked to evaluate potential trial scenarios, they found that most judges would not admit evidence regarding a woman's consensual encounters with men she met at a bar, even if that same woman was in court to testify about allegedly being raped by another man she met at a bar. Authorities commented that this type of defense tactic, which had been regularly offered and accepted into evidence in the trials under study here, was "the classic example of the type of evidence that shield laws were designed to keep out."[33] Spohn and Horney propose that their findings "reflect both a growing acceptance of sexually active single women and the educative effects of rape shield laws."[34] Conversely, presented with other potential circumstances involving victims and defendants known to each other and including details about their prior consensual sexual activities, judges also indicated a much higher likelihood of admitting such evidence during trials.[35] In spite of shield protections, rape myths still have the potential to shape the presentation of evidence in local courts.

This does not mean, however, that rape shield provisions have not repeatedly withstood constitutional challenges. In 2004 the Illinois Supreme Court upheld local shield laws and overturned an order for a new trial for Robert Santos, who had been convicted of rape in 1999. Santos had been granted a new trial after his attorney brought forward evidence that demonstrated the victim had lied, prior to her courtroom testimony, about having sexual relations with anyone besides the defendant the night of the attack. Defense counsel argued that this called into question her credibility as a prosecuting witness, and the appellate court agreed. The Illinois Supreme Court, however, reversed that decision and ruled, "What matters is whether the victim told the truth in her in-court testimony, and referring to [her] prior 'bad acts' in order to raise the inference that a witness is lying at trial is prohibited under Illinois law."[36] Buried within the legalese of the decision is a defense of the victim's privacy that rape shield legislation was originally designed to safeguard.

The transition from common law rewards to judicial rights was difficult to negotiate for Chicago residents who found themselves unwillingly engaged in the criminal justice system as either victims or perpetrators of sexual violence. Rape myths and racial stereotypes did not prevent individuals from challenging public expectations about their involvement, or lack thereof, in sexual crimes throughout the mid-twentieth century. All types of women spoke out about rape and found support for their accusations, even if that support was not always sensitive to the trauma that sexual violence imposed on them. They presented themselves as capable citizens who were not complicit in sexual attacks and who did not deserve to have their narratives dismissed by a male-dominated justice system, in spite of their race, marital status, or socioeconomic background. African American rape defendants challenged a system that discriminated against them by comparing it to Southern-style racial hierarchies with which Northern urban areas denied association. They found limited support inside the courtroom, but their arguments became embedded in the discourse of a growing civil rights movement, of which the Chicago area was an important part. In spite of the difficulties they faced, it is clear that many people spoke out against rape during a period when they enjoyed little institutionalized support to help them navigate the complexities of sex crime trials. While that support has grown in recent decades, historic myths about race, gender, and sexual violence still uncomfortably intervene in sensationalized media coverage of sex crimes and in the contemporary justice system, forcing us to continue to confront and challenge our own understandings of rape.

Appendix
Case File Data

Racial abbreviations: W = Anglo (white); B = African American (black);
O = Other (race unclear)

*Sentencing on multiple counts ran concurrently, unless otherwise indicated.
Sentencing for embedded indictments without sexual intent (including robbery,
burglary, aggravated assault, aggravated kidnapping, unlawful restraint) not listed
unless otherwise noted.

Felony Sex Crimes, 1936–1976

Year-case file	Defendant(s)	Race	Sex crime indictment(s)	Main Defense	*Sentence	Appellate decision
37-1477	Robert Conroy	W	Rape, crime v. nature	Mistaken ID	199 years	Summarily dismissed
43-1267	Samuel Wright	B	Rape	Mistaken ID	50 years	Summarily dismissed
46-1056	Harrison Stewart	B	Rape	Alibi	Life	Judgment affirmed
46-2055	Willie Lewis	B	Rape	Alibi	12 years	Summarily dismissed
48-1925	Charles Hughes	B	Assault with intent	Mistaken ID	6-8 years	Summarily dismissed
48-1949	Lorce Jones	B	Rape	Mistaken ID	35 years	Summarily dismissed
49-0064-0066 (3 counts)	Maynard McAfree	B	Rape, crime v. nature	Plea change (guilty)	25, 25 years, 5–10 years	Not eligible on appeal
49-0205	Coleman Sepe	W	Rape	Consent	35 years	Summarily dismissed
50-1545	Marvin Chukes	B	Rape	Alibi	5 years	Summarily dismissed
51-0200	John Ingraham	B	Rape	Consent	20 years	Summarily dismissed
	James Ethridge	B			30 years	
51-1709	John Jackson	B	Rape	Mistaken ID	50 years	Judgment affirmed
52-1158	Roger Williams	B	Rape	Alibi	Life	Summarily dismissed
52-1626	Harold Hiller	W	Rape	Consent	25 years	Reversed/remanded
	Ralph Liljeblad	W			25 years	
52-1976	Frank Teti	W	Rape	Consent	13 years	Judgment affirmed
	Dominic DiBiaso	W			4 years	
53-1094	Theodore Shok	W	Rape	Consent	5–10 years	Reversed/remanded
54-1294	James Jeffrey, Jr.	B	Rape	Alibi	20 years	Summarily dismissed
55-0225	Alex Ramos	W	Rape	Plea change (guilty)	20 years (each)	Not eligible on appeal
	Roy Davis	W				
	William Tortorello	W				
55-0282, 0283	Ernest Davenport	B	Rape	Plea change (guilty)	Life (each)	Not eligible on appeal
	Wesley Fields	B				
55-0881	Charles Johnson	B	Rape	Plea change (guilty)	35 years	Not eligible on appeal
55-1045	Golden McMath	B	Rape	Mistaken ID	25 years	Judgment affirmed
55-1707	Osker Hill	B	Rape	Mistaken ID	15 years	Summarily dismissed

Year-case file	Defendant(s)	Race	Sex crime indictment(s)	Main Defense	*Sentence	Appellate decision
56-0274	Michael Cirullo	W	Indecent liberties	Alibi	9 months	Judgment affirmed
56-1261–1264 (4 counts)	Donald Banks	B	Rape, crime v. nature	Mistaken ID	Life (vacated)	Reversed/remanded Acquittal
56-1829	James Wilson	B	Rape	Consent	5 years	Summarily dismissed
57-0874, 0875	Roosevelt Parker	B	Rape, crime v. nature	Alibi	30 years, 1–10 years	Summarily dismissed
57-2070	Dennis Kane	B	Crime v. nature	Consent	1–5 years	Summarily dismissed
57-2253	Johnnie Sinclair	B	Rape	Alibi	99 years	Summarily dismissed
	Robert Jackson	B		Mistaken ID	40 years	Judgment affirmed (Harvey, Jackson)
	A.C. Harvey	B		Alibi	99 years	
57-3438, 3441	Gerald Chatman	B	Rape	Alibi	60 + 60 years consecutive amended: 40–60 years 10–20 years	Reversed/remanded Sentence reduction
58-1977	Lawrence White	B	Rape	Mistaken ID	20 years	Judgment affirmed
58-2392	Charles Westbrooks	B	Rape	Mistaken ID	10 years	Judgment affirmed
58-2729	Leonard Pleasant	B	Rape	Mistaken ID	20 years	Summarily dismissed
59-0483	George Mack Sawyer	B	Rape	Consent	10 years	Judgment affirmed
59-1473	James Armstrong	B	Rape	Mistaken ID	50 years	Judgment affirmed
59-2522, 2523	William Oparka	W	Rape	Alibi	60 years	Judgment affirmed (both counts)
	Fred Oparka	W			100 years	
60-0376, 0377	Alonzo Austin	B	Rape, attempted rape	Alibi	30 years 1–14 years	Summarily dismissed
61-0763	Ronald Smith	B	Rape	Consent	50 years	Judgment affirmed
61-0918	Johnny Wilkerson	B	Rape	Consent	5 years	Summarily dismissed
61-3065	Robert Spencer	B	Rape	Alibi	3–12 years	Summarily dismissed
63-2846	Alexander Griffin	B	Rape	Consent	3–8 years	Judgment affirmed
64-0637, 0638	Sylvester Hubbard Jr.	B	Rape	Stood mute	40–60 years (each count)	Judgment affirmed

Year-case file	Defendant(s)	Race	Sex crime indictment(s)	Main Defense	*Sentence	Appellate decision
64-1864	Whitson West	B	Rape, attempted rape embedded in the indictment	Alibi	1–5 years (attempted rape only)	Judgment affirmed
64-3562	W.Q. Thompson	B	Rape	Mistaken ID	4–10 years	Judgment affirmed
65-0751	John Milton Kepler	W	Rape, deviate sexual assault	Consent	5–20 years (rape only)	Judgment reversed
65-1557	Freddie Jackson, Jr.	B	Rape	Consent	20–40 years	Judgment affirmed
65-2325	George Hankins	W	Attempted rape	Mistaken ID	4–8 years	Judgment affirmed
65-3443	Bernard Bendig	W	Deviate sexual assault	Consent	1–5 years	Judgment affirmed
65-3617	Ernest Hayes	W	Rape	False complaint	3–6 years	Judgment reversed
66-1129	Herman Burks	B	Rape	Alibi	8–13 years	Judgment affirmed
66-1515	Guarzee Gray	B	Rape	Consent	8–20 years	Judgment affirmed
66-2503	George Strong	B	Rape	Consent (solicitation)	1–5 years	Judgment affirmed
66-3506	Frank Evans	B	Attempted rape	Consent (solicitation)	5–12 years	Judgment reversed
66-3742	John Parker	B	Rape	Consent (solicitation)	15–30 years	Judgment affirmed
66-4070	Francis Oldsby	B	Deviate sexual assault, attempted rape	Consent (solicitation)	5–10 years	Judgment affirmed
67-0439	Osborn Fortson	B	Rape, deviate sexual assault	Alibi	20–40 years / 10–14 years	Judgment affirmed
67-1095	Eddie James Virgin	B	Rape	Stood mute	5–15 years	Judgment affirmed
67-1998	Frank Bruno	W	Rape	Consent	3–8 years	Judgment reversed
67-2774	Ben Murphy	B	Rape	Consent (solicitation)	2–4 years	Summarily dismissed
67-3371	Ralph Adams	B	Rape	Mistaken ID	2–4 years	Judgment affirmed
67-3569	Arne Sails	B	Rape	Mistaken ID	5–20 years	Judgment affirmed
68-0033	Kenny McCarroll	B	Deviate sexual assault	Alibi	5–7 years	Judgment affirmed
68-1207	Maurice Haynes	B	Rape	Alibi	4–10 years	Judgment affirmed
68-2351	Isaac Griggs	B	Rape	Consent (solicitation)	4–8 years	Judgment affirmed
68-4426	Eugene Hawkins	B	Rape	Consent	6–10 years	Judgment affirmed
69-0395	Roosevelt Flournoy, Jr.	B	Rape	Consent (solicitation)	5–10 years	Judgment affirmed

Year-case file	Defendant(s)	Race	Sex crime indictment(s)	Main Defense	*Sentence	Appellate decision
69-1963	Roy Young	B	Attempted rape	Mistaken ID	2–5 years	Judgment affirmed
69-2832	Herbie Wright, Jr.	B	Rape	False charge	10–20 years	Judgment affirmed
69-3380	Louis Simental	W	Rape	Consent	4–8 years	Judgment affirmed
70-1194	Henry Pointer	B	Rape, indecent liberties	False charge	4 years 1 year	Judgment affirmed
70-2878	Kenneth Dalton Samuel Ames	B B	Rape	Mistaken ID	10–20 years 8–14 years (reduced): 5–15 years 2.5–7.5 years	Judgment affirmed, sentencing modifications
71-1244	Andre Clemente	B	Rape	Alibi	7–21 years	Judgment affirmed
71-2431	Sidney Robinson	B	Rape	Mistaken ID	Not recorded	Judgment affirmed
72-0205	Paul Watts	W	Rape, indecent liberties, contributing to sexual delinquency of a minor	Consent	6–10 years: reduced to 4–10 years rape acquittal	Judgment affirmed, sentences reduced
72-1003	Karl Plewka Reginald Blakemore	W B	Rape, indecent liberties, contributing to sexual delinquency of a minor	Consent	4–8 years 5–12 years rape acquittals	Cause reduced, sentences vacated: 1 year recommended
72-1521	Roosevelt Bridges	B	Rape, etc.	Consent (solicitation)	1–3 years (robbery only) rape acquittal	Judgment affirmed
72-2404	Arthur Clay	B	Rape	Stood mute	6–18 years	Judgment affirmed
73-1091	Ricky Vanderbilt	B	Rape, deviate sexual assault	Blacked out/no recall	5–15 years, 5–15 years	Judgment reversed
73-2156	Jerry Evans Eugene Davis Versie Gilmore	B B B	Rape	Alibi	8–20 years (each)	Judgment affirmed (with dissent)
73-2991	Jerry Johnson	B	Rape	Alibi	8–24 years	Judgment affirmed

Year-case file	Defendant(s)	Race	Sex crime indictment(s)	Main Defense	*Sentence	Appellate decision
73-3324	Delbert Scott	B	Rape	Stood mute	25–50 years	Judgment affirmed
74-0154	Paul Pavlik	W	Rape	Consent	4–8 years	Judgment affirmed
74-1068	Ed Flowers	B	Rape	Alibi	4–7 years	Judgment affirmed
	David Smith	B		False Charge	5–8 years	
74-2745	Robert Leyva	O	Rape	Consent	6–12 years	Judgment affirmed
74-4611	Bobby Berry	B	Deviate sexual assault, attempted rape	Plea change (guilty)	5–10 years 1–3 years	Not eligible on appeal
74-5566	Roland Shepard	B	Rape, deviate sexual assault	Consent (solicitation)	5–10 years 5–10 years	Judgment affirmed
75-0839	Amos Shaw	B	Rape, attempted rape, deviate sexual assault, attempted deviate assault	Mistaken ID	6–18 years (each count)	Judgment affirmed
75-2542	Albert Faezell	B	Rape	Consent (solicitation)	20–40 years	Judgment affirmed
	Calvert Faezell	B			20–40 years	
75-4184	Johnny Butler	B	Attempted rape	Mistaken ID	5–15 years	Judgment affirmed
75-5771	James Dvornik	B	Rape, deviate sexual assault	False Charge	4–6 years (each count)	Judgment unknown
75-6582	Jerome Genus	B	Rape	Stood Mute	4–6 years	Judgment affirmed
75-10391	Byron Adams	B	Rape	Alibi	5–9 years	Judgment affirmed
76-2578	Edward Reed	W	Rape, deviate sexual assault	Consent	4 years (each count)	Judgment affirmed
76-4586	George Jeffers	B	Rape	Alibi	6–15 years	Judgment affirmed
76-7159	Derron Sheppard	B	Rape	Alibi	7–12 years	Judgment affirmed

Source: Criminal Felony Transcripts, Criminal Case Files (1936–1976); CCA.

Notes

Introduction

1. Hale, "Concerning the Progress of the Laws of England," 153.

2. Bevaqua, *Rape on the Public Agenda*, 59.

3. Dorr, *White Women, Rape, and the Power of Race*, 4–7.

4. Several studies trace the types of cases most likely to result in either severe punishments or potential acquittals during different periods in Anglo legal history. The majority reflect rape myth expectations in various ways. For select titles see Block, *Rape and Sexual Power*; Bourke, *Rape*; Odem, *Delinquent Daughters*.

5. The historiography on sexual violence and the American court system is vast. For select titles, see D'Cruze, *Crimes of Outrage*; Goodman, *Stories of Scottsboro*; Smith, *Sex without Consent*.

6. Brown, *Good Wives*.

7. Norton discusses the effects of regional differences and gendered assumptions about power and piety on the creation of the nation. See *Founding Mothers and Fathers*.

8. Gutman, *Black Family*, 75–76.

9. Although resistance to these beliefs was evident among African Americans (slave and free) as well as some Anglos, it was not easily accepted, especially regarding interracial unions. See Hodes, *Sex, Love, Race*.

10. See Williamson, *Crucible of Race*.

11. Bevaqua, *Rape on the Public Agenda*, 159–62.

12. The rate in Chicago was about 17 percent, with 1,973 of 11,651 reported rapes recorded as "unfounded" between 1936 and 1958. Arrest rates for forcible rapes averaged almost 67 percent during this period. See Chicago Police Department, "Annual Reports." Arrest rates for forcible rape investigations in Chicago dropped to an average of 60 percent during the 1960s and 50 percent during the 1970s. See Federal Bureau of Investigation, *Uniform Crime Reports*, 1960–76. See also Spohn and Horney, *Rape Law Reform*, 67–68.

13. Brownmiller, *Against Our Will*, 190.

14. See Grossman, *Land of Hope*; Lemann, *Promised Land*.

15. On de facto segregation, black activism, and white resistance, see Hirsch, *Making the Second Ghetto*. On civil rights in Chicago, see Anderson and Pickering, *Confronting the Color Line*; Ralph, *Northern Protest*; Reed, *Chicago NAACP*.

16. Friedman, *Crime and Punishment*, 394; Pleck, *Domestic Tyranny*, 95–98.

17. Evans, *Personal Politics*, 198–99.

18. In their comparative study of rape law reform in six urban jurisdictions, Spohn and Horney found Illinois, as represented by Chicago, to have what they characterized as "strong" reforms (36–40).

19. Epstein and Langenbahn, *Criminal Justice*, 8–9.

20. Mohr, *Doctors and the Law*, 72–73.

21. Illinois Revised Statutes, chap. 38, stat. 11–1 (hereinafter IRevS).

22. IRevS, chap. 38, stat. 11–1 through 11–3. In 1887 Illinois's legal consent age changed from ten to fourteen, and in 1905 from fourteen to sixteen. See Odem, 14.

23. Prior to 1961, forcible and statutory rapes were prosecuted under the same indictment. The 1961 revision also changed the category of crime against nature (nonconsensual sexual contact excluding vaginal intercourse) to deviate sexual assault. See IRevS, chap. 38, stat. 11–1 through 11–3.

24. Select precedents include *Bean v. People*; *Sutton v. People*; *Addison v. People*; *Donovan v. People*; *Lewis v. People*.

25. The right to waive a jury trial in Illinois came first in misdemeanor cases and, after several decades, for felony defendants. See *Zarresseller v. People*; *Harris v. People*.

26. Friedman, 388–89.

27. Select precedents include *People v. Gray*; *People v. Allen*; *People v. Eccarius*; *People v. Cieslak*.

28. Select precedents include *People v. Sciales*; *People v. Burns*; *People v. Elder*; *People v. Peters*; *People v. Langer*; *People v. Vaughn*; *People v. De Frates*; *People v. Silva*.

29. *People v. Scott*.

30. *People v. Rucker*; *People v. Schultz*; *People v. Rickey*; *People v. Fryman*.

31. Select precedents include *People v. Ardelean*; *People v. Silva*; *People v. Perez*.

32. *People v. Faulisi*; *People v. James*; *People v. Smith*.

33. See Pascoe, *Miscegenation Law*.

34. Reed, 5.

35. Friedman, 218; Bevaqua, 17–18, 89. Susan Estrich discusses the history of rape corroboration requirements and the difficulties feminists confronted when lobbying against them. See Estrich, *Real Rape*.

36. Elizabeth Anne Mills, "One Hundred Years of Fear," in Rafter and Stanko, *Judge, Lawyer, Victim, Thief*, 45. See also Robertson, "Signs, Marks, and Private Parts," 345–47.

37. Hale, quoted in Brownmiller, 413.

38. On problematic and unsuccessful prosecutions, see Clark, *Women's Silence, Men's Violence*; Arnold, "The Life of a Citizen," in Peiss and Simmons, *Passion and Power*; Dubinsky, *Improper Advances*.

39. The Chicago Police listed crimes in two classifications throughout the years under study. Part I—violent felonies; Part II—nonviolent felonies and misdemeanors. See Chi-

cago Police Department, "Annual Reports," 1936–76. On difficulties prosecuting domestic violence in American history, see Pleck, 88–121.

40. Ploscowe, *Sex and the Law.*

41. Millett, *Sexual Politics,* xiii–xiv.

42. Brownmiller, 5 (emphasis in original).

43. *Ibid.,* 4–5.

44. Davis, "Rape," in Bhavnani, *Feminism and "Race,"* 59–62.

45. See Smith, *Sex Without Consent*; Dorr, *White Rape and the Power of Race*; Block, *Rape and Sexual Power.* In a non-American context, see also Clark, *Women's Silence, Men's Violence*; Dubinsky, *Improper Advances*; Vigarello, *History of Rape.*

46. See Estrich; Bevaqua.

47. See Edwards, *Gendered Strife and Confusion*; Hodes, *White Women, Black Men.*

48. See hooks, *Ain't I a Woman*; Williams, *Alchemy of Race.*

49. See Gilmore, *Gender and Jim Crow*; Schechter, "Unsettled Business," in Brundage, *Under Sentence of Death,* 292–317; White, *Too Heavy a Load.*

50. Feimster, *Southern Horrors,* 126–27.

51. See Marshall, "From Sexual Denigration to Self-Respect."

52. On statutory rape prosecutions, see Parker, "'To Protect the Chastity of Children'"; Robertson, *Crimes against Children.* On victims of incest and family violence, see Pleck, *Domestic Tyranny*; Gordon, *Heroes of Their Own Lives.* On male victims of sexual assault, see Scarce, *Male on Male Rape*; Mezey and King, *Male Victims.*

53. See Hoff, *Law, Gender and Injustice*; Kerber, *No Constitutional Right.*

54. The revised statutes replace the category of rape with degrees of sexual assault that use gender-neutral language and recognize different levels of force. IRevS, chap. 38, stat. 12–13 through 12–18, amended 1984.

55. Friedman, 377–80; see also Mann, *Unequal Justice,* esp. 25–73.

56. Michel Foucault discussed the relationship between producing truth and access to power in a series of interviews published in 1977, in which he referenced a number of his historical inquiries about language, sexuality, medicine, and crime. See Foucault, "Truth and Power," 51–75.

57. Federal Bureau of Investigation, *Uniform Crime Reports,* compiled annually.

58. Researchers estimate that as many as 66 percent of attempted rapes and 74 percent of sexual assaults not involving intercourse go unreported annually; see Rennison, "Rape and Sexual Assault."

59. On inconsistent crime reporting in Chicago, see Ward, "Orlando W. Wilson," 98.

60. See Hart and Rennison, "Reporting Crime."

61. Davis, "Rape," 64.

62. Bart and O'Brien, *Stopping Rape,* 86–87.

63. Davis, *Violence Against Women,* 6–7; V. Smith, "Split Affinities," 272–73. See also Rennison, Violent Victimization and Race."

64. McGuire, "It Was Like All of Us Had Been Raped," 914.

65. Ninety-three transcripts between 1936 and 1976 were analyzed: seventy-six of them involved one or more defendants who were racial minorities. In only one of these cases was the minority defendant not clearly identified as African American. See Criminal

Felony Transcripts, 1936–1959/1960–1976, sampled by author; Clerk of the Circuit Court of Cook County Archives, Richard J. Daley Center, Chicago, Ill. (hereinafter CCA).

66. On masculinity and the long history of civil rights, see Bederman, *Manliness and Civilization*; Estes, *I am a Man!*

67. For close linguistic analysis of rape trials, see Matoesian, *Reproducing Rape.*

68. Key defendants' rights decisions of the Warren Court era include *Gideon v. Wainright*; *Escobedo v. Illinois*; *Miranda v. Arizona.*

69. Reagan, "Victim or Accomplice?" 313–14.

70. *Ibid.*, 331.

71. Lewis, *Gideon's Trumpet,* 97.

72. Reed, 4.

73. Felony transcript records prior to 1926 were not preserved in the CCA. Although the first preserved transcript reflects a case that began in 1937, the crime and its initial investigation took place in 1936. Thank you to Phil Costello, head archivist at the Daley Center, for clarifying how these types of records have been preserved.

74. It took several months to fully staff the new Chicago Police Sex-Homicide Division, which began investigating cases in September 1937. See "35 Policemen Put on Trail of Rapist-Killers," *Chicago Tribune,* September 23, 1937.

75. Criminal Felony Transcripts, 1936–59, CCA. The transcripts were listed under the indictment categories rape and crime against nature. Since most attempted rape indictments were subsumed under a rape indictment, an independent search of attempted rape cases yielded no transcripts to analyze. Because statutory rape was tried under the rape statute prior to 1961, and cases of incest were sometimes also tried under the rape statute, and because crime against nature charges could involve male victims, there were seven additional transcripts listed during these years that are not included in this study. Male and child victims, as well as victims of incest, raise different issues and are not numerous enough to analyze comprehensively here.

76. *Griffin v. Illinois.*

77. Criminal Felony Transcripts, 1960–1969, CCA. There are a total of 119 cases listed during these years. I read every third transcript of rape, attempted rape, and deviate sexual assault, as they were recorded chronologically on the felony transcript microfilm reels. Among these indictment categories, seven transcripts involving incest and child victims were read as part of the sample but were not systematically analyzed for this project. I thank Liz Pleck for helping me design this quantitative sampling.

78. The Criminal Felony Index records 267 cases of rape, attempted rape, and deviate sexual assault appealed during 1970–76 (inclusive). Due to legal revisions implemented in 1977, the years 1977–79 are not under consideration here, so an analysis of every eighth transcript allows for a more balanced dataset that does not weigh successful prosecutions during the 1970s more heavily than the other years under study. See Criminal Felony Transcripts, 1970–76, CCA.

79. A subject word search on "rape" resulted in 16,264 hits in the *Chicago Tribune,* 1934–76; see Proquest Historical Newspaper Database, online.

80. See Wendt, *Chicago Tribune.*

81. The controversy surrounding naming victims continues in contemporary scholarship. The Supreme Court has ruled that the first amendment protects the right of the

media to use names that are part of the public record, although it does not address the moral implications of that issue. See *Cox Broadcasting Corporation v. Cohn*

82. I thank Leslie Reagan for reminding me that this is what historians do.

83. IRevS, chap. 38, stat. 11–1 through 11–3: amended 1961; stat. 12–12 through 12–18: amended 1984.

84. *Chicago Tribune,* historical database subject search: rape, 1936–76. See also Flood, "Stormy Protest on Sex Crimes," 432–34.

85. See Breines, *Trouble Between Us*; Valk, *Radical Sisters.*

Chapter 1. Rape Victims and the Modern Justice System

1. Transcript of the rape trial of Robert Conroy, October 21–22, 1937, case #37–1477, *Illinois v. Robert Conroy* (1937), 3–18, CCA.

2. "Police Round Up Moron Suspects to Guard Women," *Chicago Tribune,* July 22, 1936.

3. "35 Policemen Put on Trail of Rapist-Killers," *Chicago Tribune,* September 23, 1937.

4. The Chicago Sex Bureau was headed by Assistant State's Attorney Samuel Papanek. "Beat and Rape Honor Pupil; New Sex Drive," *Chicago Tribune,* May 3, 1937.

5. Ramsland, *Beating the Devil's Game,* 76–79, 142–43.

6. "Beat and Rape Honor Pupil," *Chicago Tribune* May 3, 1937. On press coverage of the Brasy case, see *Chicago Tribune:* "Fish Knife Clew to Choir Singer's Moron Torturer," November 22, 1936; "Girl Fights Off Moron," November 23, 1936; "Ward Workers Join Hunt for Torture Moron," November 24, 1936.

7. Before the volume of dropped charges became too great to cover consistently, the *Chicago Tribune* reported numerous instances when sex crime charges were dropped due to faulty identifications and women withdrawing complaints or failing to appear in court to testify. Select articles include, "Teacher Fails to Appear at Rape Hearing," June 10, 1936; "Freed of Rape Charge," August 8, 1941; "Freed in Assault Case, Woman Drops Complaint," May 13, 1948; "Rape Suspect Cleared When Victim Recants," May 14, 1952; "Rape Plaintiff Recants, Suspect, 18, Dismissed," May 14, 1955; "Finds 2 Didn't Rape But Led Girl Astray," July 23, 1958.

8. Friedman, 390. The *Chicago Tribune* reported on plea bargains before they became too numerous to recount systematically. Select articles include, "Gets 6 Months after Charges Made by Girl," March 1, 1935; "Attempted Rape Charge Reduced," November 1, 1946; "Accused by Housewife Art Student Fined," June 7, 1949; "Charge of Rape Reduced Fine 'Abductor,'" April 10, 1953; "Freed in Rape Case 3 Jailed for Larceny," March 15, 1956.

9. Estrich, 8–26.

10. Prior to standardization, police districts used different methods to report crimes, making pre-1960 data inconsistent, but the only ones available. See Chicago Police Department, "Annual Reports," 1936–58. On inconsistent crime reporting in Chicago, see Chamlin and Kennedy, "The Impact of the Wilson Administration," 360.

11. Pleck, 158–59.

12. Thornock, "Military Trials of Civil Crimes," 92–94.

13. Kessler-Harris, *Out to Work,* 250–99.

14. See Hegarty, *Victory Girl.*

15. *Chicago Tribune*: "Arrest of Girls Under 21 Soars 64 Pct. In Year," September 17, 1943; "Reveals Sharp Rise in Crimes of Young Girls," October 10, 1943.

16. *Chicago Tribune*: "Crime Increase Over 1943 Cited By Commission," December 26, 1944; "War on Rapists Mapped as Sex Crimes Mount," August 17, 1945.

17. Cook County, which houses Chicago and its immediate suburbs, recorded a population growth of 29 percent, 1930–60. See U.S. Bureau of the Census, *Fifteenth/Eighteenth Census of the United States*: 1930/1960, "General Characteristics of the Population, by States," available at http://fisher.lib.virginia.edu/collections/stats/histcensus/ (accessed August 19, 2011).

18. Transcript of the rape trial of Harrison Stewart, May 16, 1946, case # 46–1056, *Illinois v. Stewart* (1946), 24, 28, CCA.

19. Transcript of the rape trial of Lorce Jones, December 21, 1948, case #48–1949, *Illinois v. Jones* (1948), 14–16, CCA.

20. Social Service Report interview with Maurice Brown, in case file #51–1709, *Illinois v. John Jackson* (1951), CCA.

21. *Chicago Tribune*: "Women Demand Action to Curb Moron Crimes," December 17, 1936; "75 Women Hear Moron Verdict Call Term Light," January 9, 1937; "Demand Action on Modernizing Sex Crime Laws," February 27, 1937; "Women Demand Harsher Terms for Sex Crimes," May 21, 1938; "Bill for Curb on Morons Put before Senate," February 1, 1939.

22. Transcript of the rape trial of Gerald Chatman, February 6, 1958, case #57–3438,3441, *IL v. Gerald Chatman* (1957), 52, CCA.

23. *Illinois v. Stewart* (1946), 57, CCA.

24. On this point, case law and legal practice did not always agree. A delayed complaint was upheld in *People v. Garafola*, establishing a precedent that was sometimes ignored, as in the case of Antonio Lopez who had rape charges against him dismissed because the alleged victim did not report the attack to police right after it happened: see "Rape Charge Dismissed," *Chicago Tribune*, July 11, 1951.

25. Transcript of the rape trial of Coleman Sepe, March 10, 1949, case #49–0205, *Illinois v. Coleman Sepe* (1949), 42, CCA.

26. Transcript of the rape trial of Harold Hiller and Ralph Liljeblad, October 7, 1952, case #52–1626, *Illinois v. Harold Hiller, Ralph Liljeblad* (1952), 57, CCA.

27. Transcript of the rape trial of Roger Williams, June 9, 1952, case #52–1158, *Illinois v. Roger Williams* (1952), 58, CCA.

28. Transcript of the rape trial of Samuel Wright, October 27, 1943, case #43–1267, *Illinois v. Samuel Wright* (1943), 6, 9–20, CCA.

29. Transcript of the rape trial of Charles Johnson, February 8–9, 1956, case #55–0881, *Illinois v. Charles Johnson* (1955), 111, CCA.

30. Ibid., 160.

31. Transcript of the rape trial of Willie Lewis, November 15, 1946—continued to January 8, 1947, case #46–2055, *Illinois v. Willie Lewis* (1946), 13–17, CCA.

32. *Illinois v. Jones* (1948), 33–36, CCA.

33. Transcript of the rape trial of Marvin Chukes, October 30, 1950, case #50–1545, *Illinois v. Marvin Chukes* (1950), 14, CCA.

34. *Illinois v. Jones* (1948), 30–42, CCA.

35. Robertson, "Signs," 346–47.

36. On wartime and postwar black migrations to Chicago, see Hirsch, *Making the Second Ghetto*; Lemann, *Promised Land*.

37. Transcript of the rape trial of Frank Teti and Dominc DiBiaso, December 1–3, 1952, case #52–1976, *Illinois v. Frank Teti, Dominic DiBiaso* (1952), 35, CCA.

38. *Illinois v. Williams* (1952), 43–45, 58, CCA.

39. IRevS, chap. 38, stat. 11–1. Gender-neutral language was not incorporated into sexual assault law in Illinois until decades later. See IRevS, chap. 38, stat. 12–12 through 12–18 (1984).

40. Medical evidence in the form of physician testimonies, stipulated medical reports, or victims mentioning hospital visits was present in 20 of the 34 (59 percent) of the transcripts analyzed during this period. See Criminal Felony Transcripts, 1937–1959, CCA.

41. F. Peterson, et al., *Legal Medicine and Toxicology*, 941–42.

42. Mohr, 72.

43. *Ibid.*, 21. On case law, see *People v. Schultz* .

44. Ramsland, 252–53.

45. Mills, "One Hundred Years of Fear," in Rafter and Stanko, 45.

46. *Illinois v. Stewart* (1946), 50–53, CCA.

47. Transcript of the rape trial of John Ingraham and James Ethridge, April 6, 1951, case #51–0200, *Illinois v. John Ingraham, James Ethridge* (1951), 46, CCA.

48. Transcript of the crime against nature trial of Dennis Kane, February 26–March 3, 1958, case #57–2070, *Illinois v. Dennis Kane* (1957), 31, CCA.

49. *Illinois v. Conroy* (1937), 139, CCA.

50. *Ibid.*, 141, CCA.

51. Transcript of the attempted rape trial of Charles Hughes, January 18, 1949, case #48–1925, *Illinois v. Charles Hughes* (1948), 3–7; CCA. On Catholic resistance to anti-Semitism in Chicago, see McGreevey, *Parish Boundaries*, 49–53.

52. *Illinois v. Hiller, Liljeblad* (1952), 5, 10, CCA.

53. Select *Chicago Tribune* articles include: "Crime and Punishment," May 5, 1937; "Death for Rapists," November 23, 1947; "Rape Charges Here Double in 5-Year Period," November 17, 1948; "Making Rape Unpopular," June 29, 1952; "Sentences for Rape," August 8, 1956.

54. Fourteen of the thirty-four transcripts analyzed during this period contained no medical evidence. See Criminal Felony Transcripts, 1936–59, CCA.

55. Medical costs varied nationally: this calculation is based on the average per-patient fee for a clinical study of venereal disease ($2), approximately 40 percent of the standard fee for a clinic visit in 1929. Jones, *Bad Blood,* 51. On minimum wage codes first set by the National Industrial Recovery Act of 1933, see Kessler-Harris, 262–63.

56. The difference in cost between emergency room visits and outpatient services accelerated by the 1930s as modern hospitals required more capital to operate. Stevens, *In Sickness and in Wealth,* 134. Rape exams might not result in an expensive hospital stay, but they always included a series of laboratory tests, each with its own cost. By 1940, for example, the cost of a single test for venereal disease, regularly performed on rape victims, was $13. Bailey and Farber, *The First Strange Place,* 101.

57. Numbers, "The Third Party," in Leavitt and Numbers, *Sickness and Health in America,* 236–39.

58. See Mills, "One Hundred Years of Fear," in Rafter and Stanko.

59. *Illinois v. Stewart* (1946), 47, CCA.

60. Leavitt, *Brought to Bed,* 40–43.

61. Reagan, "Engendering the Dread Disease," 1780–81.

62. Mills, "One Hundred Years of Fear," in Rafter and Stanko, 30.

63. *Ibid.,* 44–46; see also Mohr, 31, 73.

64. Transcript of the rape trial of Golden McMath, May 26–27, 1955, case #55–1045, *Illinois v. Golden McMath* (1955), 109, CCA.

65. *Illinois v. Teti, DiBiaso* (1952), 118, CCA.

66. Transcript of the rape trial of William and Fred Oparka, June 1–2,1960, case #s59–2522, 2523, *Illinois v. William Oparka, Fred Oparka* (1959), 115, CCA.

67. The discovery of the fisherman's knife at the scene was reported in "Fish Knife Clew to Choir Singer's Moron Torturer," *Chicago Tribune,* November 22, 1936. For police testimony about the crime scene, see *Illinois v. Conroy* (1937), 54, CCA.

68. *Illinois v. Conroy* (1937), 54, CCA.

69. *Ibid.,* 122.

70. Chicago's arrest rate for rape was somewhat lower during the years 1936–58 than was New York's, which averaged 80 percent before falling significantly after 1955. See Police Department, City of New York, "Annual Reports," 1934–1955. In both cities rape arrests were higher during these years than previously acknowledged by feminist-scholars like Brownmiller.

71. Drake and Cayton discuss the growth of Chicago's black community and white perceptions of the social dysfunction within it, including criminal activity; *Black Metropolis,* 174–213. On districts with the highest crime rates during this period, see Chicago Police Department, "Annual Reports," 1936–58.

72. *Chicago Tribune:* "Moron Rapes Girl Artist, 25, in Loop Hotel," August 16, 1937; "Move to Guard Hotel Windows against Rapist," August 17, 1937; "2 Frail Clews Spur Hunt for Nurse's Slayer," August 22, 1937; "3D Assault in 2 Days Spurs Moron Drive," August 23, 1937; "Assign Special Guard in War on Sex Crimes," August 25, 1937.

73. "35 Put on Trail of Rapist-Killers," *Chicago Tribune,* September 23, 1937. On protective aid societies in Chicago, see Pleck, *Domestic Tyranny,* 95–98.

74. Skuzinski was raped in June 1952 and identified Liljeblad from photos three weeks later but was uncertain about Hiller's identity. See *Illinois v. Hiller, Liljeblad* (1952), 22, CCA. Robinson identified the defendants from pictures two weeks after she was raped in July 1952. See *Illinois v. Teti, DiBiaso* (1952), 39, CCA.

75. *Illinois v. Chatman* (1957), 13–15, 29, 47, CCA.

76. Transcript of the rape trial of Osker Hill, September 14, 1955, case #55–1707, *Illinois v. Osker Hill* (1955), 11, CCA.

77. Select *Chicago Tribune* articles include: "Teacher Fails to Appear at Rape Hearing," June 10, 1936; "Girl Victim of Attack Attempts to End Life," August 4, 1938; "Cop Is Cleared of Rape Charge, Girl Penalized," December 1, 1943; "Plaintiff, 20, Absent, Rape Charge Dismissed," August 1, 1947; "Woman Fails Court Date, Frees Man She Accused," June 8, 1948; "Victim Won't Testify, Free Ex-Convict in Rape Case," January 8, 1954.

78. Select *Chicago Tribune* articles include: "Identity Mistaken, Taxicab Driver Freed in Rape Case," November 18, 1936; "Suspect in Rape of Sailor's Wife Exonerated," August

24, 1945; "Freed by Judge, Robber Seized in 2 Rape Cases," August 3, 1949; "Rape Suspect Cleared When Victim Recants," May 14, 1952; "Freed in Rape Case by Identification Failure," May 5, 1956.

79. Cases involving male victims were rare and were tried, exclusively, as crime against nature or deviate sexual assault. See IRevS, chap. 38, stat. 11–1 through 11–3.

80. The right of representation was nationally mandated under Supreme Court decisions during the 1960s; see *Gideon v. Wainright, Escobedo v. Illinois*. These decisions were based on the due process sections of the U.S. Constitution, pursuant to Article V, Amendment XIV, sec. I. Informing suspects of their right to "remain silent" was standardized in *Miranda v. Arizona*, based on the U.S. Constitution, pursuant to Article V, Amendment V.

81. The use of gendered language here is deliberate, as women could not be charged with rape due to the wording of the statutes. IRevS, chap. 38, stat. 11–1. The reasonable doubt standard governs criminal proceedings in the United States. See Friedman, 11.

82. The corroboration element existed throughout midcentury case law in Illinois, mirroring precedents in other states. It was up to appellate judges to determine if a victim's testimony was clear and convincing enough so as to require no additional support. Select precedents includes, *People v. Elder; People v. Langer; People v. Hiddleson; People v. Trobiani; People v. Lades*.

83. Hazard and Hodes. *The Law of Lawyering*, lxv.

84. Friedman, 12–13.

85. Other Sixth Amendment protections ensure timely adjudication, the right to be informed of criminal charges against them, and to be judged by an impartial jury of one's peers. See U.S. Constitution, pursuant to Article V, Amendment VI.

86. Taslitz, *Rape and the Culture of the Courtroom*, 9. On gendered communication patterns more broadly, see Tannen, *Gender and Discourse*.

87. Grand jury members evaluate State evidence and decide either to return or to deny criminal indictments. See Garner, *Black's Law Dictionary*, 280.

88. Select *Chicago Tribune* articles include: "Acquit Brucker Rape Suspect, Jury Denounced," November 26, 1936; "Refused to Indict 4 on Divorcee's Charge of Rape," June 10, 1942; "Acquit Parolee on Charge of Rape Attempt," November 2, 1945; "Report Refusal to Indict on Hotel Room Sex Charge," March 1, 1950; "Father of 2 Acquitted of Woman's Rape Charge," November 12, 1952; "Gary Bailiff, 69, Acquitted of Forcible Rape Charge," February 2, 1955.

89. On general conviction rates, see *Chicago Tribune*: "Chicago's Sex Crime Bureau Model for U.S.," November 25, 1938; "Rape of Girl, 20, Latest in Rising Crime Series," October 30, 1946; "Criminal Court Sentences 1062 to Penitentiary," September 6, 1948; "58 Rape Indictments Voted in County 1st 4 Months of '52," May 7, 1952. On specific convictions and sentencing, see *Chicago Tribune*, online subject search: rape 1936–59.

90. *Illinois v. Conroy* (1937), 3–4, CCA.

91. *Ibid.*, 4, 39, 44–45.

92. *Ibid.*, 5.

93. *Illinois v. Jones* (1948), 7, CCA.

94. Transcript of the rape trial of John Jackson, October 25–30, 1951, case #51–1709, *IL v. John Jackson* (1951), 5, CCA.

95. *Illinois v. Williams* (1952), 15, CCA.

96. *Illinois v. Conroy* (1937), 5, CCA.

97. *IL v. Teti, DiBiaso* (1952), 36, CCA.

98. *IL v. Jones* (1948), 79, CCA.

99. A crime against nature involved sexual acts not covered under the rape statute. The wording of the statute was changed to deviate sexual assault in 1961. See IRevS, chap. 38, stat. 11–3.

100. *Illinois v. Conroy* (1937), 5, CCA.

101. *Ibid.*, 141A.

102. *Illinois v. Sepe* (1949), 26–30, CCA.

103. Transcript of the rape trial of Theodore Shok, January 11–13, 1954; case #53–1094, *Illinois v. Theodore Shok* (1953), 16–26, CCA.

104. *Ibid.*, 36, CCA.

105. *Illinois v. Sepe* (1949), 5, CCA.

106. *Illinois v. Teti, DiBiaso* (1952), 32–33, CCA.

107. Transcript of the rape trial of Johnnie Sinclair, Robert Jackson and A. C. Harvey, December 4–10, 1957, case #57–2253, *Illinois v. Johnnie Sinclair, Robert Jackson, A. C. Harvey* (1957), 23.

108. *Illinois v. Stewart* (1946), 35, CCA.

109. *Ibid.*, 22.

110. *Illinois v. Hiller, Liljeblad* (1952), 12, CCA.

111. *Illinois v. Chukes* (1950), 7, CCA.

112. *Illinois v. Teti, DiBiaso* (1952), 38, CCA.

113. *Illinois v. Hiller, Liljeblad* (1952), 19, CCA.

114. *Illinois v. Wright* (1943), 74, CCA.

115. *Ibid.*, 5.

116. Millett, 31–32; Strong, "The Hooker," in Morgan, *Sisterhood is Powerful,* 328–33; Brownmiller, 346–47, 388–89, 402–4; Davis, *Violence Against Women,* 8–11.

Chapter 2. The Power of Racial Rape Myths after World War II

1. Meeropol, *Strange Fruit.*

2. Margolick, *Strange Fruit,* 63–64, 68, 74.

3. Chicago Fact Book Consortium, *Local Community Fact Book,* 105.

4. Margolick, 17.

5. *Ibid.*, 56, 89–91.

6. See Edwards, *Gendered Strife and Confusion;* Gilmore, *Gender and Jim Crow.*

7. See Hodes, *White Women, Black Men.*

8. The highpoint of lynch mob violence took place between approximately 1880 and 1930. See Brundage, "The Roar on the Other Side" in Brundage, *Under Sentence of Death,* 271–91.

9. Discrimination in policing was not limited to Southern jurisdictions, and black officers regularly confronted bias on the job. See Dulaney, *Black Police in America.* On Southern police forces, see Bolton and Feagin, *Black in Blue.*

10. In the nineteen available transcripts from this period, eight were interracial cases

involving white victims; seven cases were intraracial involving black victims and black defendants. White defendants were less numerous overall, appearing in only four cases during this period, only one of which involved a black victim. See Criminal Felony Transcripts, 1946–55, CCA.

11. Reed, 179–80.

12. Wabash, Englewood, and Woodlawn police districts recorded some of the highest arrest rates per thousand annually, outside the nonresidential downtown. They were located almost exclusively within historically black neighborhoods. See Chicago Police Department, "Annual Reports," 1946–1955. See also Chicago Fact Book Consortium, 109, 114, 174–75.

13. U.S. Bureau of the Census, *Seventeenth Census*, "General Population Statistics: Ethnicity/Race/Place of Birth," (1950), http://mapserver.lib.virginia.edu (accessed August 19, 2011). The Chicago police did not delineate arrest rates by race until the 1950s, when the data recorded an average of 125 white men and 146 black men arrested annually for rape. See Chicago Police Department, "Annual Reports," 1953–58.

14. Estelle Freedman, "'Uncontrolled Desires'" in Peiss and Simmons, 199–225.

15. Select *Chicago Tribune* articles include: "All-Out War upon Sex Crimes Ordered," November 2, 1946; "Kennelly Asks Strong Law on Sex Criminals," August 2, 1947; "Leniency to Rapists," February 4, 1950; "What Rapists Deserve," September 6, 1952; "Sex Criminals," September 24, 1952.

16. Chicago Police Department, "Annual Reports," 1936–55. Most of these investigations ended in plea bargains, which governed the majority of all criminal prosecutions by the early twentieth century. See Friedman, 390–93.

17. Criminal Felony Transcripts, 1946–55, CCA.

18. *Illinois v. Stewart* (1946), 17–24, CCA.

19. *Ibid.*, 17–28.

20. *Ibid.*, 24, 32.

21. *Ibid.*, 50–52.

22. *Ibid.*, 20–22.

23. IRevS, chap. 38, stat. 11–1.

24. *Illinois v. Stewart* (1946), 23, CCA.

25. Bevaqua, 9–10, 59.

26. *Illinois v. Stewart* (1946), 31, CCA.

27. *Illinois v. Jones* (1948), 4–7, 13, CCA.

28. Transcript of the sentencing hearing of Maynard McAfee, ultimately pleaded guilty to three counts of rape and crime against nature, March 14, 1949, cases 49–0064, 65, 66; *Illinois v. Maynard McAfee* (1949), 2–7, CCA.

29. *Illinois v. McMath* (1955), 41–50, 66, CCA.

30. Chicago Fact Book Consortium, 114–16, 172–77. On postwar urban migrations and shifting racial boundaries, see Hirsch, *Making the Second Ghetto*.

31. The white defendants in case #55–0225 began their trial with an alibi defense but later switched to guilty pleas. Transcript of the rape trial of Roy Davis, Alex Ramos, William Tortorello, June 23–27, 1955, case #55–0225, *Illinois v. Roy Davis, Alex Ramos, William Tortorello* (1955), 64, CCA.

32. *Illinois v. Teti, DiBiaso*, (1952), 29, CCA.

33. Of the ninety-three cases analyzed in this study, one involved white defendants accused of raping an African American victim and one involved a victim whose racial status was unclear, but possibly Latina. See case #52–1976, *Illinois v. Teti, DiBiaso* (1952); case #69–3380, *Illinois v. Louis Simental* (1969), CCA. On race and criminal sexual violence trends more broadly, see Davis, "Rape" 50–51; LaFree, *Rape and Criminal Justice.*

34. *Chicago Tribune,* online subject search: rape, 1946–55. On racial status and postwar newspaper reporting trends, see Flood, 432.

35. Although Chicago had no laws against interracial marriage as many Southern jurisdictions did, the city's residents frowned upon such unions. See Drake and Cayton, 129.

36. Of the 288 cases closely examined, Dorr found that 230 of them (87 percent) resulted in convictions. See Dorr, 5, 151–58.

37. Evelyn Brooks Higginbotham, "African-American Women's History," in Scott, *Feminism and History,* 184.

38. *Illinois v. Jackson* (1951), 22,

39. Built to address wartime housing shortages and to maintain de facto racial segregation, the Ida B. Wells Homes and the Chicago Housing Authority became postwar targets of whites who decried the growing urban crime rate, and of civil rights leaders who challenged city officials to live up to court decisions mandating open housing practices. On public housing and black activism, see Knupfer, *Chicago Black Renaissance,* 9–10, 116–35. On postwar white resistance to public housing integration, see Hirsch, "Massive Resistance," 522–60.

40. African American defendants constituted the majority of appeals during the entire period under review, appearing in 75 of the 93 transcripts analyzed between 1936–76 with an additional case involving a nonblack racial minority defendant (80.6 percent). See Criminal Felony Transcripts, 1936–59/1960–76, sampled by author, CCA. Of the fifteen available transcripts involving black defendants that took place during the immediate post–World War II decade, eleven used public defenders or court-appointed attorneys. See Criminal Felony Transcripts, 1946–55, CCA.

41. Pro bono attorneys did not regularly appear in Chicago criminal courts until the 1960s, but Cook County had established its public defender system by 1930, guaranteeing legal counsel to all criminal defendants regardless of economic status. See Friedman, 394.

42. *Illinois v. Stewart* (1946), 36, CCA.

43. Four of the eleven defendants who used public defenders during this decade retained Branion's services. See case nos. 46–2055, *Illinois v. Lewis*; 48–1949, *Illinois v. Jones*; 51–0200, *Illinois v. Ingraham, Ethridge*; 54–1294, *Illinois v. Jeffery, Jr.,* Criminal Felony Transcripts, 1946–55, CCA. On Branion's historic appointment, see D'Amato, "The Ultimate Injustice," 3.

44. Census tracts indicate that Cook County's black population doubled between 1910 and 1920, from approximately 2 percent of the total population (46,627/2,405,233) to just below 4 percent of the total population (115,238/3,053,017). See U.S. Bureau of the Census, *Thirteenth-Fourteenth Census,* "General Population: Ethnicity/Race/Place of Birth," (1910–1920), http://mapserver.lib.virginia.edu (accessed August 19, 2011).

45. African Americans constituted just over 6 percent of Cook County's total population in 1940 (249,157/4,063,342) and approximately 11.5 percent in 1950 (520,979/4,508,792). See

U.S. Bureau of the Census, *Sixteenth-Seventeenth Census,* "General Population Statistics: Ethnicity/Race/Place of Birth," (1940–1950), http://mapserver.lib.virginia.edu (accessed August 19, 2011). On the mechanization of agriculture, see Lee, *For Freedom's Sake,* 124.

46. On the National Urban League in Chicago, see Strickland, *History of the Chicago Urban League;* on the NAACP, see Reed, 5, 128–60.

47. Letter to Miss Cleola Johnson from Sidney A. Jones Jr., Chairman, Legal Redress Committee, NAACP, dated March 22, 1949. Papers of the NAACP, pt. 8: "Discrimination in the Criminal Justice System, 1910–1955—Series B," Legal Department and Central Office Records, 1940–55, reel #24, file folder frame #0329.

48. *Illinois v. Stewart* (1946), 21–22, CCA.

49. *Ibid.,* 40, CCA.

50. *Ibid.,* 36–38, CCA.

51. *Ibid.,* 40–41, CCA. When identifying a suspect, officers followed local procedures that were similar across jurisdictions. See Cahalane, *The Policeman's Guide,* 113. On Chicago police training and procedures, see Citizens' Police Committee, *Chicago Police Problems.*

52. *Illinois v. Jones* (1948), 26, 47–48, 66, CCA.

53. Chicago Fact Book Consortium, 177.

54. *Ibid.,* 109–10, 176.

55. *Illinois v. Jones* (1948), 25–29, CCA.

56. *Chicago Tribune:* "Evanston Head to File Report on Sex Crimes," September 22, 1945; "Confesses Rape of 4 Women, Attempt on 5th in Chicago Heights," October 17, 1945; "Three Evanston Women to View Rapist of Four," October 18, 1945. On racial profiling and postwar print media, see Flood, 434–35.

57. *Illinois v. Jones* (1948), 36–39, 51–52, 67–68, 97, CCA.

58. *Ibid.,* 87, CCA.

59. Select *Chicago Tribune* articles include: "1,000 Denounce Police Laxity in Rape Killing," September 3, 1946; "Alabama Rape Suspect Shot as 300 Mob Jail," May 2, 1947; "Negro Cleared of Rape Is Shot by Mob," October 29, 1947; "Florida Sends More Troops to Town in Riot," July 20, 1949.

60. *Illinois v. Jones* (1948), 17, CCA

61. Prior to 1960, six of the thirty-four cases under study for the years 1936–59 (under 20 percent) involved specific testimony about a lineup or identification through police photographs. After 1960, when court decisions began to scrutinize police procedure more strictly, 78 percent of the 59 sampled cases demonstrate that either the suspects were identified from lineups or photographs (fifteen cases) or their identity was not in question (thirty-one cases). See Criminal Felony Transcripts, 1936–59/1960–76, sampled by author, CCA.

62. Friedman, 404.

63. *Illinois v. Conroy* (1937), 3–18, CCA.

64. *Illinois v. Shok* (1954), 44–47, 108, CCA.

65. *Illinois v. McMath* (1955), 57, CCA.

66. *Illinois v. Chukes* (1950), 23, CCA.

67. Ida B. Wells-Barnett, "Southern Horrors: Lynch Law in All Its Phases" (1892) and "A Red Record: Tabulated Statistics and Alleged Causes of Lynchings in the United States, 1892–1893–1894" (1895), in Harris, *Selected Works,* 14–45, 138–252.

68. Bederman, 45–46; Brundage, "The Roar on the Other Side of Violence," in Brundage, 280–82.

69. Hall, *Revolt Against Chivalry*, 133, 201.

70. A now infamous example occurred during the U.S. Senate Judiciary Committee's confirmation hearing for African American Supreme Court nominee Clarence Thomas in 1991. Problematically, given his own privileged status, Thomas accused the exclusively white, male committee of holding a "high-tech lynching" over inquires about the sexual harassment charges brought forward against him by a former employee, Anita Hill. See Painter, "Hill, Thomas and the Use of Racial Stereotype," in Morrison, *Race-ing Justice, En-gendering Power*, 208–9.

71. *Illinois v. Stewart* (1946), 1, 23, CCA.

72. The U.S. Supreme Court upheld the right for defendants to waive their right to trial by jury in *Patton v. U.S.* .

73. Friedman, 388–89.

74. *Illinois v. Hughes* (1948), 1, CCA.

75. These defendants all waived their right to a jury trial before later changing their original not guilty pleas. See *Illinois v. McAfee* (1949), 1; transcript of the rape trial of Ernest Davenport and Wesley Fields, April 5, 1955, case #55–0082–0083, *Illinois v. Ernest Davenport, Wesley Fields* (1955), 1, CCA.

76. *Illinois v. Lewis* (1946), 2; *Illinois v. Jackson* (1951), 2; *Illinois v. Williams* (1952), 5, CCA.

77. Eleven of the fourteen cases involving black defendants during the postwar decade were heard by the bench. See case #46–1056, *Illinois v. Stewart*; #46–2055, *Illinois v. Lewis*; #48–1925, *Illinois v. Hughes*; #49–0064–0066, *Illinois v. McAfee*; #50–1545, *Illinois v. Chukes*; #51–0200, *Illinois v. Ingraham, Ethridge*; #51–1709, *Illinois v. Jackson*; #52–1158, *Illinois v. Williams*; #54–1294, *Illinois v. Jeffery, Jr.*; #55–0282–0283, *Illinois v. Davenport, Fields*; #55–1707, *Illinois v. Hill*. White defendants waived the right to be heard by a jury in three out of the five cases appealed between 1946 and 1955. See case #49–0205, *Illinois v. Sepe*; #52–1626, *Illinois v. Hiller, Liljeblad*; #55–0225, *Illinois v. Davis, Ramos, Tortorello*. Of the thirty-four total cases analyzed prior to 1960, twenty-six involved one or more black defendants and of those four (15 percent) were heard by juries, compared to four of the eight cases (50 percent) involving white defendants. On jury trials prior to 1960, see also case #37–1477, *Illinois v. Conroy*; #48–1949, *Illinois v. Jones*; #55–0881, *Illinois v. Johnson*; #55–1045, *Illinois v. McMath*; #59–1473, *Illinois v. James Armstrong*; #59–2522–2523, *Illinois v. William Oparka, Fred Oparka*, CCA.

78. On lenient sentencing, select *Chicago Tribune* articles include: "St. Charles' Inside Story," September 30, 1948; "A Judge of Real Estate," January 30, 1950; "How Stevenson Has Aided 200 Tough Convicts," July 8, 1951; "43 Defendants in Rape Cases; 20 Remain Free," December 9, 1951. On jury acquittals, select *Chicago Tribune* articles include: "7 Women 5 Men Acquit Grocer of Sex Offense," November 25, 1942; "Union Stewart Is Acquitted on Charge of Rape," November 18, 1944; "Truck Driver Cleared by Jury in Rape Trial," October 11, 1946; "3 Felons And Pal Acquitted in Rape Attack on Waitress," December 3, 1951; "Father of Two Acquitted of Woman's Rape Charge," November 12, 1952.

79. The Supreme Court found the practice of excluding potential jurors on the basis of race a violation of due process in 1935 but did not address the issue of peremptory challenges at that time. See *Norris v. Alabama*.

80. *Illinois v. McMath* (1955), 4–5, CCA.

81. *Ibid.*, 241, CCA. Peremptory challenges are allowed on both sides, but exclusion on the basis of race is constitutionally suspect today. On the legal definition, see Garner, 91. On case law, see *Batson v. Kentucky*; *Powers v. Ohio*; *Georgia v. McCollum*.

82. Drake and Cayton, 99–101; Spear, *Black Chicago*, 6.

83. O'Brien, *Color of the Law*, 89–91; Payne, *I've Got the Light of Freedom*, 427–29.

84. *Illinois v. Stewart* (1946), 4, CCA.

85. On the significance of family following World War II, see May, *Homeward Bound*; on the father as breadwinner and family protector, see Griswold, *Fatherhood in America*.

86. *Illinois v. Jones* (1948), 72–73, CCA.

87. *Illinois v. Jeffery, Jr.* (1954), 17–22, CCA.

88. *Illinois v. Johnson* (1955), 130–39, CCA.

89. The Pendleton Act (1883) created civil service reform and reflected timely professionalization trends in the United States. The Chicago police force was brought under the rubric of civil service in 1885. Although this did not end the corruption rooted in the political patronage system, it reflected national progressive impulses. See Friedman, 360.

90. Moss, *Moss' Chicago Police Manual*, 254.

91. National Commission on Law Observance and Enforcement (the Wickersham Commission), Eleventh Report, "Lawlessness in Law Enforcement" (1930).

92. Adams, *Training for the Police Service*, 55.

93. Cahalane, 87–88.

94. *Escobedo v. Illinois*.

95. *Ziang Sung Wan v. U.S.* .

96. Case #43–1467, Criminal Felony Indictment Records, CCA.

97. *Illinois v. Stewart* (1946), 10, CCA.

98. *Ibid.*, (1946), 8, CCA.

99. *Illinois v. Ingraham, Ethridge* (1951), 103, CCA.

100. *Illinois v. Johnson* (1955), 152, CCA.

101. *Chicago Defender*, online subject search: rape, 1946–55.

102. On police misconduct and judicial decisions, select *Chicago Tribune* articles include: "Woman Names Attack Suspect as Purse Thief," May 3, 1943; "Rapist Guilty Gets 25 Years in Second Trial," September 16, 1955. The series on the police department appeared in the *Chicago Tribune*: "Visitor Finds Uneasiness in Police Station," August 30, 1952; "Hyde Park Gives Up Complaints; Now Aids Cops," September 8, 1952; "Wabash Police Talk a Good Job; Records Differ," September 9, 1952.

103. On lynching numbers, see Brundage, "Introduction," in Brundage, 3–4; on interracial rape myths used to justify mob violence, see Dorr, 8.

104. Select *Chicago Defender* articles include: "Fla. Governor Denies Lynch Okay, Calls Sheriff 'Dumb' but Innocent," February 23, 1946; "Slate Whitewash Trial for Police Who Lynched Rape Charge Victim," August 9, 1947; "La. Sheriff Denies Mob Action Threat," January 15, 1949; "The Ways of White Folks," September 17, 1955.

105. Select *Chicago Tribune* articles include: "Tells of Hiding 2 Negroes from Tennessee Mob," September 28, 1946; "Hunt Negro Seized by Mob," May 24, 1947; "Mob Gathers; Rape Suspect Sped to Safety," October 13, 1947; "I Will Protect Negro Women Says Talmadge," December 4, 1948.

106. *Illinois v. McMath* (1955), 19, CCA.

107. *Illinois v. Stewart* (1946), 5, CCA.

108. *Ibid.*, 172.

109. *Ibid.*, 15–17.

110. *Brown v. Mississippi.* An expanded decision prohibiting extended suspect interrogations in federal trials was handed down in *McNabb v. U.S.* and reaffirmed in *Mallory v. U.S.* . Sometimes referred to as the Mallory Rule, these decisions collectively outlawed force to obtain confessions at the circuit level in accordance with the U.S. Constitution, Article V, pursuant to Amendment V.

111. Half-Sheet, Criminal Case File #52–1626, *Illinois v. Hiller, Liljeblad* (1952); #53–1094 *Illinois v. Shok* (1953), Criminal Case File Records, 1946–1955, CCA.

112. Half-Sheet, Criminal Case File #52–1626, *Illinois v. Hiller, Liljeblad* (1952), CCA.

113. On Chicago employment statistics in the first half of the twentieth century, see Drake and Cayton, 214–62. For national trends on racial discrimination in employment, see Kelley, *Race Rebels,* 164–65.

114. *Illinois v. Johnson* (1955), 128–39, CCA.

115. *Illinois v. Jeffery, Jr.* (1954), 37, CCA.

116. *Illinois v. Stewart* (1946), 132–38, CCA.

117. *Ibid.*, 131, 145.

118. *Ibid.*, 147–48.

119. *Ibid.*, 148.

120. *Illinois v. McMath* (1955), 174–76, CCA.

121. *Illinois v. Chukes* (1950), 56–57, CCA.

122. *Ibid.*, 59.

123. *Ibid.*, 61–62.

124. See Spiegel, *Make Room for TV.*

125. *Illinois v. Chukes* (1950), 80, CCA.

126. Case #48–1925 for attempted rape that carried a one- to ten-year maximum sentence, *Illinois v. Hughes* (1948), 168; case #50–1545 involved a youthful offender, *Illinois v. Chukes* (1950), 80, CCA. Sentences listed in Appendix.

127. *Illinois v. McAfee* (1949), 8; *Illinois v. McMath* (1955), 241; *Illinois v. Sepe* (1946), 128; *Illinois v. Jones* (1948), 108; *Illinois v. Stewart* (1946), 36; *Illinois v. Davenport, Fields* (1955), 13, CCA. Averages tabulated by author, sentences listed in Appendix.

128. Roger Williams was sentenced to life after being convicted of rape in 1952. See *Illinois v. Williams* (1952), 83. On sentencing in the rest of the cases, see *Illinois v. Lewis* (1946), 66; *Illinois v. Ingraham, Ethridge* (1951), 138; *Illinois v. Jackson* (1951), 52; *Illinois v. Jeffery, Jr.* (1954), 49; *Illinois v. Johnson* (1955), 194; *Illinois v. Hill* (1955), 64, CCA. Averages tabulated by author, sentences listed in Appendix.

129. *Illinois v. Hiller, Liljeblad* (1952), 235; *Illinois v. Teti, DiBiaso* (1952), 385; *Illinois v. Shok* (1953), 268; *Illinois v. Davis, Ramos, Tortorello* (1955), 6–8, CCA. Averages tabulated by author, sentences listed in Appendix.

130. *Chicago Tribune,* online subject search: rape, 1946–55.

131. Kelley, *Freedom Dreams,* 159–62. See also Margolick, *Strange Fruit.*

Chapter 3. Black Victims and Postwar Trial Strategies

1. Transcript of the rape trial of Lawrence White, February 18, 1959, case #58–1977, *Illinois v. Lawrence White* (1958), 10, CCA.

2. *Ibid.*, 13–15.

3. *Ibid.*, 15.

4. *Ibid.*, 62–64.

5. Transcripts of the motions hearing for Lawrence White, May 5, 1959, case #58–1977, *Illinois v. Lawrence White* (1958), 33, CCA.

6. *Illinois v. White* (1958), 8; see also, *Illinois v. White* (1958), motions hearing, 33, CCA.

7. *Illinois v. White* (1958), 22, CCA.

8. There is a long historiography on black women's resistance to sexual stereotypes and the system's denial of their claims of sexual victimization, especially if raped by white men. See Rennie Simpson, "The Afro-American Female," in Snitow, et al., *Powers of Desire*, 230–33; Davis, *Violence Against Women*; Bevaqua, 11, 21–26; White, *Dark Continent of Our Bodies*, 33–37.

9. African Americans constituted nearly 12 percent of Cook County's population in 1950 and almost 17 percent in 1960. See U.S. Bureau of the Census, *Seventeenth-Eighteenth Census*, "General Population Statistics: Ethnicity/Race/Place of Birth," (1950–60), http://mapserver.lib.virginia.edu (accessed August 19, 2011).

10. Case #37–1477, *Illinois v. Conroy* (1937), and #49–0205, *Illinois v. Sepe* (1949), both involved a white victim and a white defendant. Case #46–2055, *Illinois v. Lewis* (1946), involved a black victim and black defendant. See Criminal Felony Transcripts, 1936–49, CCA.

11. A single trial saw an African American woman testify against two white defendants in case #52–1976, *Illinois v. Teti, DiBiaso* (1952), CCA.

12. Interracial cases involving white victims were fewer than 12 percent of those appealed between 1950 and 1959. See case #50–1545, *Illinois v. Chukes* (1950); #55–0282–0283, *Illinois v. Davenport, Fields* (1955); #55–1045, *Illinois v. McMath* (1955), CCA.

13. *Chicago Tribune:* "Freed of Rape Charge after 4 Years in Jail," March 24, 1956; "Judge Frees 3 Juveniles in Rape Attack," May 28, 1958; "Police Probe Clears Park Rape Suspect," July 7, 1956.

14. Davis, *Violence Against Women*, 6–7; Rennison, "Violent Victimization and Race." See also Free, *Racial Issues in Criminal Justice*, 12.

15. Statistics cited by the National Bar Association, an organization of and for African American attorneys founded in 1925, indicate that by the end of World War II there were just over 1,000 African American bar-certified, practicing attorneys throughout the United States. Statistically, few black attorneys could have appeared in any Chicago trials during the 1950s because there were so few of them. See National Bar Association, "History," http://www.nationalbar.org (accessed August 19, 2011).

16. "Citizens' Group to Hear Panel on W. Side Crime," *Chicago Tribune*, December 7, 1952. On black women's activism in mid-twentieth-century Chicago more broadly, see Knupfer, *The Chicago Black Renaissance*.

17. White, *Too Heavy a Load*, 183, 255; also see Hendricks, *Gender, Race and Politics*.

18. White, *Too Heavy a Load,* 198. On prominent women in the Southern movement, see Payne, 68–77, 79–105, 265–83.

19. On the life and politics of Daley, see Biles, *Richard J. Daley*; Cohen and Taylor, *American Pharaoh.*

20. Hirsch, *Making the Second Ghetto,* 68–99, 219–26.

21. Spinney, *City of Big Shoulders,* 213–40.

22. On Daley's maintenance of de facto racial segregation within Chicago, see Spinney, 204–8; Hirsch, *Making the Second Ghetto,* 12–16, 35, 186, 196. On the growth and decline of black political support for Daley, see Grimshaw, *Bitter Fruit,* 91–140.

23. Select *Chicago Tribune* articles include: "Hiring of 150 Cops Pledged in Sex Drive," April 5, 1950; "Declares Rape Reports Grow, Attacks Fewer," October 26, 1950; "City Rewards Urged to Curb Sex Offenders," October 23, 1953; "Convict 89 Pct. of All Tried as Sex Offenders," December 24, 1954.

24. "The Victims of Rape," *Chicago Tribune,* October 13, 1951. The *Tribune* was not always resolute in this policy, but after a 1947 lawsuit in a neighboring state, editors adhered to it. On the controversy, see "Editor in Court for Using Name of Rape Victim," *Chicago Tribune,* November 21, 1947; "Law Shielding Names of Rape Victims Is Declared Invalid," February 4, 1948; "High Court OK's Wisconsin Curb on Rape News," July 2, 1948; "Dismiss Charge of Publishing Name in Rape," October 8, 1948; "Badger High Court Refuses to Review Acquittal," April 13, 1949; "Wisconsin Assembly OK's Bill Broadening Ban in Morals Cases," May 28, 1949. On victim naming in Illinois, see also *Chicago Tribune:* "War on Rapists Mapped as Sex Crimes Mount," August 17, 1945, and "Police Protection of Young Criminals," March 2, 1956.

25. Flood, 444–48.

26. A subject search: "rape" + "black women" in the *Chicago Defender,* 1936–76, had fifty-three hits, only six printed before the 1970s, when black women's groups in Chicago began speaking out about the rapes of black women. See Proquest Historical Newspaper Database, online.

27. "Youth Who Went Berserk in Court Gets 120-Yr. Term," *Chicago Defender,* February 15, 1958.

28. *Ibid.*; see also *Illinois v. Chatham* (1957), 118, CCA.

29. Lerner, *Black Women,* 163.

30. IRevS, chap. 38, stat. 11–1.

31. White, *Too Heavy a Load,* 22–23.

32. Gilmore, 102–5; see also Giddings, *When and Where I Enter,* 7.

33. See Davis, *Blues Legacies and Black Feminism.*

34. White, *Too Heavy a Load,* 127–28.

35. Transcript of the rape trial of Roosevelt Parker, July 1–2, 1957, case #57-0874,0875, *Illinois v. Roosevelt Parker* (1957), 6–14, CCA.

36. *Ibid.*, 136–137.

37. *Ibid.*, 15–16, 59–62.

38. *Ibid.*, 114, 118.

39. *Ibid.*, 15–16, 58.

40. *Illinois v. Jackson* (1951), 38–40, CCA.

41. *Illinois v. Jeffery, Jr.* (1954), 16–17, CCA.

42. *Illinois v. Sinclair, Jackson, Harvey* (1957), 21–22, CCA.

43. *Ibid.*, 36, 143, 218.

44. *Illinois v. Johnson* (1955), 12; *Illinois v. Chatham* (1957), 5, 99, CCA.

45. *Illinois v. Sinclair, Jackson, Harvey* (1957), 598–99, CCA.

46. *Illinois v. Parker* (1957), 200, CCA.

47. *Ibid.*, 201.

48. *Ibid.*, 206; see also *Illinois v. Sinclair, Jackson, Harvey* (1957), 605, 615, 618, CCA. Sentences listed in Appendix.

49. *Illinois v. Teti, DiBiaso* (1952), 46–47, CCA.

50. *Ibid.*, 33–35.

51. *Ibid.*, 316.

52. *Ibid.*, 343–44.

53. *Illinois v. Kane* (1957), 22–24, CCA.

54. *Ibid.*, 96. Extensive case law cited the significance of immediate complaints and the corroboration requirement. See especially *People v. De Frates.*

55. *Illinois v. Teti, DiBiaso* (1952), 48, CCA.

56. *Ibid.*, 48, 77.

57. In legal terms, nonresponsive means the witness did not answer a question posed to him or her and is grounds for sustaining an objection. See Garner, 449.

58. Transcript of the rape trial of Charles Westbrooks, September 9–10, 1958, case #58–2392, *Illinois v. Charles Westbrooks* (1958), 36, CCA.

59. *Ibid.*, 36, 111.

60. *Illinois v. Jeffery, Jr.* (1954), 14–15, CCA.

61. *Illinois v. Sinclair, Jackson, Harvey* (1957), 51, 256, CCA.

62. *Illinois v. Johnson* (1955), 34, 68, CCA.

63. Transcript of the rape trial of James Wilson, October 25 continued to November 9, 1956, case #56–1829, *Illinois v. James Wilson* (1956), 14–22, CCA.

64. *Ibid.*, 22, 92–95.

65. *Ibid.*, 249–56, 262–65, 277–78.

66. *Ibid.*, 38–39, 271, 314.

67. *Illinois v. Sepe* (1949), 111, CCA.

68. Mumford, *Interzones,* 94–96.

69. *Illinois v. Wilson* (1956), 316, CCA.

70. *Ibid.*, 36.

71. *Illinois v. White* (1958), 88, CCA.

72. Transcript of the rape trial of Leonard Pleasant, October 28, 1958, *Illinois v. Leonard Pleasant* (1958), 171, CCA.

73. *Illinois v. Sepe* (1949), 114, CCA.

74. *Chicago Tribune:* "Girl Accuser's Story Frees 3 in Rape Cases," July 8, 1943; "Union Stewart Is Acquitted on Charge of Rape," November 18, 1944; "Truck Driver Cleared by Jury in Rape Trial," October 11, 1946; "Four Freed in Rape Charge," August 22, 1947; "Probation Granted Man Accused by Young Woman," November 20, 1947; "Gets 8 Months in Morals Case Involving Girl 17," November 19, 1949.

75. Of the twenty-six available transcripts for this period, eight cases involved white victims and two of these used consent defenses. See case #52–1626, *Illinois v. Hiller, Liljeblad* (1952); #53–1094, *Illinois v. Shok* (1953), CCA.

76. Select *Chicago Tribune* articles include: "Chicago Checks Rape Increase Survey Shows," October 25, 1950; "Cover Up And Be Safe," August 2, 1951; "Urges Death for Rapists in Vicious Cases," December 29, 1953; "Juvenile Rapists," April 20, 1955; "Sentences for Rape," August 8, 1956.

77. IRevS, chap. 38, stat. 11–1.0 ("futility of resistance"), stat. 11–1.5 ("voluntary submission").

78. *People v. Scott.*

79. *Illinois v. Hill* (1955), 4–6, CCA.

80. *Ibid.*, 56.

81. Transcript of the rape trial of George Mack Sawyer, April 20, 1959, case #59–0483, *Illinois v. George Mack Sawyer* (1959), 14–16, CCA.

82. *Ibid.*, 51–52.

83. Chicago Fact Book Consortium, 82.

84. Hirsch, *Making the Second Ghetto*, 35.

85. Relevant case law is typically grouped under the *Shelley* decision, but the Court heard several restricted covenant cases simultaneously. See *Sipes v. McGhee*; *Shelley v. Kraemer*; *Hurd v. Hodge.*

86. Hirsch, *Making the Second Ghetto*, 12–16, 35, 186, 196. See also Drake and Cayton, 182–90. On civil rights activism outside the South during this period, see Sugrue, *Sweet Land of Liberty.*

87. Chicago Police Department, "Annual Reports," 1951. Chicago's black population grew by 65 percent during the 1950s, from 520,979 residents to 861,146 residents. U.S. Bureau of the Census, *Seventeenth-Eighteenth Census*, "General Population Statistics: Ethnicity/Race/Place of Birth," (1950–60), http://mapserver.lib.virginia.edu (accessed August 19, 2011). On racial transitioning on the west side, see also Chicago Fact Book Consortium, 70–83.

88. Reed, 4–5. On criminal bias against the underclass, see also Mann, 166–219; Friedman, 377–79.

89. Reiman, *The Rich Get Richer*; Kelley, *Race Rebels*, 206–7.

90. *Illinois v. White* (1958), 20–22, 30, CCA.

91. *Ibid.*, 24–25, 33.

92. *Ibid.*, 47–50.

93. *Ibid.*, 62–66.

94. *Ibid.*, 77–86.

95. White had previously been convicted of armed robbery and was sentenced to 3–5 years. *Ibid.*, 92.

96. *Illinois v. White* (1958), motions hearing, 4–5, CCA.

97. *Ibid.*, 19, 27–28, 33.

98. Michel, *Children's Interests/Mothers' Rights*, 170–71; See also Gordon, *Pitied But Not Entitled*, 111–44.

99. *Illinois v. White* (1958), motions hearing, 34–35, CCA.

100. *Illinois v. Westbrooks* (1958), 8–14, CCA.

101. *Ibid.*, 34.

102. *Illinois v. Pleasant* (1958), 12, CCA.

103. *Illinois v. Westbrooks* (1958), 163–64, CCA.

104. Illinois Sex Offenders Commission Report, folder 339–13: Illinois Sex Offenders Commission (1951–52), box 339: Metropolitan Welfare Collection, Chicago Historical Society, Chicago (hereinafter CHS).

105. Illinois Sex Offenders Commission Report, Area V: Prevention; folder 339–13: Illinois Sex Offenders Commission (1951–52), box 339, Metropolitan Welfare Collection, CHS.

106. Illinois Sex Offenders Commission Report, Area I: The Nature of the Sex Offender, 9; Folder 339–13: Illinois Sex Offenders Commission (1951–52), box 339, Metropolitan Welfare Collection, CHS.

107. *Illinois v. Chatham* (1957), 130–31. The case was reversed, remanded, and retried before a jury. Chatham was convicted a second time and sentenced to forty to sixty years on one count of rape and ten to twenty years on one count of attempted rape, to run concurrently with credit for time served. The second trial took place in 1967, after psychiatrists found the defendant competent to stand trial again. See William Haines, "Behavioral Examination, Report to the Court," March 28, 1967, case #57–3438, 3441, *Illinois v. Chatham* (1957), case file, CCA.

108. Jackson received a lighter sentence than his co-defendants because trial evidence never linked him to the gun used in the attack and because the victim's medical exam failed to reveal the presence of a venereal disease that Jackson suffered from, thus calling into question the possibility he had forced intercourse with her. See *Illinois v. Sinclair, Jackson, Harvey* (1957), 616–18, CCA.

109. *Illinois v. Pleasant* (1958), 175, 180, CCA.

110. *Illinois v. Wilson* (1956), 340, CCA.

111. *Illinois v. Kane* (1957), 97, CCA.

112. I found fifty-seven articles detailing the conviction and sentencing of African American men for sex crimes in Chicago between 1950–59. Aside from seven defendants sentenced to life in prison or 199 years—the latter being the maximum possible sentence for rape in Illinois at the time—the average sentence was twenty-four years. White defendants during this period were also sentenced to a wide range of prison terms, with four life sentences included among the ninety-five articles I found that featured sentence terms published during the 1950s. Excluding life sentences, the average prison term assigned to convicted white defendants was thirteen to fifteen years. See *Chicago Tribune,* online subject search: rape, 1950–59. Averages tabulated by author.

113. See Pierce-Baker, *Surviving the Silence*; McGuire, *At the Dark End of the Street.*

114. Transcripts produced for appeal do not always record closing arguments. In the nineteen of twenty-six cases appealed during the 1950s that did, ten suggested that police investigations were technically flawed and that prosecutors hid these flaws in the presentation of their cases. See Criminal Felony Transcripts, 1950–59, CCA.

Chapter 4. Order in the Court

1. U.S. Constitution, pursuant to Article V, Amendments V, XIV. See also Lewis, 93–97.

2. *Gideon v. Wainright.*

3. *Escabedo v. Illinois*; *Miranda v. Arizona*.

4. Chicago's first public legal aid society began operations in 1905. See Pleck, 98. An expanded Public Defender's office opened in Chicago in 1930. See Friedman, 394.

5. See Free.

6. Between 1966 and 1969, inclusive, the average forcible rape risk rate was recorded at 29 per 100,000 women nationally with the core city risk rate averaging 60 per 100,000 women. Chicago's risk/arrest/indictment rates were comparable to other major cities, including New York and Los Angeles. See Federal Bureau of Investigation, *Uniform Crime Reports*.

7. The sample includes cases of rape, attempted rape, and deviate sexual assault as listed chronologically on the Criminal Felony Transcripts Reels, 1960–69, CCA. Deviate sexual assault replaced the indictment category crime against nature in 1961. See IRevS, chap. 38, stat. 11–3.

8. The sample includes eighteen black intraracial cases; six white intraracial cases; eight interracial cases involving white victims and black defendants, exclusively. See Criminal Felony Transcript Reels, 1960–69, sampled by author. In the remaining case sampled the victim's race was not clear, but possibly was Latina. See transcript of the rape trial of Louis Simental, January 15 and January 18, 1971, case #69–3380, *Illinois v. Louis Simental* (1969), CCA.

9. See Lindberg and Sykes, *Shattered Sense of Innocence*.

10. Rice, "Black Radicalism on Chicago's West Side," 31.

11. Lindberg, *To Serve and Collect*, 295–317.

12. DeGrazio appealed his suspension. The Illinois Supreme Court found DeGrazio's conduct unbecoming of a police officer and upheld his suspension. See *DeGrazio v. Civil Service Commission of Chicago*.

13. Ward, 68.

14. *Ibid.*, 9–10.

15. Wilson served in Kansas, 1928–39. See *Ibid.*, 23–51.

16. *Ibid.*, 81, 96.

17. Isserman and Kazin, *America Divided*, 227; see also Jeffrey Haas, *The Assassination of Fred Hampton*.

18. *Griffin v. Illinois*.

19. *People v. Mays*.

20. *People v. Elder*; *People v. Peters*; *People v. Langer*; *People v. Vaughn*; *People v. Trobiani*; *People v. Ladas*; *People v. Walden*; *People v. Mack* ; *People v. Stagg*.

21. Quote taken from *People v Szybeko*. Additional case law includes *People v. Reaves*; *People v. Rossililli*; *People v. White*.

22. Garner, 90.

23. "Chicago Crime Lab: Best in The US," *Chicago Tribune*, October 22, 1967. On reports of police incompetence, select *Chicago Tribune* articles include: "Cops Face Lie Quiz in Theft," January 7, 1962; "2 Ex-Deputies Jailed 1–3 Yrs. for $20 Bribe," February 8, 1963; "Error Frees Rape Suspect," October 2, 1963; "Rise in Crime Due to Drought, Wilson Says," June 1, 1967; "Suspect Freed Of Burglary, Rape Charges," May 24, 1969.

24. Transcript of the rape, deviate sexual assault trial of Frank Bruno, March 21–22, 1968, case #67–1998, *Illinois v. Frank Bruno* (1967), 83, CCA.

25. *Ibid.*, 84–85.

26. Transcript of the attempted rape, deviate sexual assault trial of Francis Oldsby, June 26, 1967, case #66–4070, *Illinois v. Francis Oldsby* (1966), 85, CCA.

27. *Ibid.*, 86.

28. Medical testimony was presented or stipulated in 59 percent of cases appealed between 1937 and 1959. See Criminal Felony Transcripts, 1936–59, CCA. On both corroborative and skeptical medical testimony in rape cases more broadly, see Robertson, "Signs, Marks and Private Parts," 345–88; Mills, "One Hundred Years of Fear," in Rafter and Stanko, 32–33.

29. Transcript of the rape trial of Eugene Hawkins, March 4–5, 9, 1970, case #68–4426, *Illinois v. Eugene Hawkins* (1968), 236–37, CCA.

30. Transcript of the deviate sexual assault trial of Bernard Bendig, January 26–27, 1966, case #65–3443, *Illinois v. Bernard Bendig* (1965), 77, CCA.

31. Transcript of the rape trial of Ernest Hayes, March 25, 1966, case #65–3617, *Illinois v. Ernest Hayes* (1965), 41, CCA.

32. *Ibid.*, 43–57.

33. Mohr, 21.

34. Transcript of the rape, etc. trial of Guarzee Gray, August 15, 1966, case #66–1515, *Illinois v. Guarzee Gray* (1966), 121, CCA.

35. Transcript of the rape trial of Herbie Wright Jr., March 16, 1970, case #69–2832, *Illinois v. Herbie Wright Jr.* (1969), 21, 45, CCA.

36. Transcript of the rape, etc. trial of W. Q. Thompson, February 2, 1965, case #64–3562, *Illinois v. W. Q. Thompson* (1964), 89, CCA.

37. Transcript of the rape, etc. trial of Whitson West, October 14–15, 1964, case #64–1864, *Illinois v. Whitson West* (1964), 156, CCA.

38. Citizens' Police Committee, vii.

39. Seventy-five of the ninety-three transcripts analyzed between 1937 and 1976 (80 percent) involve one or more African American men on trial for both intra- and interracial sex crimes. See Criminal Felony Transcripts, 1936–59/1960–76 sampled by author, CCA.

40. Rice, 121.

41. Police violence against African American urban residents was not exclusive to Chicago, although murder conspiracies put forth by black power leaders were not easily determined. See Epstein, "Black Panthers and the Police," 45–48, 51–77. One could also argue that even a single police murder of radical activists was unwarranted, violent, unfair, and constituted a conspiracy to preserve a discriminatory status quo during the period. See Pearson, *The Shadow of the Panther.*

42. The State dropped the rape indictment (#68–0032) against McCarroll, who was ultimately convicted of a single count of deviate sexual assault. See transcript of the deviate sexual assault trial of Kenny McCarroll, October 27–31, 1969, case #68–0033, *Illinois v. Kenny McCarroll* (1968), 851, CCA.

43. Transcript of the attempted rape trial of Roy Young, September 2–3, cont. October 1, 1970, case #69–1963, *Illinois v. Roy Young* (1969), 175–78, CCA.

44. *Ibid.*, 81.

45. *Ibid.*, 237.

46. Transcript of the rape trial of Herman Burks, June 15–17, 1966, case #66–1129, *Illinois v. Herman Burks* (1966), 37, CCA.

47. *Ibid.*, 179.

48. "It's a Crime Wave Only on Paper, Wilson Says," *Chicago Tribune*, August 19, 1960; see also *Chicago Tribune:* "Crime Up 50% in New System of Tabulating," July 16, 1960; "Chicago Crime Rises 90%, but Only on Paper," January 21, 1961.

49. Transcript of the rape trial of Eddie James Virgin, January 26–27, 1971, case #67–1095, *Illinois v. Eddie James Virgin* (1967), 273–74, CCA.

50. The motion was denied. See *ibid.*, 58, 346–47.

51. *Illinois v. Burks* (1966), 146, CCA.

52. *Illinois v. Virgin* (1967), 432, CCA.

53. *Illinois v. Hayes* (1965), 52–61, CCA.

54. Transcript of the attempted rape trial of George Hankins, October 14, 1965, case #65–2325, *Illinois v. George Hankins* (1965), 75–76, CCA.

55. *Ibid.*, 179.

56. *Illinois v. Burks* (1966), 187, CCA.

57. *Illinois v. Virgin* (1967), 457, CCA.

58. In the cases sampled during the 1960s, four circuit-level convictions were reversed, but none of the appellate opinions cited police discrimination as a basis for reversal. See case #65–0751, *Illinois v. John Milton Kepler* (1965); case #65–3617, *Illinois v. Ernest Hayes* (1965); case #66–3506, *Illinois v. Frank Evans* (1966); case #67–1998, *Illinois v. Frank Bruno* (1967). Criminal Felony Transcripts, 1960–69, sampled by author, CCA.

59. Transcript of the rape, deviate sexual assault trial of Osborn Fortson, June 5–7, 1967, case #67–0439, *Illinois v. Osborn Fortson* (1967), 37, CCA.

60. *Ibid.*, 49.

61. *Illinois v. McCarroll* (1968), 1036, CCA.

62. Chicago officials convened a commission to investigate the violence, which concluded that officers had conducted a police riot during the convention. See Walker, *Rights in Conflict*, vii.

63. Select *Chicago Tribune* articles include: "Wilson Backs Cops in Holding Suspects," October 27, 1963; "Tell How Acts of High Court Impede the Police," August 10, 1964; "Inbau Backs Interrogation by Policemen," March 14, 1965; "Handcuffed Police," July 14, 1966; "The Protection Denied the Law-Abiding," September 14, 1966.

64. *Illinois v. McCarroll* (1968), 839, CCA.

65. Transcript of the attempted rape trial of Frank Evans, February 3, 6, 1967, case #66–3506, *Illinois v. Frank Evans* (1966), 277–78, CCA.

66. *Illinois v. Hawkins* (1968), 131, CCA.

67. *Ibid.*, 143–44.

68. *Ibid.*, 149.

69. *Ibid.*, 169–70.

70. In camera means outside the presence of a jury and trial spectators. Only attorneys and testifying witnesses are permitted in court during in camera hearings. See Garner, 303.

71. Pretrial discovery, where the defense is allowed access to the plaintiff's case through official investigative documents, was created to encourage civil court settlements: it was

extended to criminal cases in the 1930s. See Friedman, 386. Written work produced during criminal investigations, including police and attorneys' personal notes, are classified as "work product" and are not open to pretrial discovery. See *Hickman v. Taylor.*

72. *Illinois v. Bendig* (1965), 46, CCA.

73. *Ibid.*, 50.

74. *Illinois v. Fortson* (1967), 103–4, CCA.

75. The military's wartime anti-VD campaign expanded public health efforts initially created in New York during the 1930s. See Brandt, *No Magic Bullet,*122–70. The Kinsey Reports revolutionized the study of sexuality with an objective "count and catalog" approach to research on human sexual practices. See Kinsey, et al. *Male*; Kinsey, et al., *Female.*

76. D'Emilio and Freedman, *Intimate Matters,* 281–82, 302–3.

77. *Griswold v. Connecticut.* The vast historiography on contraception in the United States is beyond the scope of this study. On select titles, see Gordon, *Woman's Body, Woman's Right*; Watkins, *On the Pill*; Tone, *Devices and Desires.*

78. U.S. Constitution, pursuant to Article V, Amendment VI.

79. The use of the male pronoun here is deliberate, as none of the judges appearing in the transcripts analyzed were women. By 1978, only 5.8 percent of all judges nationwide—at circuit, district, state, or federal levels—were women. See Flynn, "Women as Criminal Justice Professionals," in Rafter and Stanko, 311. On the rules of appeal, see Friedman, 256.

80. Laws preventing broad interrogations of women's sexuality during rape trials were not codified in Illinois until 1978. IRevS, chap. 38, stat. 11–1 through 11–3, sec. 117(a), (1978). On reform proposals, see NOW Task Force Newsletter, "The Drive for Rape Law Reform" (October 1974), 11, folder 7: Legal Reform, box 1: Madison Rape Crisis Center Papers, Wisconsin State Historical Society Archives, Madison (hereinafter WHS). Black victims began appearing in the cases analyzed here with more regularity by the mid-1950s. For the entire period under study, African American and/or Latina victims appear in fifty-six of the ninety-three cases (60 percent). See Criminal Felony Transcripts, 1936–59/1960–76 sampled by author, CCA.

81. Transcript of the rape trial of Ben Murphy, May 14, 1968, case #67–2774, *Illinois v. Ben Murphy* (1967), 55–58, CCA.

82. IRevS, chap. 38, stat. 11–1 (1934).

83. *Illinois v. Murphy* (1967), 68, CCA.

84. *Ibid.*, 15, 132–40.

85. Transcript of the rape trial of Isaac Griggs, February 3, 1969, case #68–2351, *Illinois v. Isaac Griggs* (1968), 21, CCA.

86. *Ibid.*, 28.

87. *Illinois v. Murphy* (1967), 163; *Illinois v. Griggs* (1968), 81, CCA. Averages tabulated by author, sentences listed in Appendix.

88. See Criminal Felony Transcripts, 1936–59, CCA. Averages tabulated by author, defense strategies, and corresponding sentences listed in Appendix.

89. On scrutiny of women's general character and its admissibility, see *People v. Gray*; *People v. Allen*; *People v. Eccarius*; *People v. Cieslak*; *People v. Fitzgibbons*; *People v. Kazmierczyk.*

90. Deutsch, *The Psychology of Women.*

91. Criminal Felony Transcripts, 1936–59/1960–69, sampled by author, CCA. Defense strategies listed in Appendix.

92. Transcript of the rape trial of Alexander Griffin, September 17, 1964, case #63–2846, *Illinois v. Alexander Griffin* (1963), 12–15, CCA.

93. *Ibid.*, 26.

94. *Ibid.*, 86–87.

95. *Ibid.*, 87.

96. Transcript of the rape trial of John Milton Kepler, August 16, 1965, case #65–0751, *Illinois v. John Milton Kepler* (1965), 59–64, CCA.

97. *Ibid.*, 60.

98. *Ibid.*, 60.

99. *Illinois v. Bendig* (1965), 54–55, CCA.

100. *Ibid.*, 55.

101. Legally categorized as criminal sexual solicitation, prostitution was (and still is) prohibited in Illinois and most other U.S. jurisdictions. See IRevS, chap. 38, stat. 11–15 through 11–19. Limited exceptions include Rhode Island, and areas of Nevada. See Rhode Island Revised Statues, chap. 11, stat. 34.1–34.11; Nevada Revised Statutes, title 15: chap. 200, stat. 295–400.

102. See Criminal Felony Transcripts, 1960–69, sampled by author, CCA.

103. *Illinois v. Strong* (1966), 82, CCA.

104. *Ibid.*, 87, 92–94.

105. *Ibid.*, 121–122.

106. *Ibid.*, 120.

107. *Illinois v. Flournoy, Jr.* (1969), 49, CCA.

108. *Ibid.*, 60.

109. *Illinois v. Oldsby* (1966), 43–46, CCA.

110. *Ibid.*, 97–101.

111. *Ibid.*, 49–50.

112. Chicago Fact Book Consortium, 114–15.

113. *Illinois v. Oldsby* (1966), 54, CCA.

114. Chicago Fact Book Consortium, 114; Peterson, *Report on Chicago Crime,* 4.

115. *Illinois v. Oldsby* (1966), 111, CCA.

116. *Ibid.*, 110.

117. *Ibid.*, 111–12.

118. *Illinois v. Bendig* (1965), 91, CCA.

119. *Illinois v. Kepler* (1965), 140–141, CCA.

120. *Illinois v. Griffin* (1963), 89, CCA.

121. *Illinois v. Fortson* (1967), 118, CCA.

122. Case #52–1626, *Illinois v. Hiller, Liljeblad* (1952): Fifth Amendment violations over statements made under duress; case #53–1094, *Illinois v. Shok* (1953): Sixth Amendment violations over facing one's accuser due to the denial of an interpreter to assist the immigrant victim's testimony; case #56–1261–1264, *Illinois v. Banks* (1956): Sixth and Seventh Amendment violations over improper rejection of jury instructions proposed by the defense; case #57–3438, 3441, *Illinois v. Chatham* (1957): Eighth Amendment violations

of cruel and unusual punishment and improper denial of a psychiatric examination. See Criminal Case Files, 1936–59, CCA.

123. On summary dismissal, see Lewis, 15, 35. The half-sheet included with every case file notes legal motions and their results: the absence of notation beyond an initial motion of appeal means the case was summarily dismissed. The Illinois First District Court of Appeals heard arguments in sixteen of the thirty-four cases analyzed before 1960 (67 percent) and upheld convictions, either by judgment or dismissal, in thirty of them. See Criminal Case Files, 1936–59, CCA. Appellate decisions listed in Appendix.

124. Criminal Case Files, 1960–69, sampled by author, CCA. Appellate decisions listed in Appendix.

125. *Ibid.* Appellate decisions listed in Appendix.

126. *People of the State of Illinois v. Ernest V. Hayes,* March 20, 1968, Appellate Opinions, comp. *Illinois Appellate Court Records,* 203.

127. *Illinois v. Evans* (1966), 26; see also case file half-sheet, case #67–1998, CCA.

128. Case file half-sheet, case #65–0751, *Illinois v. Kepler* (1965), CCA.

129. *Illinois v. Bruno* (1967), 3–4, 64, CCA.

130. Case file half-sheet, case #67–1998, *Illinois v. Bruno* (1967), CCA.

131. *Illinois v. Virgin* (1967), 258, CCA.

132. *Illinois v. Flournoy Jr.* (1969), 15, CCA.

133. *Illinois v. Wright Jr.* (1969), 50–51, CCA.

134. Transcript of the rape trial of Maurice Haynes, January 6–7, 1969, case #68–1207, *Illinois v. Maurice Haynes* (1968), 30, CCA.

135. Evans, 195–98.

136. *Ibid.,* 199.

137. Brownmiller, 431–35; Millett, 61–64.

138. Transcript of the rape trial of Freddie Jackson Jr., November 10, 12, 1965, case #65–1557, *Illinois v. Freddie Jackson, Jr.* (1965), 164, CCA.

Chapter 5. Second-Wave Feminists (Re)Discover Rape

1. Transcript of the rape trial of James Dvornik, May 11–13, 26–27, 1977, case #75–5771, *Illinois v. James Dvornik,* 149–183, CCA.

2. Barbara Ellingson-Waugh, "'Practical' Solutions Don't Solve Rape Crisis," *Capital Times,* December 15, 1972; folder 1: Rape Crisis Center 1972–73, Janet Heller Papers, WHS. On victim blaming and the difficulties of prosecuting rape, see also Estrich, esp. 19–22; Bevacqua, 9–10.

3. Letter from Patricia Russion to Madison, Wis., Chief of Police, dated December 15, 1972; folder 1: Rape Crisis Center 1972–73, Janet Heller Papers, WHS.

4. Bevaqua, 55.

5. Echols, *Daring to Be Bad,* 188.

6. Brownmiller, quoted in "Revolt against Rape," *Time* 106 (October 13, 1975), 54.

7. In review indices, the contrast between entries for *Against Our Will* and for other publications is startling. Thirty-four entries for that book, plus twenty-six additional reviews are listed under the author's name for a second title, *Femininity.* Other titles averaged three reviews. See Tarbet and Beach, *Book Review Index,* 704.

8. Robin Morgan, "Review," *Ms.* 6 (July 1977), 34. Ann Marie Cunningham, "Spotlight on Rape," *Progressive* 40 (January 1976), 53.

9. Criticisms taken from *New Yorker* 51 (November 3, 1975), 172; Jerrold K. Footluck, "A Feminist's View," *Newsweek* 86 (November 10, 1975), 72. Almost all reviews repeated Brownmiller's now-famous central thesis about rape (5; emphasis in original).

10. Select reviews include Mary Ellen Gale, "Review of *Against Our Will*," *New York Times Book Review*, October 12, 1975; Mary Leonard, "An 'Instant' Classic on Rape Mixes Anger and Scholarship," *National Observer* 14 (November 15, 1975), 25; Helene E. Schwartz, "Man, Woman and Rape," *The Nation* 221 (November 29, 1975), 566; Amanda Heller, "Short Reviews," *Atlantic Monthly* 236 (November 1975), 118; Edna O'Hern, "Review," *America* 134 (January 31, 1976), 78.

11. Diana Loercher, "The Problem of Rape: One Woman's View," *Christian Science Monitor* 68 (January 14, 1976), 18; M. J. Sobran Jr., "Boys Will Be Rapists," *National Review* 28 (March 5, 1976), 220.

12. Jean Stafford, "Brownmiller on Rape: A Scare Worse than Death," *Esquire* 84 (November 1975), 50 (emphasis in original).

13. Andrew Greeley, "Rape Book a Feminist Ms.-take," *Chicago Tribune,* November 18, 1975.

14. Davis, *Violence Against Women,* 3–13.

15. D.C. Rape Crisis Center, "How to Start a Rape Crisis Center" (1972), revised and expanded August 1977, 18; folder 2: Rape Papers, Women's Collection, Northwestern University Archives, Evanston, Ill. (hereinafter WC/NUE).

16. During the mid-twentieth century, 1,973 of 11,651 forcible rapes were recorded as unfounded (17 percent) compared to 541 of 6,265 murder and non-negligent homicides so recorded (9 percent). See Chicago Police Department, "Annual Reports," 1936–58. Brownmiller argued that the differential unfounded rate for rape versus that of other violent crimes proved investigators did not take rape seriously (435).

17. Federal Bureau of Investigation, *Uniform Crime Reports,* 1970–79. Average tabulated by author.

18. Carol Kleiman, "A Helping Hand for Rape Victims," *Chicago Tribune,* May 21, 1973. On the unfounded rate for rape, see Chicago Police Department, "Annual Reports," 1935–58.

19. Chicago Legal Action for Women, "Lay Advocate Training Manual: A Guide to Assist Rape Victims" (1974), 2, folder 1, Rape Papers, WC/NUE.

20. Reagan, *When Abortion Was a Crime,* 221.

21. "Feminist News: A Newsletter by and for Women at the University of Chicago" May 7, 1974, 2; folder 1: Rape Crisis Center, 1972–73, Janet Heller Papers, WHS.

22. Chicago Legal Action for Women, "Lay Advocate Training Manual: A Guide to Assist Rape Victims" (1974), 1; folder 1: Rape Papers, WC/NUE.

23. D.C. Rape Crisis Center, "How to Start a Rape Crisis Center" (1972), revised and expanded, August 1977, 31; folder 2: Rape Papers; WC/NUE.

24. Rosen, *The World Split Open,* 227–39. On social reform organization more broadly, see McCarthy and Wolfson, "Consensus Movements, Conflict Movements," in Morris and Mueller, *Frontiers in Social Movement Theory,* 273–97.

25. Chicago Legal Action for Women, "Lay Advocate Training Manual" (1974), 13; folder 1: Rape Papers, WC/NUE.

26. *Ibid.*, 11.

27. Roman Pucinski, "Let Women Punish Rapists," *Chicago Tribune,* August 23, 1973. See also, *Chicago Tribune:* "Pucinski Urges New Plan in Rapes," August 16, 1973; Edward Schreiber, "Policewomen's Unit Is Urged for Rape Cases," September 14, 1973.

28. Chicago Legal Action for Women, "Lay Advocate Training Manual" (1974), 29–30; folder 1: Rape Papers, WC/NUE.

29. William Juneau, "Carey's Top Aide CLAWed," *Chicago Tribune,* October 26, 1974.

30. Charles Mount, "Carey Steps Up Reform on Rape," *Chicago Tribune,* November 9, 1974.

31. William Juneau, "Epstein to Head Rape Task Force," *Chicago Tribune,* December 24, 1974.

32. Ronald Katulak, "Erasing the Emotional Scars of Rape," *Chicago Tribune,* December 11, 1972.

33. Pamela Lakes Wood, "The Victim in a Forcible Rape Case: A Feminist View," *American Criminal Law Review* 11 (Winter 1973), 351–52; Folder 6/I: Criminal Justice System, Box 1: Madison Rape Crisis Center Papers, WHS.

34. Chicago Hospital Council, *Guidelines for the Treatment of Suspected Rape Victims* (adopted, March 1974), 4 (emphasis in original).

35. Chicago Citizens Advisory Committee on Rape, "Report, of the Hospital Subcommittee on Rape" (March 1974), cover page; folder 1: Rape Papers, WC/NUE.

36. *Ibid.*, 1.

37. *Ibid.*, 3–11.

38. *Ibid.*, 1.

39. *Ibid.*, 13, 15. On case law and the resistance standard, see *People v. Rossililli; People v. James; People v. Smith.*

40. Chicago Citizens Advisory Committee on Rape, "Report of the Hospital Subcommittee on Rape" (March 1974), 14–15; folder 1: Rape Papers, WC/NUE.

41. *Ibid.*, 17.

42. *Ibid.*, 15.

43. Chicago Hospital Council, *Guidelines.*

44. *Chicago Tribune:* Edward Schreiber, "Rape Case Units Proposed," April 18, 1974; "Foes of Rape Set Major Goals," April 25, 1974; Sharon Mooney-Prokep, "Hospitals and Rape," June 5, 1974.

45. Transcript of the rape trial of Roosevelt Bridges, February 21–22, 1973, case #72–1521, *Illinois v. Roosevelt Bridges* (1972), 76–77, CCA.

46. Transcript of the rape trial of Ed Flowers and David Smith, March 17–April 25, 1975, case #74–1068, *Illinois v. Ed Flowers, David Smith* (1974), 86–88, CCA.

47. Transcript of the rape trial of Edward Reed, March 7, 9, 1977, case #76–2578, *Illinois v. Edward Reed* (1976), 106, CCA.

48. On gendered authority and conflict in American medical institutions, see Melosh, *The Physician's Hand.*

49. *Illinois v. Dvornik* (1975), 183, 185, CCA.

50. *Ibid.*, 311–12.

51. Transcript of the rape trial of Roberto Leyva, January 13–21, 1975, case #74–2745, *Illinois v. Roberto Leyva* (1974), 304, CCA.

52. Transcript of the rape trial of George Jeffers, May 1–10, 1978, case #76–4586, *Illinois v. George Jeffers* (1976), 102, CCA.

53. U.S. Bureau of the Census, *Nineteenth Census*, "General Population: Race and Ethnic Origins," (1970). See also Chicago Fact Book Consortium, 6–7, 274.

54. Gordon, *All Our Lives*.

55. Gamble, *Making a Place for Ourselves*, 131–43.

56. "About Loretto Hospital/History," http://www.lorettohospital.org/History.htm (accessed August 19, 2011); see also Hirsch, *Making the Second Ghetto*.

57. The National Association of Colored Graduate Nurses was founded in 1908. See Darlene Clark Hine, "Mabel K. Staupers and the Integration of Black Nurses into the Armed Forces," in Leavitt, *Women and Health*, 498.

58. National Black Nurses Association, "About NBNA: NBNA Mission," http://www.nbna.org/ (accessed August 19, 2011).

59. Breines, *Trouble Between Us*, 58–59.

60. Bart and O'Brien; Hine, "Rape and the Inner Lives of Black Women,"912–20.

61. Breines, *Trouble Between Us*, 62–63.

62. Established in 1876, the Loop YWCA first extended its services to Chicago's African American women in 1915. By World War II it had racially integrated service programming and an interracial board of directors and was recognized by the Mayor's Commission on Human Relations in 1946. See Knupfer, 136–49. On Loop YWCA feminism and anti-rape efforts, see also *Chicago Tribune*: Carol Kleiman, "Why the Y Is Fem-land," January 1, 1974; "Rape Conference Planned," November 14, 1974; Carol Kleiman, "Sisterhood Alive, Well in Loop," December 29, 1974.

63. Springer, *Living for the Revolution*,53–56.

64. "Racism Charged in Rape Cases," *Chicago Tribune*, March 24, 1974. See also select *Chicago Tribune* articles: Luci Horton, "Stereotype of Black Women Is Target of Organization," March 12, 1972; Jeannye Thorton, "Black Women Fighting Hanrahan," November 3, 1972; "Foes of Rape Set Major Goals," April 25, 1974. See also select *Chicago Defender* articles: "Rape Theme of Special Panel," November 8, 1973; "Women Launch Fight on Crime," February 25, 1974; "Women Host Rape Confab," April 22, 1974; "What to Do in Case of Rape," March 8, 1975.

65. See Bart and O'Brien, *Stopping Rape*.

66. NOW Rape Task Force Newsletter, "The Drive for Rape Law Reform" (October 1975), 11; folder 7: Legal Reform, box 1, WHS.

67. "State Will Provide Free Treatment for Rape Victims," *Chicago Tribune*, March 11, 1976.

68. Robert Davis, "City Council Unit OKs Crime Victim Bill," *Chicago Tribune*, April 6, 1976.

69. Braen, *The Rape Examination*, 3.

70. *Ibid.*, 4. See also "State Will Provide Free Treatment," *Chicago Tribune*, March 11, 1976.

71. On the history of medico-legal jurisprudence and professional debates, see Mohr, 197–212.

72. Braen, 15.

73. Select *Chicago Tribune* articles include: Leanita McClain, "Rape Panel Hears Victims' Testimony," February 3, 1974; Pat Colandar, "The Police: Answering the Rape Victim's

Call," October 27, 1975; Pat Colandar, "The Trial and Trauma of Prosecuting Rapists," October 28, 1975; Pat Colander, "Erasing the Aftershock of Rape," October 30, 1975; Linda Reinshagen, "Leniency to Rapists," December 16, 1975.

74. D.C. Rape Crisis Center, "How to Start a Rape Crisis Center" (1972) revised and expanded August 1977, 17; folder 2: Rape Papers, WC/NUE.

75. Chicago Legal Action for Women, "Lay Advocate Training Manual" (1974), 29; folder 1: Rape Papers, WC/NUE. See also "Report of the Citizens Advisory Committee on Rape to State's Attorney Bernard Carey, Cook County (March 1975), 7; folder 1: Rape Papers, WC/NUE.

76. Edward Schreiber, "N.Y. Cop Tells of Success with Her Rape Unit," *Chicago Tribune*, September 15, 1973.

77. Ronald Kotulak, "Mental Scars Feared," *Chicago Tribune*, June 17, 1974.

78. "Rape Case Investigations Hit," *Chicago Tribune*, August 18, 1974.

79. The department hired its first woman in 1910 and created a separate "Women's Division" to oversee the training and activities of female officers and police matrons in 1947. See Chicago Police Department, "Commissioner's Report," Annual Report (1951), 35. On the expansion of female appointments, see also *Chicago Tribune*: Patricia Leeds, "Retired Cop Wears Frills, but Says 'I Miss My People,'" June 19, 1975; Patricia Leeds, "Yes Sir, Sergeant, Er Ma'am," October 13, 1975; Edith Herman, "Police Women," August 31, 1976.

80. *Illinois v. Leyva* (1974), 167, CCA.

81. Transcript of the rape trial of Roland Sheppard, October 23, 1975, case #74–5566, *Illinois v. Roland Sheppard* (1974), 47, CCA.

82. Transcript of the rape trial of Amos Shaw, September 26–29, 1977, case #75–0839, *Illinois v. Amos Shaw* (1975), 320, 464, CCA.

83. *Illinois v. Dvornik* (1995), 208–22, CCA.

84. Transcript of the rape, etc., trial of Karl Plewka and Reginald Blakemore, July 24, 1972, case #72–1003, *Illinois v. Karl Plewka and Reginald Blakemore* (1972), 225–26, CCA. The appellate court affirmed the convictions but vacated the original sentences as too severe in light of the rape acquittal. See *Illinois v. Karl Plewka, Reginald Blakemore*, 27 Ill. App. 3d 553; 327 N.E.2d 457 (1975). Sentences listed in Appendix.

85. *Illinois v. Plewka, Blakemore* (1972), 216, CCA.

86. Select articles include, *Chicago Tribune*: "Dentist Freed in Evanston Rape Charge," May 12, 1970; "Hanrahan Aides Hit in Rape Case," October 27, 1972; "Freed, Then Charged in Rape Case," December 1, 1973; "Rape Jury Takes 18 Hrs. to Acquit," September 1, 1976.

87. Transcript of the rape trial of Sidney Robinson, June 13–17, 1974, case #71–2431, *Illinois v. Sidney Robinson* (1971), 129, CCA.

88. IRevS, chap. 38, stat. 11–1. On the history of rape as a crime against male property, see Block, *Rape and Sexual Power*.

89. Transcript of the rape trial of Albert and Calvert Faezell, January 27–February 3, 1976, case #75–2542, *Illinois v. Albert and Calvert Faezell* (1975), 58, CCA.

90. Carol Kleiman, "Rape: The Terror Only a Woman Can Understand," *Chicago Tribune*, June 27, 1973. On the longer history of this myth see also Brownmiller, *Against Our Will*; Bevaqua, *Rape on the Public Agenda*; Freedman, "Uncontrolled Desires" in Peiss and Simmons, 199–225.

91. Transcript of the rape trial of Jerry Johnson, May 15–16, 1974, case #73–2991, *Illinois v. Jerry Johnson* (1973), 281, CCA.

92. *People v. De Frates*; *People v. Scott*. See also "Forcible and Statutory Rape: An Exploration of the Operation and Objectives of the Consent Standard," *Yale Law Journal* 62, no. 1 (December 1952), 55–83.

93. "Nightscene" radio broadcast (WTMJ, 620 AM) March 6, 1973, folder 1: Rape Crisis Center, 1972–73, Janet Heller Papers, WHS.

94. *Chicago Tribune*: Bernard Gavzer, "Screaming May Be a Woman's Best Defense," September 28, 1970; "Protecting Yourself against RAPE," January 17, 1971; Jack Mabley, "A Rape Victim? Need Help? Scream 'Fire!,'" May 5, 1974; "Campus' Whistle War on Rape Set," November 27, 1974; Pat Colander, "Self-Defense—What You Should Know," July 20, 1975.

95. *Illinois v. Leyva* (1974), 296–97, CCA.

96. *Ibid.*, 307.

97. Prior to 1970, fifty-one of the sixty-seven cases analyzed (76 percent) were heard by the bench. Of the twenty-six cases sampled between 1970 and 1976, eleven (42 percent) were jury trials. Of these, two involved defendants who were not black. See case #72–0205, *Illinois v. Paul Watts* (1972); case #74–2745, *Illinois v. Roberto Leyva* (1974), CCA.

98. Haas, 93.

99. *Ibid.*, 125.

100. *Ibid.*, 344–47.

101. Dulaney, 74–76.

102. *Ibid.*, 75.

103. Select *Chicago Tribune* articles include: Jack Houston, "Fear Still Waits on CTA Platforms as Night Falls," November 8, 1970; Gerald West and Patricia Krizmis, "Law Should Be Same for All—But It Isn't, Blacks Report." December 5, 1971; Peter Negronida, "Police Task Force: Main Target of Blacks' Criticism," May 15, 1972; Vernon Jarrett, "Law and Order: Selective Worry," December 22, 1972; "Study Shows More Crime in Mostly Black Districts," September 5, 1975.

104. *Illinois v. Dvornik* (1975), 681–682, CCA.

105. *Illinois v. Jeffers* (1976), 432, CCA.

106. Spohn and Horney, 20–21.

107. Pending in 1975, the revision was enacted through House Bill 760 that went into effect in 1978. See NOW Rape Task Force Newsletter, "The Drive for Rape Law Reform" (October 1975), 11, Folder 7: Legal Reform, Box 1: Madison Rape Crisis Center Papers, WHS. See also Colleen M. Loftus, "The Illinois Rape Shield Statue: Privacy at Any Cost?" *John Marshall Law Review*, vol. 15 (Winter 1982), 162–163.

108. NOW Rape Task Force Newsletter, "The Drive for Rape Law Reform," (October 1975), 11: Folder 7: Legal Reform, Box 1: Madison Rape Crisis Center Papers, WHS.

109. Spohn and Horney, 36–37.

110. *Ibid.*, 57.

111. *Chicago Tribune*: Edith Herman, "Legislators Draft New Rape Laws," February 4, 1975; John Elmer, "Illinois House Approves Bill Limiting Rape Case Evidence," March 20, 1975; Deborah Nexon, "Human Rape Bill," April 15, 1975; "Senate Bill to Aid Victims of Rape," May 28, 1975; John McCarron, "Women: Daley Killed Anti-Rape Bills," July 1, 1975.

112. Brown, "Historical Perspective," 95.

113. Loftus, 164–66.

114. *Illinois v. Sheppard* (1974), 21–23, CCA.

115. *Illinois v. Reed* (1976), 2–6, CCA.

116. Garner, 654.

117. *Illinois v. Reed* (1976), 2–20, CCA.

118. *People v. Wilcox.* The attorney cited this case in *Illinois v. Reed* (1976), 19–20, CCA.

119. *Illinois v. Reed* (1976), 223; *Illinois v. Dvornik* (1975), 782, CCA. Sentences listed in Appendix.

120. The averages account for reductions imposed at the appellate level. See Criminal Felony Transcripts, 1970–76, sampled by author, CCA. Averages tabulated by author, sentences listed in Appendix.

121. Felony Criminal Transcripts, 1936–59/1960–69, sampled by author, CCA. Averages tabulated by author, sentences listed in Appendix.

122. *Illinois v. Albert, Calvert Faezell* (1975), 721, CCA.

123. Transcript of the rape, etc., trial of Delbert Scott, November 4, 6, 1974, case #73–3342, *Illinois v. Delbert Scott* (1973), 182–83, CCA. The merged sentence for aggravated kidnapping was reversed and remanded on appeal, and the convictions on all counts and the remaining sentences were affirmed. See *Illinois v. Scott* 45 Ill. App. 3d.487; 359 N.E.2d 878 (1975).

124. *Chicago Tribune,* online subject search: rape, 1960–69.

125. *Chicago Tribune,* online subject search: rape, 1970–76.

126. Federal Bureau of Investigation, *Uniform Crime Annual Reports,* 1960–76.

127. Entman and Rojecki, *The Black Image in the White Mind,* xi–xii.

128. Transcript of the rape, etc., trial of Kenneth Dalton and Samuel Ames, December 28–30, 1970, case #70–2878, *Illinois v. Kenneth Dalton, Samuel Ames* (1970), 434, 451–52, CCA.

129. Case file half-sheet, case #70–2878, *Illinois v. Dalton, Ames* (1970), CCA. Sentences listed in Appendix.

130. Transcript of the rape, etc., trial of Richard (Ricky) Vanderbilt, June 21, 1973, case #73–1091, *Illinois v. Richard Vanderbilt* (1973), 11–14, 83, CCA.

131. R. A. Reifman, Pyschiatric Evaluation Report, case file notes, case #73–1091, *Illinois v. Vanderbilt* (1973), CCA.

132. *Illinois v. Vanderbilt* (1973), 3–6, CCA. Term limits are based on the right to a speedy trial, as outlined in the U.S. Constitution, pursuant to Article III, Amendment VI.

133. Case file half-sheet, case #73–1091, *Illinois v. Vanderbilt* (1973), CCA.

134. Transcript of the rape, etc., trial of Paul Watts, September 5–7, 1972, case #72–0205, *Illinois v. Paul Watts* (1972), 670–71; *Illinois v. Plewka, Blakemore* (1972), 225–26, CCA.

135. *Illinois v. Watts,* 19 Ill. App. 3d 733; 312 N.E.2d 672 (1974). Sentences listed in Appendix.

136. *Illinois v. Plewka, Blakemore,* 27 Ill. App. 3d. 553; 327 N.E.2d 457 (1975).

137. *Ibid.*

138. *Illinois v. Bridges* (1972), 201–6, CCA.

139. Appellate judgment recorded, August 27, 1974, case file notes, case #72–1521, *Illinois v. Bridges* (1972), CCA.

140. Seven of the sixty-seven cases (10 percent) analyzed between 1936 and 1969 were reversed. See Criminal Case Files, Felony Transcripts, 1936–59/1960–69 sampled by author, CCA.

141. Seven of the twenty-six cases sampled saw modifications upon appeal. See Criminal Felony Transcripts, 1970–76, sampled by author, CCA.

142. Spohn and Horney, 37.

Conclusion

1. Hancock, "Wolf Pack," 38–42.

2. See Smith, "Central Park Revisited."

3. Nick Ravo, "Marchers and Brooklyn Youths Trade Racial Jeers," *New York Times,* August 27, 1989.

4. Sydney H. Schanberg, "A Journey through the Tangled Case of the Central Park Jogger," *Village Voice,* November 19, 2002.

5. Williams, "Reasons for Doubt," 10.

6. Chancer, *High-Profile Crimes,* 29–60.

7. U.S. Bureau of Justice Statistics, "National Crime Victimization Survey," http://bjs .ojp.usdoj.gov/index.cfm?ty=dcdetail&iid=245 (accessed August 19, 2010).

8. Meili, Interview. See also Meili, *I Am the Central Park Jogger.*

9. See Benedict, *Virgin or Vamp*; Entman and Rojecki, *Black Image in the White Mind.*

10. IRevS, chap. 38, stat. 11–1; revised, chap. 38, stat. 12–13 through 12–18 (1984).

11. Pascoe, 48.

12. Wilson and Marcur, "2 Duke Athletes Are Arrested and Charged," *New York Times,* April 18, 2006.

13. Wilson and Glater, "Files from Duke Rape Case Give Details but No Answers," *New York Times,* August 25, 2006.

14. *Ibid.*

15. *Ibid.*

16. "Former Duke Lacrosse Rape Case D.A. to Resign," *Associated Press,* June 15, 2007.

17. Wilson and Glater, "Files."

18. See Taylor and Johnson, *Until Proven Innocent*; Yaeger and Pressler, *It's Not About the Truth*; Baydoun and Good, *A Rush to Injustice.*

19. Barber, "Crystal Magnum Goes for 'Grace," August 22, 2008, http://www .lashawnbarber.com/archives/2008/08/22/crystal-mangum-goes-for-grace (accessed October 21, 2008), online review of Magnum, et al., *Last Dance for Grace: The Crystal Mangum Story* (New York: fire! Films and Books, 2008).

20. Reginald Daye died two weeks after allegedly being stabbed by Mangum on April 3, 2011. Durham County authorities indicted her for one count of first-degree murder and two counts of theft on April 18, 2011. "Duke Lacrosse Accuser Crystal Mangum Charged with Murder," *Associated Press,* April 19, 2011. See also Deconto, "Crystal Mangum Indicted in Boyfriend's Death," *Durham News Observer,* April 18, 2001; Graham and Conant, "Duke Lacrosse Accuser's New Trouble," *Newsweek,* April 4, 2011.

21. American Medical Association, "Billing Guidelines for Sexual Assault Examinations," (2007).

22. Illinois Crime Victim's Compensation Program, (July 2006) 2–4, 9–12.

23. American Medical Association, "Billing Guidelines," 7–8. Averages tabulated by author.

24. Mary Pemberton, "Wasilla Rape Victims Billed When Palin Was Mayor," *Associated Press,* September 12, 2008.

25. Braen, 8.

26. Carlos Sadovi, "Money Found for Rape-Kit Testing," *Chicago Tribune,* January 14, 2004.

27. "The Price of DNA Delay," *Chicago Tribune,* May 4, 2009; "New State Rape Kit Law Sets Precedent," *Chicago Tribune,* July 7, 2010.

28. Kari Lydersen, "Law Came Too Late for Some Rape Victims," *New York Times,* July 8, 2010.

29. *Ibid.*

30. Feldberg, "Defining the Facts of Rape," 90–114.

31. Kate Stone Lombardi, "A New Effort to Speed Rape Exam Procedures," *New York Times,* November 10, 1996.

32. The SANE program was first authorized through the Illinois Criminal Justice Information Authority. See Ninety-First Illinois General Assembly, Public Act #91-0529 (1999).

33. Spohn and Horney, 145.

34. *Ibid.,* 153.

35. *Ibid.,* 154–56.

36. *People v. Santos.*

Bibliography

Archival Sources

Chicago Historical Society, Chicago, Ill.:
 Metropolitan Welfare Collection
Clerk of the Circuit Court of Cook County, Ill, Richard J. Daley Center, Chicago, Ill.:
 Criminal Felony Transcripts
 Police Case Files
National Association for the Advancement of Colored People Papers [microfilm]
Northwestern University Archives, Northwestern University, Evanston, Ill.:
 Women's Collection
Wisconsin Historical Society, Madison, Wis.:
 Janet Heller Papers
 Madison Rape Crisis Center Papers
 Women Against Violence Against Women Papers

Published Primary Sources

NEWSPAPERS:

Associated Press
Chicago Tribune
Chicago Defender
Chicago Sun
New York Times
Village Voice

Adams, O. D. *Training for the Police Service*. Washington D.C.: Government Printing Office, 1938.
Block, Kenneth, comp. *A Report on Chicago Crime*. Chicago: Chicago Crime Commission, 1969.

Braen, G. Richard. *The Rape Examination.* Chicago: Abbott Laboratories, 1976.

Brownmiller, Susan. *Against Our Will: Men, Women and Rape.* New York: Bantam, 1975.

Cahalane, Cornelius F. *The Policeman's Guide: A Manual of Study and Instruction.* New York: Harper, 1952.

Chicago Hospital Council. "Guidelines for the Treatment of Suspected Rape Victims," 1974.

Citizens' Police Committee, eds. *Chicago Police Problems.* Chicago: University of Chicago Press, 1931.

Cunningham, Ann Marie. "Spotlight on Rape," *Progressive* 40 (January 1976): 52–53.

Drake, St. Clair, and Horace R. Cayton. *Black Metropolis: A Study of Negro Life in a Northern City, Volume One.* New York: Harper and Row, 1945.

Footluck, Jerrold K. "A Feminist's View," *Newsweek* 86 (November 10, 1975): 72.

Gale, Mary Ellen. "Review of *Against Our Will,*" *New York Times Book Review,* October 12, 1975, sec. 7: 1–3.

"General Review." *New Yorker* 51 (November 3, 1975): 171–72.

Hale, Sir Matthew. "Concerning the Progress of the Laws of England after the Time of King William I until the Time of King Edward II," in *The History of the Common Law,* 4th ed., edited by Charles Runnington. London: Strahan and Woodfall, 1779.

Heller, Amanda. "Short Reviews," *Atlantic Monthly* 236 (November 1975): 118.

Hopkins, Ernest J. *Our Lawless Police: A Study of the Unlawful Enforcement of the Law.* New York: Viking, 1931.

Kinsey, Alfred J. *Sexual Behavior in the Human Female.* Philadelphia: Sanders, 1953.

———. *Sexual Behavior in the Human Male.* Philadelphia: Sanders, 1948.

Leonard, Mary. "An 'Instant' Classic on Rape Mixes Anger and Scholarship," *National Observer* 14 (November 15, 1975): 25.

Loercher, Diana. "The Problem of Rape: One Woman's View," *Christian Science Monitor* 68 (January 14, 1976): 18.

Meeropol, Abel [Lewis Allan, pseud.] *Strange Fruit,* Billie Holiday. Commodore 78: 1939.

Millett, Kate. *Sexual Politics.* New York: Ballantine, 1969.

Morgan, Robin. "Review," *Ms.* 6 (July 1977): 34.

Morgan, Robin, ed. *Sisterhood Is Powerful: An Anthology of Writings from the Women's Liberation Movement.* New York: Vintage, 1970.

Moss, Stewart P., comp. *Moss' Chicago Police Manual.* Chicago: Flood, 1923.

National Commission on Law Observance and Enforcement (Wickersham Commission). Eleventh Report. "Lawlessness in Law Enforcement," 1930.

O'Hern, Edna. "Review," *America* 134 (January 31, 1976): 77–78.

Peterson, Frederick, et al., eds. *Legal Medicine and Toxicology.* Philadelphia: Saunders Company, 1923.

Peterson, Virgil W., comp. *A Report on Chicago Crime.* Chicago: Chicago Crime Commission Reports, 1954–68.

"Revolt Against Rape," *Time* 106 (October 13, 1975): 54.

Schwartz, Helen E. "Man, Woman and Rape," *The Nation* 221 (November 29, 1975): 566–68.

Sobran, M. J., Jr. "Boys Will Be Rapists," *National Review* 28 (March 5, 1976): 220+.

Stafford, Jean. "Brownmiller on Rape: A Scare Worse than Death," *Esquire* 84 (November 1975): 50+.

Walker, Daniel. *Rights in Conflict: Convention Week in Chicago, August 25–29, 1968.* New York: Dutton, 1968.

Government Publications

Bachman, Ronet, and Linda E. Saltzman. "Violence Against Women: Estimates from the Redesigned Survey," Special Report (NCJ-154348). Washington D.C.: U.S. Department of Justice, Bureau of Justice Statistics, August 1995.

Epstein, Joel, and Stacie Langenbahn. "The Criminal Justice and Community Response to Rape" (OJP-89-C-009). Washington D.C.: U.S. Department of Justice, National Institute of Justice, May 1994.

Hart, Timothy C., and Callie M. Rennison. "Reporting Crime to the Police, 1992–2000," Special Report (NCJ-195710). Washington D.C.: U.S. Department of Justice, Bureau of Justice Statistics, March 2003.

Rennison, Callie M. "Rape and Sexual Assault: Reporting to Police and Medical Attention, 1992–2000," Select Findings (NCJ-194530). Washington D.C.: U.S. Department of Justice, Bureau of Justice Statistics, August 2002.

———. "Violent Victimization and Race, 1993–98," Special Report (NCJ 176354). Washington D.C.: U.S. Department of Justice, Bureau of Justice Statistics, March 2001.

United States Bureau of Justice Statistics, comp. "National Crime Victimization Survey." Tabulated annually.

United States Census Bureau, comp. *Fifteenth-Twentieth Census,* "Population Statistics." (1930–80).

United States Constitution.

United States Federal Bureau of Investigation, comp. *Uniform Crime Reports.* Tabulated annually.

Court Opinions (Federal and State), Legal Codes, Published Crime Statistics

Addison v. People, 62 N.E. 296, 179 Ill. 405 (1901).
Batson v. Kentucky, 476 U.S. 79, 106 S. Ct. 1712, 90 L. Ed. 2d 69 (1986).
Bean v. People, 16 N.E. 656, 124 Ill. 576 (1888).
Bradwell v. Illinois, 16 Wallace 130 (1873).
Brown v. the Board of Education of Topeka, KS, 347 U.S. 483 (1954).
Brown v. Mississippi, 297 U.S. 278 (1936).
Cox Broadcasting Company v. Cohn, 420 U.S. 469 (1975).
DeGrazio v. Civil Service Commission of Chicago, 202 N.E.2d 522 (1964).
Donovan v. People, 74 N.E. 772, 215 Ill.520 (1905).
Duren v. Missouri, 439 U.S. 357 (1979).
Escobedo v. Illinois, 378 U.S. 478 (1964).
Florida Star v. B.J.F., 491 U.S. 524 (1989).
Georgia v. McCollum, 505 U.S. 42, 112 S. Ct. 2348, 120 L. Ed. 2d 33 (1992).
Gideon v. Wainwright, 372 U.S. 335 (1963).
Griffin v. Illinois, 351 U.S. 12 (1956).
Griswold v. Connecticut, 381 U.S. 479 (1965).
Harris v. People, 21 N.E. 563, 128 Ill. 585 (1889).
Hickman v. Taylor, 329 U.S. 495, 510–511 (1947).
Hurd v. Hodge, 334 U.S. 24 (1948).
J.E.B. v. Alabama, 511 U.S. 127 (1994).

Lewis v. People, 96 N.E. 1005, 252 Ill. 281 (1911).

Mallory v. U.S., 354 U.S. 449 (1957).

McNabb v. U.S., 318 U.S. 332 (1943).

Miranda v. Arizona, 384 U.S. 436 (1966).

Norris v. Alabama, 294 U.S. 297 (1935).

O'Callahan v. Parker, 395 U.S. 258 (1969).

Patton v. U.S., 281 U.S. 276 (1930).

People v. Allen, 124 N.E. 329, 289 Ill. 218 (1919).

People v. Ardelean, 13 N.E.2d 976, 368 Ill. 274 (1938).

People v. Burns, 4 N.E.2d 26, 364 Ill. 49 (1936).

People v. Cieslak, 149 N.E. 815, 319 Ill. 221 (1925).

People v. De Frates, 70 N.E.2d 591, 395 Ill. 495 (1947).

People v. Dravilles, 152 N.E. 212, 321 Ill. 390 (1926).

People v. Eccarius, 136 N.E. 651, 305 Ill. 62 (1922).

People v. Elder, 47 N.E.2d 694, 382 Ill. 388 (1943).

People v. Faulisi, 185 N.E.2d 211, 25 Ill.2d 457 (1962).

People v. Fitzgibbons, 174 N.E. 848, 343 Ill. 69 (1931).

People v. Fryman, 122 N.E.2d 573, 4 Ill.2d 224 (1954).

People v. Garafola, 16 N.E.2d 741, 369 Ill. 237 (1938).

People v. Gray, 96 N.E. 268, 251 Ill. 431 (1911).

People v. Hiddleson, 59 N.E. 2d. 639, 389 Ill. 293 (1945).

People v. James, 210 N.E.2d 804, 62 Ill.2d 225 (1965).

People v. Kazmierczyk, 192 N.E. 657, 357 Ill. 592 (1934).

People v. Lades, 146 N.E.2d 56, 12 Ill.2d 290 (1958).

People v. Langer, 52 N.E.2d. 194, 384 Ill. 608 (1944).

People v. Mack, 185 N.E.2d 154, 25 Ill.2d 416 (1962).

People v. Mays, 179 N.E.2d 654, 23 Ill.2d 520 (1962).

People v. Perez, 107 N.E.2d 749, 412 Ill. 425 (1952).

People v. Peters, 48 N.E.2d 352, 382 Ill. 549 (1943).

People v. Reaves, 183 N.E.2d 169, 24 Ill.2d 380 (1962).

People v. Rickey, 31 N.E.2d 973, 375 Ill. 525 (1941).

People v. Rossililli, 181 N.E.2d 114, 24 Ill.2d 341 (1962).

People v. Rucker, 79 N.E. 606, 224 Ill. 131 (1906).

People v. Santos, 286 Ill. Dec. 102, 211 Ill.2d 395, 813 N.E.2d 159 (2004).

People v. Schultz, 102 N.E. 1045, 260 Ill. 35 (1913).

People v. Sciales, 187 N.E. 169, 353 Ill. 169 (1933).

People v. Scott, 95 N.E.2d 315, 407 Ill 301 (1950).

People v. Silva, 89 N.E.2d 800, 405 Ill. 158 (1950).

People v. Smith, 203 N.E.2d 879, 32 Ill.2d 88 (1965).

People v. Stagg, 194 N.E.2d 342, 29 Ill.2d 415 (1963).

People v. Szybeko, 181 N.E.2d 176, 24 Ill.2d 335 (1962).

People v. Trobiani, 106 N.E.2d. 367, 412 Ill. 235 (1952).

People v. Vaughn, 61 N.E.2d 546, 390 Ill. 360 (1945).

People v. Walden, 169 N.E.2d 241, 19 Ill.2d 602 (1960).

People v. White, 186 N.E.2d 351, 26 Ill.2d 199 (1962).

People v. Wilcox, 33 Ill. App. 3d 432, 435, 337 N.E.2d 211, 215 (1975).

Powell v. Alabama, 287 U.S. 45 (1932).

Powers v. Ohio, 499 U.S. 400, 111 S. Ct. 1364, 113 L. Ed. 2d 411 (1991).

Shelley v. Kraemer, 334 U.S. 1 (1948).

Sipes v. McGhee, 316 Mich. 614; 25 N.W. (2d) 638 (1947).

Strauder v. West Virginia, 100 U.S. (1880).

Sutton v. People, 34 N.E. 420, 145 Ill.279 (1893).

Taylor v. Louisiana, 419 U.S. 522 (1975).

U.S. v. Ballard, 329 U.S. 187 (1946).

Zarresseller v. People, 17 Ill. 101 (1855).

Ziang Sung Wan, v. U.S., 266 U.S. 1 (1924).

Appellate Opinions, comp. *Illinois Appellate Court Records,* series 2d. vols. 93, 103. Mundelein, Ill.: Callaghan, 1968.

Chicago Police Department. "Annual Reports," 1934–58.

Chicago Police Department. "A Report of Progress, 1960–64."

Illinois General Assembly, comp. *Laws of Illinois.* Springfield, Ill.: General Assembly, various years.

———. "Illinois Criminal Justice Information Authority." Ninety-First Illinois General Assembly, Public Act #91-0529 (1999).

Nevada Revised Statutes, title 15: chap. 200, stat. 295–400.

Police Department, City of New York. "Annual Reports." New York: Bureau of Printing, 1934–55.

Rhode Island Revised Statues, chap. 11, stat. 34.1–34.11.

Smith-Hurd, ed. *Illinois Annotated Statutes,* chap. 37, "Courts," and chap. 38, "Criminal Law and Procedure," stat. 11.1–14, 12.12–18. St. Paul, Minn.: West, 1979.

Secondary Sources

BOOKS

Adler, Jeffrey S. *First in Violence, Deepest in Dirt: Homicide in Chicago, 1875–1920.* Cambridge, Mass.: Harvard University Press, 2006.

Anderson, Alan B., and George W. Pickering. *Confronting the Color Line: The Broken Promise of the Civil Rights Movement in Chicago.* Athens: University of Georgia Press, 1986.

Bailey, Beth, and David Farber. *The First Strange Place: Race and Sex in World War II Hawaii.* Baltimore: Johns Hopkins University Press, 1992.

Bart, Pauline B., and Patricia H. O'Brien. *Stopping Rape: Successful Survival Strategies.* New York: Pergamon, 1985.

Baydoun, Nader, and R. Stephanie Good. *A Rush to Injustice: How Power, Prejudice, Racism and Political Correctness Overshadowed Truth and Justice in the Duke Lacrosse Rape Case.* Nashville, Tenn.: Thomas Nelson, 2007.

Bederman, Gail. *Manliness and Civilization: A Cultural History of Gender and Race in the United States, 1880–1917.* Chicago: University of Chicago Press, 1995.

Bell, Catherine. *Ritual Theory, Ritual Practice.* New York: Oxford University Press, 1992.

Benedict, Helen. *Virgin or Vamp: How the Press Covers Sex Crimes.* New York: Oxford University Press, 1992.

Bevaqua, Maria. *Rape on the Public Agenda: Feminism and the Politics of Sexual Assault.* Boston: Northeastern University Press, 2000.

Biles, William Roger. *Big City Boss in Depression and War: Mayor Edward J. Kelley of Chicago.* DeKalb: Northern Illinois University Press, 1984.

———. *Richard J. Daley: Politics, Race, and the Governing of Chicago.* DeKalb: Northern Illinois University Press, 1995.

Block, Sharon. *Rape and Sexual Power in Early America.* Chapel Hill: University of North Carolina Press, 2006.

Bolton, Ken Jr., and Joe R. Feagin. *Black in Blue: African-American Police Officers and Racism.* New York: Routledge, 2004.

Bourke, Joanna. *Rape: Sex, Violence, History.* London: Virago, 2007.

Brandt, Allan. *No Magic Bullet: A Social History of Venereal Disease in the United States since 1880.* New York: Oxford University Press, 1987.

Breines, Winifred. *Young, White and Miserable: Growing Up Female in the Fifties.* Boston: Beacon, 1992.

———. *The Trouble Between Us: An Uneasy History of White and Black Women in the Feminist Movement.* New York: Oxford University Press, 2006.

Brown, Kathleen M. *Good Wives, Nasty Wenches, and Anxious Patriarchs: Gender, Race, and Power in Colonial Virginia.* Chapel Hill: University of North Carolina Press, 1996.

Brown, Peter Megargee. *The Art of Questioning: Thirty Maxims of Cross-Examination.* New York: Macmillan, 1987.

Brundage, W. Fitzhugh, ed. *Under Sentence of Death: Lynching in the New South.* Chapel Hill: University of North Carolina Press, 1997.

Blum, John Morton. *V Was for Victory: Politics and American Culture during World War II.* New York: Harcourt Brace Jovanovich, 1976.

Butler, Judith. *Gender Trouble: Feminism and the Subversion of Identity.* New York: Routledge, 1990.

Carson, Clayborne. *In Struggle: SNCC and the Black Awakening of the 1960s.* Cambridge, Mass.: Harvard University Press, 1981).

Chancer, Lynn S. *High-Profile Crimes: When Legal Cases Become Social Causes.* Chicago: University of Chicago Press, 2005.

Chicago Fact Book Consortium, eds. *Local Community Fact Book: Chicago Metropolitan Area.* Chicago: Chicago Review Press, 1984.

Clark, Anna. *Women's Silence, Men's Violence: Sexual Assault in England, 1770–1845.* New York: Pandora, 1987.

Clement, Elizabeth. *Love for Sale: Courting, Treating, and Prostitution in New York City, 1900–1945.* Chapel Hill: University of North Carolina Press, 2006.

Cohen, Adam, and Elizabeth Taylor. *American Pharaoh: Richard J. Daley—His Battle for Chicago and the Nation.* New York: Back Bay Books, 2001.

Davis, Angela Y. *Blues Legacies and Black Feminism: Gertrude "Ma" Rainey, Bessie Smith, and Billie Holiday.* New York: Pantheon, 1998.

———. *Violence Against Women and the Ongoing Challenge to Racism.* Latham, N.Y.: Kitchen Table/Women of Color Press, 1985.

Dayton, Cornelia Hughes. *Women before the Bar: Gender, Law, and Society in Connecticut, 1639–1789.* Chapel Hill: University of North Carolina Press, 1995.

D'Cruze, Shani. *Crimes of Outrage: Sex, Violence, and Victorian Working Women.* DeKalb: Northern Illinois University Press, 1998.

D'Emilio, John, and Estelle B. Freedman. *Intimate Matters: A History of Sexuality in America.* 2nd ed. Chicago: University of Chicago Press, 1997.

Deutsch, Helene. *The Psychology of Women: A Psychoanalytic Interpretation.* New York: Grune & Stratton, 1944.

Doreski, Carole K. *Writing America Black: Race Rhetoric in the Public Sphere.* New York: Cambridge University Press, 1998.

Dorr, Lisa Lindquist. *White Women, Rape, and the Power of Race in Virginia, 1900–1960.* Chapel Hill: University of North Carolina Press, 2004.

Douglas, Susan J. *Where the Girls Are: Growing Up Female with the Mass Media.* New York: Random House, 1994.

Dubinsky, Karen. *Improper Advances: Rape and Heterosexual Conflict in Ontario, 1880–1929.* Chicago: University of Chicago Press, 1993.

Dulaney, J. Marvin. *Black Police in America.* Bloomington: Indiana University Press, 1996.

Echols, Alice. *Daring to Be Bad: Radical Feminism in America, 1967–1975.* Minneapolis: University of Minnesota Press, 1989.

———. *Scars of Sweet Paradise: The Life and Times of Janis Joplin.* New York: Holt, 1999.

Edwards, Laura F. *Gendered Strife and Confusion: The Political Structure of Reconstruction.* Urbana: University of Illinois Press, 1997.

Entman, Robert M., and Andrew Rojecki. *The Black Image in the White Mind: Media and Race in America.* Chicago: University of Chicago Press, 2000.

Estes, Steve. *I Am a Man! Race, Manhood, and the Civil Rights Movement.* Chapel Hill: University of North Carolina Press, 2005.

Estrich, Susan. *Real Rape: How the Legal System Victimizes Women Who Say No.* Cambridge, Mass.: Harvard University Press, 1987.

Evans, Sara. *Personal Politics: The Roots of Women's Liberation in the Civil Rights Movement and the New Left.* New York: Vintage, 1979.

Feimster, Crystal N. *Southern Horrors: Women and the Politics of Rape and Lynching.* Cambridge, Mass.: Harvard University Press, 2009.

Finegold, Kenneth. *Experts and Politicians: Reform Challenges to Machine Politics in New York, Cleveland and Chicago.* Princeton, N.J.: Princeton University Press, 1995.

Fout, John C., and Maura Shaw Tantillo, eds. *American Sexual Politics: Sex, Gender, and Race since the Civil War.* Chicago: University of Chicago Press, 1990.

Fox-Genovese, Elizabeth. *Within the Plantation Household: Black and White Women of the Old South.* Chapel Hill: University of North Carolina Press, 1988.

Free, Marvin D. *Racial Issues in Criminal Justice: The Case of African Americans.* Monesy, N.Y.: Criminal Justice Press, 2004.

Fremon, David K. *Chicago Politics Ward by Ward.* Bloomington: Indiana University Press, 1988.

Friedman, Lawrence M. *Crime and Punishment in American History.* New York: Basic, 1993.

Gamble, Vanessa Northington. *Making a Place for Ourselves: The Black Hospital Movement 1920–1945.* New York: Oxford University Press, 1995.

Garner, Bryan A., ed. *Black's Law Dictionary.* New pocket ed. New York: West, 1996.

Genovese, Eugene. *Roll Jordan, Roll: The World the Slaves Made.* New York: Pantheon, 1974.

Giddings, Paula. *When and Where I Enter: The Impact of Black Women on Race and Sex in America.* New York: Morrow, 1984.

Gilmore, Glenda Elizabeth. *Gender and Jim Crow: Women and the Politics of White Supremacy in North Carolina, 1896–1920.* Chapel Hill: University of North Carolina Press, 1996.

Goodman, James. *Stories of Scottsboro: The Rape Case that Shocked 1930s America and Revived the Struggle for Equality.* New York: Pantheon, 1994.

Gordon, Linda. *Heroes of Their Own Lives: The Politics and History of Family Violence, Boston, 1880–1960.* New York: Viking, 1988.

———. *Pitied But Not Entitled: Single Mothers and the History of Welfare, 1890–1935.* New York: Free Press, 1994.

———. *Woman's Body, Woman's Right: Birth Control in America.* Rev. ed. New York: Penguin, 1990.

Gordon, Sarah. *All Our Lives: A Centennial History of Michael Reese Hospital and Medical Center, 1881–1981.* Chicago: Hospital and Medical Center Press, 1981.

Grimshaw, William J. *Bitter Fruit: Black Politics and the Chicago Machine, 1931–1991.* Chicago: University of Chicago Press, 1992.

Griswold, Robert L. *Fatherhood in America: A History.* New York, Basic, 1993.

Grossman, James R. *Land of Hope: Chicago, Black Southerners, and the Great Migration.* Chicago: University of Chicago Press, 1989.

Gutman, Herbert G. *The Black Family in Slavery and Freedom, 1750–1925.* New York: Pantheon, 1976.

Haas, Jeffrey. *The Assassination of Fred Hampton: How the FBI and the Chicago Police Murdered a Black Panther.* Chicago: Lawrence Hill, 2010.

Hall, Jacquelyn Dowd. *Revolt Against Chivalry: Jessie Daniel Ames and the Women's Campaign against Lynching.* New York: Columbia University Press, 1979.

Harris, Trudier, ed. *Selected Works of Ida B. Wells-Barnett.* New York: Oxford University Press, 1991.

Hazard, Geoffrey C., and W. William Hodes. *The Law of Lawyering: A Handbook on the Model Rules of Professional Conduct.* New York: Aspen Law and Business, 1997.

Hegarty, Marilyn E. *Victory Girls, Khaki-Wackies, and Patriotutes: The Regulation of Female Sexuality During World War II.* New York: New York University Press, 2008.

Hendricks, Wanda A. *Gender, Race, and Politics in the Midwest: Black Club Women in Illinois.* Bloomington: Indiana University Press, 1998.

Higgenbotham, Evelyne Brooks. *Righteous Discontent: The Women's Movement in the Black Baptist Church, 1880–1920.* Cambridge, Mass.: Harvard University Press, 1993.

Hirsch, Arnold R. *Making the Second Ghetto: Race and Housing in Chicago, 1940–1960.* Rev. ed. Chicago: University of Chicago Press, 1998.

Hodes, Martha, ed. *Sex, Love, Race: Crossing Boundaries in North American History.* New York: New York University Press, 1999.

———. *White Women, Black Men: Illicit Sex in the Nineteenth Century South.* New Haven, Conn.: Yale University Press, 1997.

Hoff, Joan. *Law, Gender, and Injustice: A Legal History of U.S. Women.* New York: New York University Press, 1991.

hooks, bell. *Ain't I a Woman: black women and feminism.* Boston: South End, 1981.

Isserman, Maurice, and Michael Kazin. *America Divided: The Civil War of the 1960s.* New York: Oxford University Press, 2000.

Jones, Jacqueline. *Labor of Love, Labor of Sorrow: Black Women, Work, and Family under Slavery.* New York: Basic, 1985.

Jones, James H. *Bad Blood: The Tuskegee Syphilis Experiment.* New York: Free Press, 1981.

Kelley, Robin D. G. *Race Rebels: Culture, Politics, and the Black Working Class.* New York: Free Press, 1994.

———. *Freedom Dreams: The Black Radical Imagination.* Boston: Beacon, 2002.

Kennedy, David M. *Freedom from Fear: The American People in Depression and War, 1929–1945.* New York: Oxford University Press, 1999.

Kerber, Linda. *No Constitutional Right to Be Ladies: Women and the Obligations of Citizenship.* New York: Hill and Wang, 1998.

Kessler-Harris, Alice. *Out to Work: A History of Wage-Earning Women in the United States.* New York: Oxford University Press, 1982.

Knupfer, Anne Meis. *The Chicago Black Renaissance and Women's Activism.* Urbana: University of Illinois Press, 2006.

LaCapra, Dominick, ed. *The Bounds of Race: Perspectives on Hegemony and Resistance.* Ithaca, N.Y.: Cornell University Press, 1991.

LaFree, Gary D. *Rape and Criminal Justice: The Social Construction of Sexual Assault.* Belmont, Calif.: Wadsworth, 1989.

Lawson, Steven. *Black Ballots: Voting Rights in the South, 1944–1946.* New York: Columbia University Press, 1985.

Leavitt, Judith Walzer. *Brought to Bed: Child-Bearing in America, 1750–1950.* New York: Oxford University Press, 1986.

———, ed. *Women and Health in America: Historical Readings.* Madison: University of Wisconsin Press, 1984.

Leavitt, Judith Walzer, and Ronald L. Numbers, eds. *Sickness and Health in America: Readings in the History of Medicine and Public Health.* 2nd rev. ed. Madison: University of Wisconsin Press, 1985.

Lee, Chana Kai. *For Freedom's Sake: The Life of Fannie Lou Hamer.* Urbana: University of Illinois Press, 1999.

Lemann, Nicholas. *The Promised Land: The Great Black Migration and How It Changed America.* New York: Vintage, 1992.

Lerner, Gerda, ed. *Black Women in White America: A Documentary History.* New York: Vintage, 1972.

———. *The Majority Finds Its Past.* New York: Oxford University Press, 1979.

Lewis, Anthony. *Gideon's Trumpet.* New York: Random House, 1964.

Lindberg, Richard C. *To Serve and Collect: Chicago Politics and Police Corruption from the Lager Beer Riot to the Summerdale Scandal.* New York: Praeger, 1991.

Lindberg, Richard C., and Gloria Jean Sykes. *Shattered Sense of Innocence: The 1955 Murders of Three Chicago Children.* Carbondale: Southern Illinois University Press, 2006.

Mangum, Crystal Gail, et al. *Last Dance for Grace: The Crystal Mangum Story.* New York: fire! Films and Books, 2008.

Mann, Coramae Richey. *Unequal Justice: A Question of Color.* Bloomington: Indiana University Press, 1993.

Margolick, David. *Strange Fruit: Billie Holiday, Cafe Society, and an Early Cry for Civil Rights*. Philadelphia: Running Press, 2000.

Marsh, Jeanne, et al. *Rape and the Limits of Law Reform*. Boston: Auburn House, 1982.

Matoesian, Gregory M. *Reproducing Rape: Domination through Talk in the Courtroom*. Cambridge, U.K.: Polity, 1993.

Matthews, Nancy A. *Confronting Rape: The Feminist Anti-Rape Movement and the State*. New York: Routledge, 1994.

May, Elaine Tyler. *Homeward Bound: American Families in the Cold War Era*. Rev. ed. New York: Basic, 1999.

McGreevey, John T. *Parish Boundaries: The Catholic Encounter with Race in the Twentieth-Century Urban North*. Chicago: University of Chicago Press, 1996.

McGuire, Danielle L. *At the Dark End of the Street: Black Women, Rape, and Resistance— A New History of the Civil Rights Movement from Rosa Parks to the Rise of Black Power*. New York: Knopf, 2010.

McMullen, Richie J. *Male Rape: Breaking the Silence of the Last Taboo*. London: GMP, 1990.

Meili, Trisha. *I Am the Central Park Jogger: A Story of Hope and Possibility*. New York: Scribner, 2004.

Melosh, Barbara. *The Physician's Hand: Work, Culture, and Conflict in American Nursing*. Philadelphia: Temple University Press, 1982.

Meyerowitz, Joanne, ed. *Not June Cleaver: Women and Gender in Postwar America, 1945– 1960*. Philadelphia: Temple University Press, 1994.

Mezey, Gillian C., and Michael B. King, eds. *Male Victims of Sexual Assault*. New York: Oxford University Press, 2000.

Michel, Sonya. *Children's Interests/Mothers' Rights: The Shaping of America's Child Care Policy*. New Haven, Conn.: Yale University Press, 1999.

Miller, Vivien M. L. *Crime, Sexual Violence, and Clemency: Florida's Pardon Board and Penal System in the Progressive Era*. Gainesville: University Press of Florida, 2000.

Mohr, James. *Doctors and the Law: Medical Jurisprudence in Nineteenth-Century America*. New York: Oxford University Press, 1993.

Monkkonen, Eric H. *Murder in New York City*. Berkeley: University of California Press, 2001.

Moore, Brenda L. *To Serve My Country, To Serve My Race: The Story of the Only African-American WACS Stationed Overseas during World War II*. New York: New York University Press, 1996.

Morantz-Sanchez, Regina Markell. *Sympathy and Science: Women Physicians in American Medicine*. New York: Oxford University Press, 1985.

Morris, Aldon. *The Origins of the Civil Rights Movement: Black Communities Organizing for Change*. New York: Free Press, 1984.

Morrison, Toni, ed. *Race-ing Justice, En-gendering Power: Essays on Anita Hill, Clarence Thomas, and the Construction of Social Reality*. New York: Pantheon, 1992.

Mumford, Kevin J. *Interzones: Black/White Sex Districts in Chicago and New York in the Early Twentieth Century*. New York: Columbia University Press, 1997.

Norton, Mary Beth. *Founding Mothers and Fathers: Gendered Power and the Forming of American Society*. New York: Knopf, 1996.

O'Brien, Gail Williams. *The Color of the Law: Race, Violence, and Justice in the Post–World War II South.* Chapel Hill: University of North Carolina Press, 1999.

Odem, Mary E. *Delinquent Daughters: Protecting and Policing Adolescent Female Sexuality in the United States, 1885–1920.* Chapel Hill: University of North Carolina Press, 1995.

Payne, Charles M. *I've Got the Light of Freedom: The Organizing Tradition and the Mississippi Freedom Struggle.* Berkeley: University of California Press, 1995.

Pearson, Hugh. *The Shadow of the Panther: Huey Newton and the Price of Black Power in America.* New York: Perseus, 1994.

Peiss, Kathy, and Christina Simmons, eds. *Passion and Power: Sexuality in History.* Philadelphia: Temple University Press, 1989.

Peiss, Kathy. *Cheap Amusements: Working Women and Leisure in Turn-of-the-Century New York.* Philadelphia: Temple University Press, 1986.

Pierce-Baker, Charlotte. *Surviving the Silence: Black Women's Stories of Rape.* Reprint, New York: Norton, 2000.

Pleck, Elizabeth. *Domestic Tyranny: The Making of American Social Policy against Family Violence from Colonial Times to the Present.* New York: Oxford University Press, 1987.

Ploscowe, Morris. *Sex and the Law.* New York: Prentice-Hall, 1951.

Rafter, Nicole Hahn, and Elizabeth Anne Stanko, eds. *Judge, Lawyer, Victim, Thief: Women, Gender Roles, and Criminal Justice.* Boston: Northeastern University Press, 1982.

Ralph, James R. Jr. *Northern Protest: Martin Luther King Jr., Chicago, and the Civil Rights Movement.* Cambridge, Mass.: Harvard University Press, 1993.

Ramsland, Katherine. *Beating the Devil's Game: A History of Forensic Science and Criminal Investigation.* New York: Berkley, 2007.

Reagan, Leslie J. *When Abortion Was a Crime: Women, Medicine, and the Law in the United States, 1867–1973.* Berkeley: University of California Press, 1997.

Reed, Christopher Robert. *The Chicago NAACP and the Rise of Black Professional Leadership, 1910–1966.* Bloomington: Indiana University Press, 1997.

Reiman, Jefferey. *The Rich Get Richer and the Poor Get Prison: Ideology, Class, and Criminal Justice.* 2nd ed. New York: Wiley, 1984.

Robertson, Stephen R. *Crimes Against Children: Sexual Violence and Legal Culture in New York City, 1880–1960.* Chapel Hill: University of North Carolina Press, 2005.

Rosen, Ruth. *The World Split Open: How the Modern Women's Movement Changed America.* New York: Penguin, 2000.

Rosenberg, Charles E. *The Care of Strangers: The Rise of America's Hospital System.* New York: Basic, 1987.

Scarce, Michael. *Male on Male Rape: The Hidden Toll of Stigma and Shame.* New York: Insight, 1997.

Schudson, Michael. *Discovering the News: A Social History of American Newspapers.* New York: Basic, 1978.

Scott, Joan Wallach, ed. *Feminism and History.* New York: Oxford University Press, 1996.

Smith, Merrill D., ed. *Sex Without Consent: Rape and Sexual Coercion in America.* New York: New York University Press, 2001.

Snitow, Ann, et al., eds. *Powers of Desire: The Politics of Sexuality.* New York: Monthly Review, 1983.

Spear, Alan H. *Black Chicago: The Making of a Negro Ghetto, 1890–1920.* Chicago: University of Chicago Press, 1967.

Spigel, Lynn. *Make Room for TV: Television and the Family Ideal in Postwar America.* Chicago: University of Chicago Press, 1992.

Spinney, Robert G. *City of Big Shoulders: A History of Chicago.* DeKalb: Northern Illinois University Press, 2000.

Spohn, Cassia, and Julie Horney. *Rape Law Reform: A Grassroots Revolution and Its Impact.* New York: Plenum, 1992.

Springer, Kimberly. *Living for the Revolution: Black Feminist Organizations, 1968–1980* Durham, N.C.: Duke University Press, 2005.

Stevens, Rosemary. *In Sickness and In Wealth: American Hospitals in the Twentieth Century.* New York: Basic, 1989.

Strickland, Arvarh E. *History of the Chicago Urban League.* Urbana: University of Illinois Press, 1966.

Sugrue, Thomas J. *Sweet Land of Liberty: The Forgotten Struggle for Civil Rights in the North.* New York: Random House, 2008.

Tannen, Deborah. *Gender and Discourse.* New York: Oxford University Press, 1996.

Tarbet, Gary C., and Barbara Beach, eds. *Book Review Index: A Master Accumulation, 1965- 1984.* Vol. 1: A–B. Detroit: Gale Research, 1985.

Taslitz, Andrew E. *Rape and the Culture of the Courtroom.* New York: New York University Press, 1999.

Taylor, Stuart., and K.C. Johnson. *Until Proven Innocent: Political Correctness and the Shameful Injustice of the Duke Lacrosse Rape Case.* New York: Thomas Dunne, 2007.

Tone, Andrea. *Devices and Desires: A History of Contraceptives in America.* New York: Hill and Wang, 2002.

Tuttle, William M., Jr. *Race Riot: Chicago in the Red Summer of 1919.* New York: Atheneum, 1970.

Turner, Patricia. *I Heard It Through the Grapevine: Rumor in African-American Culture.* Berkeley: University of California Press, 1993.

Valk, Anne M. *Radical Sisters: Second-Wave Feminism and Black Liberation in Washington, DC.* Urbana: University of Illinois Press, 2008.

Vigarello, Georges. *A History of Rape: Sexual Violence in France from the 16th to the 20th Century.* Trans. Jean Birrell. Malden, Mass.: Blackwell, 2001.

Walsh, Mary Roth. *Doctors Wanted, No Women Need Apply: Sexual Barriers in the Medical Profession, 1835–1975.* New Haven, Conn.: Yale University Press, 1977.

Watkins, Elizabeth Siegel. *On the Pill: A Social History of Oral Contraceptives, 1950–1970.* Baltimore: Johns Hopkins University Press, 2001.

Wendt, Lloyd. *Chicago Tribune: The Rise of a Great American Newspaper.* New York: Rand McNally, 1979.

West, Robin. *Caring for Justice.* New York: New York University Press, 1997.

White, Deborah Gray. *Too Heavy a Load: Black Women in Defense of Themselves, 1894–1994.* New York: Norton, 1999.

White, E. Frances. *Dark Continent of Our Bodies: Black Feminism and the Politics of Respectability.* Philadelphia: Temple University Press, 2001.

Williams, Patricia J. *The Alchemy of Race and Rights: Diary of a Law Professor.* Cambridge, Mass.: Harvard University Press, 1991.

Williamson, Joel. *The Crucible of Race: Black-White Relations in the American South since Emancipation.* New York: Oxford University Press, 1984.

Wynn, Neil. *The Afro-American and the Second World War.* New York: Holmes and Meier, 1976.

Yaeger, Don, and Mike Pressler. *It's Not About the Truth: The Untold Story of the Duke Lacrosse Case and the Lives It Shattered.* New York: Threshold, 2007.

ARTICLES

Brown, Kenneth M. "Historical Perspective: Rape Shield Law." *New Hampshire Bar Journal* 24, no. 4 (July 1982): 95–108.

Call, Jack E., David Nice, and Susette M. Talarico. "An Analysis of State Rape Shield Laws." *Social Science Quarterly* 72, no. 4 (December 1991): 774–788.

Chamlin, Mitchell B. and Mary Baldwin Kennedy. "The Impact of the Wilson Administration on Economic Crime Rates." *Journal of Quantitative Criminology* 7 no. 4 (1991): 357–72.

Cohen, Daniel A. "Social Injustice, Sexual Violence, Spiritual Transcendence: Constructions of Interracial Rape in Early American Crime Literature, 1767–1817." *William and Mary Quarterly* 56 no. 3 (July 1999): 481–526.

D'Amato, Anthony. "The Ultimate Injustice: When a Court Misstates the Facts." *Cardozo Law Review* 11 (1990): 1313.

Davis, Angela Y. "Rape, Racism, and the Myth of the Black Rapist." In *Feminism and 'Race,'* edited by Kum-Kum Bhavnani, 50–64. New York: Oxford University Press, 2001.

Donat, Patricia L. N. and John D'Emilio. "A Feminist Redefinition of Rape and Sexual Assault: Historical Foundations and Change." *Journal of Social Issues* 48, no. 1 (1992): 9–22.

Epstein, Edward Jay. "The Black Panthers and the Police: A Pattern of Genocide?" *New Yorker* February 13, 1971, 45–48+.

Feldberg, Georgina. "Defining the Facts of Rape: The Uses of Medical Evidence in Sexual Assault Trials." *Canadian Journal of Women and the Law* 9, no. 1 (Winter 1997): 90–114.

Flood, Dawn Rae. "Stormy Protests on Sex Crimes: Local Debates about Race and Rape in Postwar Chicagoland." *Journal of the Illinois State Historical Society* 102, no. 3–4 (Fall-Winter 2009): 429–58.

"Forcible and Statutory Rape: An Exploration of the Operation and Objectives of the Consent Standard." *Yale Law Journal* 62, no. 1 (December 1952): 55–83.

Foucault, Michel. "Truth and Power." In *The Foucault Reader,* edited by Paul Rabinow, 51–75. New York: Random House, 1984.

Hancock, Lynnell. "Wolf Pack: The Press and the Central Park Jogger." *Columbia Journalism Review* 41, no. 5 (January/February 2003): 38–42.

Hine, Darlene Clark. "Rape and the Inner Lives of Black Women in the Middle West: Preliminary Thoughts on the Culture of Dissemblance." *Signs: Journal of Women and Culture in Society* 14 (Summer 1989): 912–20.

Hirsch, Arnold R. "Massive Resistance in the Urban North: Trumbull Park, Chicago, 1953–1966." *Journal of American History* 82, no. 2 (September 1995): 522–50.

Johnson, Marilyn. "Gender, Race, and Rumours: Re-examining the 1943 Race Riots." *Gender and History* 10, no. 2 (August 1998): 252–77.

Lindemann, Barbara S. "To Ravish and Carnally Know: Rape in Eighteenth-Century Massachusetts." *Signs: Journal of Women in Culture and Society* 10, no. 1 (1984): 63–82.

Loftus, Colleen M. "The Illinois Rape Shield Statute: Privacy at Any Cost?" *John Marshall Law Review* 15 (Winter 1984): 157–75.

Marshall, Annecka. "From sexual denigration to self-respect: resisting images of Black female sexuality," in *Reconstructing Womanhood, Reconstructing Feminism: Writings on Black Women,* edited by Delia Jarrett-Macauley, 5–35. New York: Routledge, 1996.

McCarthy, John D. and Mark Wolfson. "Consensus Movements, Conflict Movements, and the Cooptation of Civic and State Infrastructures," in *Frontiers in Social Movement Theory,* edited by Aldon D. Morris and Carol McClurg Mueller, 273–297. New Haven, Conn.: Yale University Press, 1992.

McGuire, Danielle L. "'It Was Like All of Us Had Been Raped': Sexual Violence, Community Mobilization, and the African American Freedom Struggle." *Journal of American History* 91, no. 3 (December 2004): 906–31.

Meyer, Leisa D. "Creating G.I. Jane: The Regulation of Sexual Behavior in the Women's Army Corps during World War II." *Feminist Studies* 18, no. 3 (Fall 1992): 581–601.

Mormino, Gary. "G.I. Joe Meets Jim Crow: Racial Violence and Reform in World War II Florida." *Florida Historical Quarterly* 73, no. 1 (1994): 23–42.

Onkst, David. "First a Negro . . . Incidentally a Veteran: Black World War II Veterans and the G.I. Bill of Rights in the Deep South, 1944–1948." *Journal of Social History* 33, no. 3 (1998): 517–43.

Parker, Kathleen R. "'To Protect the Chastity of Children Under Sixteen': Statutory Rape Prosecutions in a Midwest County Circuit Court, 1850–1950." *Michigan Historical Review* 20, no.1 (Spring 1994): 49–79.

Pascoe, Peggy, "Miscegenation Law, Court Cases, and Ideologies of 'Race' in Twentieth Century America." *Journal of American History* 83, no. 1 (June 1996): 44–69.

Reagan, Leslie J. "Engendering the Dread Disease: Women, Men and Cancer." *American Journal of Public Health* 87 (November 1997): 1779–87.

———. "Victim or Accomplice?" Crime, Medical Malpractice, and the Construction of the Aborting Woman in American Case Law, 1860s-1970." *Columbia Journal of Gender and Law* 10, no. 2 (2001): 311–31.

Robertson, Stephen. "Signs, Marks, and Private Parts: Doctors, Legal Discourses, and Evidence of Rape in the United States, 1823–1930." *Journal of the History of Sexuality* 8, no. 3 (1998): 345–88.

Smith, Chris. "Central Park Revisited." *New York Magazine,* October 14, 2002.

Smith, Valerie. "Split Affinities: The Case of Interracial Rape." In *Conflicts in Feminism,* edited by Marianne Hirsch and Evelyn Fox Keller, 271–87. New York: Routledge, 1990.

Thornock, Major John R. "Military Trials of Civil Crimes." *Military Review* 51, no. 12 (December, 1971): 88–96.

Williams, Patricia J. "Reasons for Doubt." *The Nation* 275 (December 30, 2002): 10.

Williamson, Joel. "Wounds, Not Scars: Lynching, the National Conscience and the American Historian." *Journal of American History* 83, no. 4 (March 1997): 1221–53.

UNPUBLISHED DISSERTATIONS

Rice, Jon Frank. "Black Radicalism on Chicago's West Side: A History of the Illinois Black Panther Party." PhD diss., Northern Illinois University, 1998.

Ward, Bernard James. "Orlando W. Wilson and the Development of His Education and Training Policies while Superintendent of the Chicago Police Department, 1960–1967." PhD diss., Loyola University Chicago, 2000.

ONLINE AND MEDIA RESOURCES

"About Loretto Hospital/History" at http://www.lorettohospital.org/History.htm (accessed August 19, 2011).

American Medical Association. "Billing Guidelines for Sexual Assault Examinations," (2007) at http:www.lni.wa.gov/IPUB/800–100–000.pdf (accessed September 29, 2011).

Barber, La Shawn. "Crystal Mangum Goes for 'Grace'" (posts for August 22/25, 2008) at http://www.lashawnbarber.com/archives/2008/08/22/crystal-mangum-goes-for-grace (accessed October 21, 2008).

Deconto, Jesse James. "Crystal Mangum Indicted in Boyfriend's Death." *Durham News Observer* (April 18, 2011), available at http://www.newsobserver.com/2011/04/18/1138586/crystal-mangum-indicted-for-boyfriends.html (accessed September 29, 2011).

Graham, David A. and Eve Conant. "Duke Lacrosse Accuser's New Trouble." *Newsweek* (April 4, 2011) available at http://www.thedailybeast.com/articles/2011/04/05/duke-lacrosse-rape-accusers-new-trouble-crystal-mangum-arrested.html (accessed September 29, 2011).

Illinois Crime Victim's Compensation Program (July 2006), available at http://www.cyberdriveillinois.com/publications/pdf_publications/cc94.pdf (accessed September 29, 2011).

Meili, Trisha. Televised interview with Katie Couric, *Dateline: NBC*. April 6, 2003.

National Bar Association. "Our History" at http://www.nationalbar.net/node/2 (accessed August 19, 2011).

National Black Nurses Association. "About NBNA: NBNA Mission" at http://www.nbna.org (accessed September 28, 2011).

Index

Page numbers in *italics* followed by *m* indicate maps and those followed by *t* indicate tables.

DAWN RAE FLOOD is an assistant professor
of history at Campion College at the University
of Regina, Canada.

Women in American History

Radical Sisters: Second-Wave Feminism and Black Liberation in Washington, D.C.
  Anne M. Valk
Feminist Coalitions: Historical Perspectives on Second-Wave Feminism in the
  United States   *Edited by Stephanie Gilmore*
Breadwinners: Working Women and Economic Independence, 1865–1920
  Lara Vapnek
Beauty Shop Politics: African American Women's Activism in the Beauty Industry
  Tiffany M. Gill
Demanding Child Care: Women's Activism and the Politics of Welfare, 1940–1971
  Natalie M. Fousekis
Rape in Chicago: Race, Myth, and the Courts   *Dawn Rae Flood*

The University of Illinois Press
is a founding member of the
Association of American University Presses.

Composed in 10.5/13 Adobe Minion
by Jim Proefrock
at the University of Illinois Press
Manufactured by Sheridan Books, Inc.

University of Illinois Press
1325 South Oak Street
Champaign, IL 61820-6903
www.press.uillinois.edu

Berkeley College

CAMPUSES: Brooklyn, NY * New York, NY * White Plains, NY
Newark, NJ * Paramus, NJ * Woodbridge, NJ * Woodland Park, NJ
* Berkeley College Online *

PLEASE KEEP DATE DUE CARD IN POCKET